Resettling Displaced Communities

Crossing Borders in a Global World: Applying Anthropology to Migration, Displacement, and Social Change

Series Editors: Raúl Sánchez Molina (ersanchez@fsof.uned.es)
Nancy Anne Konvalinka (nkonvalinka@fsof.uned.es)

Advisory Board: Maria Eugenia Bozzoli, Adi Bharadwaj, Monica Bonaccorso, Lucy M. Cohen, Yasmine Ergas, Andrés Fábregas Puig, Carles Feixa, Ubaldo Martínez Veiga, Marit Melhuus, Alicia Re Cruz, Amy Speier, Meenakshi Thapan, and María Amelia Viteri

Mission Statement

By crossing political, social, cultural, and identity borders current migrants, refugees, and travelers meet challenges of globalization in their processes of displacement, incorporation, and adaptation to new settlements. These circumstances open up opportunities for anthropologists and members of related disciplines to work together with migrants, residents, and communities seeking to contribute to knowledge and action. This series seeks to address these challenges and their intersections with national, ethnic, gender, and generational identities by providing a range of interdisciplinary theoretical and methodological frameworks of how scholars and practitioners can approach not only knowledge but also application. In addition, this series aims to show models of collaboration and interaction in economy, policy, social and physical reproduction, health, labor market, education, and other social institutions. In doing so, the series should be of value to scholars studying historical and contemporary issues in displacement, migration, immigration, and development studies as well as advanced undergraduate and graduate students and practitioners interested in the impact of displacements, migration, and social and cultural changes in contemporary societies. Some examples of specific movements are migrants from less to more affluent areas, migrants escaping violence in their home contexts, migrants sent abroad by their companies, and people seeking medical and reproductive treatments unavailable at home.

Books in Series

Resettling Displaced Communities: Applying the International Standard for Involuntary Resettlement, by William L. Partridge and David B. Halmo
Identities on Trial in the United States: Asylum Seekers from Asia, by ChorSwang Ngin
The Crux of Refugee Resettlement: Rebuilding Social Networks, edited by Andrew Nelson, Alexander Rödlach, and Roos Willems

Resettling Displaced Communities

Applying the International Standard for Involuntary Resettlement

William L. Partridge and David B. Halmo

LEXINGTON BOOKS

Lanham • Boulder • New York • London

Published by Lexington Books
An imprint of The Rowman & Littlefield Publishing Group, Inc.
4501 Forbes Boulevard, Suite 200, Lanham, Maryland 20706
www.rowman.com

6 Tinworth Street, London SE11 5AL, United Kingdom

British Library Cataloguing in Publication Information Available

Library of Congress Cataloging-in-Publication Data

Names: Partridge, William L., author. | Halmo, David B., author.
Title: Resettling displaced communities : applying the international standard for involuntary resettlement / William L. Partridge and David B. Halmo.
Description: Lanham : Lexington Books, [2020] | Series: Crossing borders in a global world: applying anthropology to migration, displacement, and social change | Includes bibliographical references and index. | Summary: "The goal of resettlement must be the sustainable social, economic and human development of displaced communities. The provisions and directives entailed in resettlement policies and current performance standards constitute the I.S.I.R. Case examples from Asia, Africa and the Americas illustrate the praxis required for improving outcomes"—Provided by publisher.
Identifiers: LCCN 2020031561 (print) | LCCN 2020031562 (ebook) |
  ISBN 9781793624024 (cloth) | ISBN 9781793624048 (pbk)
  ISBN 9781793624031 (epub)
Subjects: LCSH: Forced migration—Government policy. | Forced migration—International cooperation. | Refugees—International cooperation. | Refugees—Government policy.
Classification: LCC HV640 .P367 2020 (print) | LCC HV640 (ebook) |
  DDC 363.5/83—dc23
LC record available at https://lccn.loc.gov/2020031561
LC ebook record available at https://lccn.loc.gov/2020031562

This book is dedicated to the trailblazers, the pioneers of resettlement social science—David Brokensha, David Butcher, Elizabeth Colson, Thayer Scudder, Alfonso Villa Rojas, Fernando Camara Barbachano, Salomon Nahmad, Robert Chambers, Michael Cernea—and to all those who followed and will follow, for pouring their minds, skills, and careers into the betterment of displaced and resettled peoples' lives. And to all those displaced and resettled, in support of your struggles to achieve social and economic justice.

Contents

Acknowledgments

This book began as an article manuscript to honor the legacy of Elizabeth Colson, distinguished professor of anthropology, trailblazing social activist, and pioneer of involuntary resettlement social science. The bulk of the book has been written while in lockdown in the midst of the global novel coronavirus pandemic, in which hundreds of thousands of people have lost their lives, and millions of people have been economically displaced, many of whom will end up having lost their livelihoods permanently. We can only hope that they will be assisted in establishing new livelihoods and rebuilding their lives, which is a central theme of this book, by their communities, their societies, and their governments around the world.

Bill Partridge would like to thank David for accepting the challenge of working with him on this book and for the splendid and singular contributions he has made. Bill would also like to acknowledge and give thanks to Michael M. Cernea, good friend and colleague at the World Bank, for his tutelage and wise counsel; to Professor Thayer Scudder, who started him on this journey and never failed to provide insight and encouragement over the years; and to María Clara Mejía, his loving spouse and soul mate, an internationally recognized and widely respected anthropologist and resettlement specialist, and his constant source of inspiration.

David would like to thank Bill Partridge—professor, mentor, thesis committee chairman, friend—for his invitation to collaborate on the book; Ted and Carmen Downing for their continued encouragement and support; Brooke Wilmsen and Susanna Price for generously sharing their recent published work upon request; and finally, but most importantly, his sister Susan for her constant love and support, as well as her tolerant patience with a stubborn anthropologist brother.

We both would like to express our gratitude to Corporacion Antioquia Presente, Medellin, Colombia and its Executive Director, Marcela Ochoa Bernal, for permitting us to reprint photographs from their Salinas and La Pintada projects on the front cover as well as Alvaro Salgado for designing the front cover.

Finally, we both would like to thank Kasey Beduhn, Associate Acquisitions Editor at Lexington Books, for taking an interest in and encouraging the expansion of the early draft article manuscript into a full-length book, and for all her efforts in guiding us and shepherding the book manuscript through the publication process. Many thanks also to Monica Sukumar for her diligent efforts in accommodating our many requests for making last minute corrections to the manuscript.

Any errors of fact or interpretation are the authors' own, and in no way should be otherwise attributed to any other individuals, organizations, or institutions mentioned in the book.

List of Acronyms

ADB	Asian Development Bank
AfDB	African Development Bank
AIIB	Asian Infrastructure Investment Bank
AIPP	Asia Indigenous Peoples Pact
BINGO	Big International Nongovernmental Organization
BOOT	Build-Own-Operate-Transfer
BP	Bank Procedure
BRI	Belt Road Initiative
CAO	Compliance Advisor Ombudsman
CHESF	Companhia Hidreletrica do Valle do Sao Francisco
CSO	Civil Society Organization
DFAT	Department of Foreign Affairs and Trade
DFDR	Development-Forced Displacement and Resettlement
DPL	Development Policy Loan
DPU	Development Planning Unit
DRM	Disaster Risk Management
DRR	Disaster Risk Reduction
EBRD	European Bank for Reconstruction and Development
ECA	Export Credit Agency
EIR	Extractive Industries Review
ELETROBRAS	Centrais Eletricas Brasileiras, S. A.
EP	Equator Principles
ESCP	Environmental and Social Commitment Plan
ESF	Environmental and Social Framework
ESS	Environmental and Social Standard
ESSD	Environmentally and Socially Sustainable Development

FLACSO	Facultad Latinoamericano de Ciencias Sociales
GEF	Global Environment Facility
GFDRR	Global Fund for Disaster Risk Reduction
GN	Guidance Note
GP	Good Practice
GTZ	German Technical Cooperation Agency
ICDP	Integrated Conservation and Development Project
IDB	Inter-American Development Bank
IDMC	Internal Displacement Monitoring Centre
IDP	Internally Displaced Persons
IED	Independent Evaluation Department
IEG	Independent Evaluation Group
IFC	International Finance Corporation
IIHS	Indian Institute for Human Settlements
INI	Instituto Nacional Indigenista
IOM	International Organization for Migration
IPLC	Indigenous People and Local Communities with Customary Tenure
IRR	Involuntary Risks and Reconstruction Model
ISAGEN	Colombia National Electricity Agency
IUCN	Worldwide Fund for Nature
JICA	Japan International Cooperation Agency
LARR	The Right to Fair Compensation and Transparency in Land Acquisition, Rehabilitation and Resettlement Act
MDFI	Multilateral Development Finance Institution
MFDR	Mining-Forced Displacement and Resettlement
NDB	New Development Bank
NGO	Nongovernmental Organization
NPC	National Power Corporation
NRC	Norwegian Refugee Council
NT2	Nam Theun 2
OD	Operational Directive
OECD	Organization for Economic Cooperation and Development
OMS	Operational Manual Statement
OP	Operational Policy
OPIC	Overseas Private Investment Corporation
OPR	Office of Population Relocation
P4R	Projects for Results
PANAMIN	Presidential Assistant on National Minorities
PAP	Project-Affected Persons/People

PAR	Poverty Alleviation Resettlement
POE	Panel of Experts
PR	Performance Requirement
PS	Performance Standard
RAP	Resettlement Action Plan
SEZ	Special Economic Zone
SHDRI	Second Highway Design and Research Institute
SIA	Social Impact Analysis/Assessment
UN	United Nations
UNDP	United Nations Development Programme
UNHCR	United Nations High Commission for Refugees
UNPFII	United Nations Permanent Forum on Indigenous Issues
USAID	United States Agency for International Development
VGGT	Voluntary Guidelines on Responsible Governance of Tenure
VRA	Volta River Authority
WB	World Bank
WBG	World Bank Group
WCD	World Commission on Dams

Introduction

As the third decade of the twenty-first century begins, all indications are that the number of people forcibly displaced by events both planned and unplanned will continue to increase, thus necessitating their resettlement. The estimated number of physically displaced people continues to grow on an annual basis; the number of those economically displaced drastically exceeds the number of those physically displaced. The globalized neoliberal economic ideology, with its emphasis on unrestrained growth, continues to expand and entrench itself around the world. Emerging market economies are investing billions of dollars into programs of national development that entail the planning and construction of new infrastructure, urban upgrading and expansion, and special economic zones dedicated to free trade. Such huge programs of construction require the acquisition, expropriation, or concession of enormous amounts of land and, consequently, the displacement of millions of people.

Countries and corporations struggling to compete successfully in the global market economy are investing billions in the extraction and conversion of natural resources into sources of energy, technology, and other commodities. Free-flowing rivers are impounded to generate electricity. Large areas of substrates rich in mineral and metal resources are mined to convert those substances into energy, and their component parts are used for the ever-growing varieties of new technologies. Large areas of forest are cleared for the timber to be converted into commercial commodities, or the cleared land is used for the industrial production of cash crops, oil and fiber by-products, and a variety of animals for food. These extractive industries require the acquisition or concession of expansive tracts of land and the displacement of millions of people.

Almost ironically, at the same time, it has long been recognized that large areas of the earth's biosphere are unique enough in the diversity of plants, animals, and other natural resources to warrant protection from exploitation. There has emerged, consequently, a global system of national and international parks, reserves, sanctuaries, and other protected areas. Gazetting or demarcating these protected areas requires the cordoning off of hundreds of thousands of hectares of land and prohibiting or restricting access to it and its resources to people who formerly resided in and around the areas and utilized such resources for their livelihoods. In other words, in many instances globally, the establishment of protected areas requires the physical and economic displacement of hundreds of thousands, if not millions, of people.

The recent resurrection of populist, nationalist ideologies has exacerbated the already entrenched beliefs that certain types of people, political and religious systems, and economic philosophies are superior to others. These insidious ideologies have translated into the xenophobic persecution of and systematic discrimination against various kinds of "minority" populations, in some cases by refusing to recognize them as citizens. At its most extreme, such persecution takes the form of ethnic cleansing and genocide. More often, it takes the forms of government-sponsored bans, "sweeps" or raids and roundups, detentions, imprisonment, pogroms, and evictions by force of arms, this last resulting in the involuntary displacement of millions. Ultimately, inimical philosophies and worldviews have led to campaigns of armed conflict that may last for decades, displacing millions more. Many continue to languish in refugee camps, without a place to call home.

A growing number of world-renown physical and climate scientists have reached a consensus conclusion that human activities, primarily the burning of fossil fuels, has led to unprecedented warming of the planet. Many warn that official denial and foot-dragging on the issue over the past decades now precludes the resolution of the problem. Climate change is real; its concomitant extreme weather events, increasing in frequency and intensity, are resulting in the displacement of millions due to disasters such as floods, hurricanes, typhoons, tornados, and wildfires stemming from such events. At the same time, population growth and environmental aesthetics have led larger numbers of people to settle in relatively more hazard-prone and risky environments. There is, by most accounts, a global shift of population to the coasts; this is certainly true in the United States. People who crave vistas reside in more remote mountain forests and canyons and along attractive seacoasts, only to be displaced by the increasing and seemingly annual lightning-sparked wildfires and hurricane- and severe storm-generated flooding. In other countries as well as the West, millions of people live on steep slopes, in toxic towns and villages in proximity to chemical and other poisonous waste dumps, and in otherwise polluted and hastily built slums on the outskirts of cities. These populations

are at an increasingly greater risk of being displaced and losing their livelihoods, if not their lives, to industrial accidents, earthquakes, and other catastrophes. Millions of people are displaced annually by such disasters.

It should be clear to the reader by now that the common denominator in all
these events and processes is the involuntary or forced physical and economic
displacement of millions upon millions of people. This book, however, is not
so much about involuntary or forced displacement per se. Rather, the book
focuses on what we can hope to achieve, utilizing the social science knowledge base accumulated over seventy years of empirical, practical experience
on the ground, in assisting the successful *resettlement* of displaced communities and their subsequent social, economic, and human development.
Experience has shown that displaced people can be resettled so they are
able to live sustainable, productive lives, improve their living standards, and
experience well-being, however they themselves define it. Involuntary displacement is devastating and traumatic, to be sure, and there is a vast literature describing it in detail. Empirical and project-level experience, however,
demonstrates that adequately financed resettlement, conducted in a socially
and culturally compatible manner in full collaboration with those displaced,
combined with creative thinking and innovative solutions deriving from the
knowledge input of all participants, opens up possibilities for new opportunities for subsequent social and economic development once the bases of
reestablishing displaced communities have been achieved. Our focus here
is on "resettlement with development," in a context where "development"
entails "the freedom to choose among opportunities for realizing one's human
potential" (Sen 1999).

RESETTLEMENT WITH DEVELOPMENT

Because community displacement destroys a previous way of life, all involuntary resettlement operations must be conceived and implemented as development projects designed to build new livelihoods. It is impossible to restore,
reconstruct, or reestablish the culture and community that have been erased
by forced displacement and resettlement (Downing and Garcia-Downing
2009; Oliver-Smith 2018, 28). Too often those directing or advising resettlement operations have focused their efforts upon restoring what went before,
the traditional, the known, rather than recognizing what the displaced can see
facing them right before their eyes—that they are being swept up in dramatic,
unpredictable, often frightening, all-encompassing processes of social, economic, political, and environmental change.

Much of the experience over the last few decades with involuntary resettlement has been negative. Resettlement conceptualization, planning, and

implementation have usually been deficient, many resettlement operations becoming failures to the point of impoverishing the affected communities. Much of the reason for such failure is the too frequent focus on restoring a previous way of life, reestablishing what administrators, planners, and others responsible imagine the traditional way of life to be. Such a misperception fails to recognize and respect the active agency of displaced people, their capacity for adaptation, creativity, learning, and innovation.

The social costs of involuntary resettlement that fails to respect the dignity, integrity, capabilities, and worth of the displaced people are enormous. Much of our experience over the last few decades has shown that too often resettlement planning and implementation have been deficient to the point of impoverishing the affected families. This conclusion is based on the accumulated evidence of independent research by anthropologists, economists, and others that shows poor resettlement results in lifetimes of investment and achievement being swept away, socioeconomic production systems and incomes being destroyed, social organization and social structure being dismantled, and attitudes of hostility and sullen resentment of authorities responsible for the disaster quickly coming to dominate the public culture of the displaced (Cernea 1997; Cernea and Guggenheim 1993; Oliver-Smith 2009; Partridge 1989).

Yet when involuntary resettlement does respect the dignity, integrity, capabilities, and worth of the affected families, the outcomes are often positive. That is the subject of this book. Positive outcomes occur where affected people are made full participants in resettlement operations that have as their objectives rebuilding livelihoods and improving standards of living. Independent research by anthropologists, economists, and others has documented the positive results of reestablishing livelihoods through resettlement from lands subject to frequent flooding, from unstable slopes prone to landslides, from low-lying areas polluted by runoff of human and animal waste, from locales devastated by volcanic eruptions, hurricanes, or other disasters, from regions victimized by armed conflict, and from areas expropriated for large-scale economic development projects like dams.

Much of the documentation of resettlement outcomes by independent researchers is from large-scale development projects financed by the World Bank, the Inter-American Development Bank, the International Finance Corporation, and the Asian Development Bank. That is because in the 1980s, these multilateral development finance institutions took the lead in establishing involuntary resettlement policies that are broadly similar and which apply to all their operations. Taken together, the involuntary resettlement policies of the Multilateral Development Finance Institutions (MDFIs) can be considered widely accepted international standards (African Development Bank 2003; Asian Development Bank 1995, 2003, 2009; Inter-American

Development Bank 1997a; International Finance Corporation 2006, 2007, 2012; Organization for Economic Cooperation and Development 1992; World Bank 1980, 1990, 2001, 2013). The MDFIs fomented much of the research on resettlement not only to provide practical guidance to member countries based on experience but also to document the utility and efficacy of the international standards for future operations. These policies have, in turn, stimulated some countries, such as China, India, Kenya, and others, to follow suit, to establish their own national policies and legal frameworks to regulate involuntary resettlement.

ORGANIZATION OF THE BOOK

The central feature of this book is the presentation of lessons learned, both positive and negative, in the recent past about involuntary resettlement in development projects. It gathers together and summarizes selected, well-documented cases from Latin America, East Asia, South Asia, and Africa. It is to be hoped that some, if not most, of these lessons will be instructive as practitioners, policymakers, and scholars in the future come to grapple with increases in massive displacement of communities due to development, resource extraction, conflict, disasters, and climate change. Prior to the presentation of cases, however, we discuss the larger historical, policy, and project contexts within which they are embedded.

The book is organized into three parts. Part I summarizes the background, history, and recent developments regarding the issue of involuntary displacement and resettlement and consists of three chapters. Chapter 1 identifies the current trends and major drivers or causes of involuntary displacement. Chapter 2 presents an abbreviated history of the early resettlement failures and the resulting outrage of project-affected people and the larger civil society, which led to the promulgation of a resettlement safeguard policy, innovated by World Bank social scientists and consultants. The chapter traces the evolution and refinement of that policy and its implementation, or lack thereof, throughout the 1980s, 1990s, and into the 2000s and the internal social, political, and institutional dynamics at play during those periods. It then briefly addresses what many experts perceive as the recent dilution and weakening of the most recent World Bank resettlement policy, OP 4.12, replaced by an Environmental and Social Framework (ESF) consisting of an overarching Environmental and Social Policy and accompanying performance standards (ESS), including a standard for involuntary resettlement (Environmental and Social Standard, or ESS 5). The new framework and standards seem to those critical of the latest conversion to abdicate the World Bank from responsibility and transfer to borrowers increased responsibility and obligation to meet the standard. Chapter 3 summarizes the diffusion of World Bank resettlement policy provisions and directives internationally to other MDFIs, bilateral institutions, and private sector lenders, the culmination of which currently provides resettlement experts with a substantial body of policy proscriptions, directives, and provisions which, when considered as a combined whole, constitute what we call the *International Standard for Involuntary Resettlement*, a global standard for dealing effectively with involuntary resettlement. The concept of the "International Standard for Involuntary Resettlement" is defined as *that body of provisions and directives, derived from decades of empirical observation and results on the ground, comprised of and subsumed within both prior safeguard policies and current performance standards of development finance institutions, both multilateral and bilateral, public and private.* While the concept is inclusive of all prior policy provisions and current standards of the MDFIs, we argue that the concept is best exemplified by WB OD 4.30 of 1990, which we, along with Scudder (2005, 278), believe to be the strongest policy statement on involuntary resettlement to date. The concept necessarily excludes various sets of guidelines set forth by international agencies, research institutions, nongovernmental organizations, and think tanks. As immensely important, valuable, and worthy of application as they are, they are guidelines, and thus voluntary, not binding on anyone. The chapter subsequently takes stock of the current state of borrower countries' legal and policy frameworks for handling involuntary resettlement.

Chapter 3 concludes with the explication of our position, following the eminent economist Amartya Sen (1999, 2009), regarding the moral responsibility and obligation, on the part of country governments and their constituent ministries, financing institutions, including managers and staffs, specialists and consultants, as well as nongovernmental organizations, and any others responsible for conducting resettlement operations, where they cannot be avoided or when they are necessary to save lives, in a socially and culturally appropriate manner in close and constant collaboration with the affected people as full partners and fellow citizens. Project-affected people must be fairly and justly compensated for *all* their losses, both material and economic, provided with adequate land and security of tenure, infrastructure, and public services to reconstitute their communities, and the necessary training, education, and other assistance to enhance successful adaptation and for rebuilding their livelihoods in the new environment and conditions. Wherever possible, they must be entitled *with priority*, over and above compensation and other forms of restitution, to receive a fair proportion of project revenues as full beneficiaries (Cernea 2007, 2008, his emphasis). Most importantly, resettled people must be given the *freedom to choose* among alternative opportunities which may arise in the aftermath of resettlement. The ultimate objectives of resettling forcibly displaced communities must be their *sustainable social, economic, and human development, improvement in standards of living,* and *achieving well-being as defined by them.* In short and in other words, resettlement operations should be carried out *in accordance with the strongest directives and provisions of both prior safeguard policies and current standards,* that is to say, in accordance with what we define here as the International Standard for Involuntary Resettlement.

Part II explores the application of effective international standards and best practices in contemporary resettlement operations. It bears mentioning that we do not compare and contrast or evaluate the merits and faults of the various resettlement theories or models formulated based on both field and policy research experience (e.g., Scudder and Colson's "stage" model, Cernea's IRR model, de Wet's spatial and complexity model, or Downing and Garcia-Downing's routine/dissonant culture and psycho-socio-cultural model). The proponents of each model have published extensively on them in comparison to the others (Cernea 1999, 2000, 2018; Scudder 2005, 2009; de Wet 2006, 2009; Scudder and Colson 1982; Downing 1996; Downing and Garcia-Downing 2009), and they have recently been subjected to critical evaluation (e.g., Hay, Skinner, and Norton 2019; Kircherr and Charles 2016; Wilmsen, Adjartey, and van Hulten 2018). We direct the reader to that literature.

Proper planning, design, and implementation of resettlement operations require a deeper understanding of the human communities facing displacement and resettlement beyond simplistic characterizations as "poor," "marginalized," "peasant," and such. Community life and culture, and people's daily interaction with both, is very much more complex. Chapter 4 lays out our understanding of community life and culture and its complexity, grounded in empirical social anthropological research, highlighting those elements that are critical to sound planning, design, and implementation of resettlement operations.

Chapters 5 through 9 present case examples of good practices in implementing the International Standard for Involuntary Resettlement, the major provisions and directives of which are contained within both earlier international safeguard policies and the performance standards currently in force, along with a few in which implementation of the directives contained in the International Standard were ignored, bypassed, or resulted in unintended consequences due in part to lack of foresight. The cases are drawn from global experience with involuntary resettlement of the World Bank, the International Finance Corporation, the Inter-American Development Bank, the Asian Development Bank, as well as the experiences of other multilateral and bilateral government finance institutions. While they highlight good practices, it should be emphasized that the case examples do not imply that the projects cited were free of flaws or exemplary in all respects.

Part III concludes the book by addressing the challenges ahead in achieving sustainable social, economic, and human development of communities in the wake of involuntary resettlement, as discussed in chapter 10. The chapter argues that social science knowledge and practice are key to achieving that objective. We argue that achieving resettlement with development will require a praxis of ethical commitment to taking politically effective actions to empower displaced communities, accepting the challenge of designing and negotiating project-specific resettlement policy, planning, and implementation together with all stakeholders in community, organizational, and institutional contexts. We argue that such praxis is required to achieve successful resettlement, whether those responsible be national or international nongovernmental organizations, administrative and service agencies of government at all levels, private and public sector business firms, or transnational and multilateral institutions, to confront and correct policy and legal frameworks that deepen exclusion, oppression, poverty, and other forms of exploitation. Such praxis requires dealing with the powerful as well as the powerless in working toward leveling the playing field to permit the active, direct participation of displaced people in the design and execution of their own resettlement, which is the only way to achieve sustainable social, economic, and human development.

We, along with many others, and in accordance with the first provision of all previous and current international standards, advocate the avoidance and/or minimization of involuntary displacement and resettlement as a first matter of priority. But the plain, unavoidable, and incontrovertible fact of the matter is that population resettlement will continue to be necessary due to mega-projects, disasters, climate change, urban development, and armed conflict. Indeed, it is highly likely that the remainder of the century will see the incidence and scale of population displacement dramatically increase compared to that experienced in the past. The present volume simply confronts that fact head-on and, it is hoped, by virtue of presenting empirically documented case examples, makes some instructive contributions to improving the planning, design, implementation, and outcomes of resettlement operations as sustainable social, economic, and human development projects.

Part I

BACKGROUND, HISTORY, AND RECENT DEVELOPMENTS

Chapter 1

Dimensions of Involuntary Displacement and Resettlement

Involuntary displacement is caused by many different events and processes, both planned and unplanned. Research into these causes strongly suggests that the numbers of people involuntarily displaced, by whatever cause, will continue to increase significantly. Considering for the moment the case of development-forced displacement and resettlement, in the hydropower sector alone an estimated 3,700 major dams were under construction or being planned as of 2014, some 847 of which would have a capacity of over 100 megawatts each (Zarfl et al. 2014). Planned hydropower development will be concentrated in major river basins of Southeast Asia, South America, and Africa (up to and over 100 dams each), and to a lesser extent, the Balkans, Caucasus, and Anatolia (26 to 100 dams; Zarfl et al. 2014).

Social scientists specializing in disaster research have documented the dramatic increase in both technological and weather-related disasters, the latter intensifying even more so due to climate change. Disaster- and climate change–forced displacement may perhaps overtake DFDR as the major driver of displacement and resettlement in the coming decades (de Sherbinin, et al. 2011; Oliver-Smith 2018; Oliver-Smith and de Sherbinin 2014).

The displacement and resettlement caused by extractive industries and conservation have become major areas of focus for resettlement scholars and practitioners. The displacement impacts of new lands settlement, colonization schemes, and the expansion of corporate industrial plantation agriculture have long been studied, as have refugees and other internally displaced persons (IDPs) forced to abandon their homes due to armed conflict and other humanitarian crises.

This chapter examines what we know of the incidence and magnitude of forced displacement and resettlement due to all of the aforementioned causes. The first section briefly reviews global trends in the displacement of populations. This is followed by summaries of the events and processes that drive, or cause, forced displacement. For each, examples are provided along with some of the more relevant literature analyzing the actual and potential displacement impacts. We note here that the social science literature on all forms of involuntary displacement and resettlement is voluminous and rapidly growing; thus it is beyond the scope of this book and our expertise to provide a comprehensive literature review of each category of driver involving displacement and resettlement. Consequently, we limit our citations for the most part to sources which we view as significant or exemplary treatments of the drivers and their displacement effects.

GLOBAL TRENDS

There exist no firm, reliable numbers of people displaced by development, resource extraction, disaster, and other causes. One very recent study analyzing data from twenty-nine large dam projects concludes that data regarding the numbers of displaced and resettled people are "greatly dispersed" and that "data in the dam industry and resettlement data must be treated with caution" (Kircherr et al. 2019, 208). An analysis of a 2012–2014 World Bank portfolio review found that the best indicator of the accelerating trend in forced displacement is the number of projects that trigger the Bank's Involuntary Resettlement Policy. Findings show more than a doubling in the proportion of projects triggering the policy over a twenty-year period, from 12 percent of 431 closed projects to 29 percent of 747 active projects. When the 41 percent of the 245 projects still in the pipeline is added, it increases the growing trend to 3.5 times (Cernea and Maldonado 2018, 5–6). Astonishingly, Cernea and Maldonado (2018 38, n. 3) point out that no other MDFI that they know of has published portfolio reviews on resettlement performance, despite having policies on transparency, accountability, and information disclosure.

It is distressing that the World Bank and other MDFIs are unable to provide solid numbers of people displaced and/or resettled by the projects which they finance with any precision, especially since they pride themselves at quantifying in excruciating detail other things they consider important. This may, perhaps, be due to the all too common finding, usually after construction has already begun that planning and appraisal calculations most often tend to greatly *underestimate and undercount* the number of people projected to be displaced and/or resettled by any given project.

Consequently, the best numbers at our disposal are mere estimates from a variety of sources. In terms of development-forced displacement (DFDR), the World Bank, for example, in 1994 estimated that ten million people per year were displaced by hydropower, urban, and transport projects during the decade of the 1990s, for a total of 100 million people. Between 2001–2010, it is estimated that fifteen million people per year were displaced, totaling 150 million. The estimate for 2011–2020 exceeds twenty million per year, for a total of 200 million or more (Cernea and Maldonado 2018, 4). They point out that these are very likely conservative estimates.

The World Commission on Dams (WCD) in 2000 estimated that eighty million people were displaced by dams in the last century; Scudder (2011) estimated more than 200 million people displaced by all infrastructure development in the past century, with 40 percent of that total displaced by dams alone. In terms of economic displacement, dam construction negatively affects a staggering 472 million people worldwide estimated to be living downstream from dams (Richter et al. 2010). On a national scale, Cernea (2004) estimated that 22.5 million people had been displaced by dams in China. Shi (2018, 144) calculates that over eighty million people were displaced by all development projects in China between 1950 and 2015; over twenty million by dams and reservoirs, sixteen million by communications and transportation projects, and forty-four million by urban and other projects. For India, Mathur (2013, 2016) reports an estimated sixty million or more displaced by development in the last sixty years, some being displaced multiple times, and a projected drastic increase in scale and magnitude.

There is no global or reliable estimate of people displaced by mining. The best that can be said is that the number is significant and growing (Downing 2002; Owen and Kemp 2015). The UN High Commissioner for Refugees (UNHCR 2018) estimates that a record high of 68.5 million people were displaced by war, violence, and persecution in 2017. Various reports estimate that tens of millions of people have been displaced by the establishment of parks, refuges, and other protected areas for conservation purposes, a figure that is highly contested (Agrawal and Redford 2009, 1). A 2015 report by the Norwegian Refugee Council (NRC) and Internal Displacement Monitoring Centre (IDMC) estimates that, on average, 26.4 million people have been displaced by disasters each year since 2008. An estimated 17.5 million people were displaced by weather-related disasters and 1.7 million displaced by geophysical hazards in 2014. Asian countries, China, India, and the Philippines in particular, accounted for 87 percent of the people displaced by disasters in 2014, with an estimated total of 16.7 million displaced.

DRIVERS/CAUSES OF DISPLACEMENT

UN-Habitat listed five major causes of involuntary resettlement—urban development, large-scale infrastructure projects, disasters and climate change, mega-events, and the global financial crisis (du Plessis 2011; Farha 2011). To this list can be added several additional drivers or causes of displacement. Each is discussed subsequently.

Development

By far the most significant driver of forced displacement and resettlement is the execution of planned development projects in several sectors. It is safe to say that development undertakings have caused the physical and economic displacement of hundreds of millions of people. As has been well documented, the vast majority of those displaced has been, and continues to be, poor and minority ethnic groups, including indigenous and tribal peoples.

Infrastructure, Energy, and Public Works

Large-scale infrastructure development projects such as hydroelectric and irrigation dams, airports, roads and expressways, transmission lines, industrial parks, and the like displace tens of millions of people every year (see above). Such displacement is usually justified as serving a public good, which is the case for only certain segments of the public. Land is usually acquired or expropriated for such massive undertakings through the use (and abuse) of "eminent domain," which allows the state to take private properties for some public purpose or public good. Infrastructure projects include significant capital investment from corporations and other private sector actors in addition to public resources. People displaced by development projects, if unassisted to reestablish their livelihoods, inevitably have no choice but to migrate to the city slums, exacerbating already miserable conditions. In the case of dams, downstream populations often suffer more long-term adverse impacts on their lives and livelihoods due to overall decreased flow combined with erratic and unpredictable flooding generated by water releases from the dam. In addition, they may face the additional threat of dam collapse, most recently exemplified by the Xe Pian-Xe Namnoy Dam in southern Laos, which collapsed in January 2018, killing seventy-one and destroying thousands of homes and hectares of farmland, possibly due to construction company corner-cutting for the maximization of profit (Inclusive Development International and International Rivers 2019).

Urban Development and Expansion

Urban development continues to be a major cause of involuntary displacement and resettlement (Koenig 2009). In China and countries of Latin America, for example, the number of projects financed and located in urban areas has dramatically increased, surpassing projects in rural areas (McDonald 2006; Mejia 1999). Recent reports document that cities are increasingly the destination of people displaced by conflict, violence, and other humanitarian crises (IDMC 2019; World Bank 2019). Five percent of the population of Bogota, Colombia, for example, consists of 386,000 IDPs, an estimated 238,000 fleeing the recent crisis in Venezuela (IDMC 2019, 77). Over and above the increasing influx of IDPs and other migrants, cities are rapidly increasing in population around the world, and this rapid urban growth is often unplanned, unmanaged, and insufficient in terms of the provision of land, housing, services, and basic infrastructure. The result is a significant increase in the number of slum dwellers, with nearly one billion people now living in urban slums, most without secure tenure. Governments have responded by instituting master plans for urban development that usually incorporate forced displacement as a means of clearing land to make it available to private investors for profitable development as well as for parks and recreation areas and expressways and their interchanges, and for the beautification of urban landscapes. Most such displacement occurs from areas with low incomes, poor housing, and without secure tenure—obvious targets for government authorities looking for cheap land to expropriate—disproportionately affecting the poor, minority groups, indigenous people, and female-headed households.

Free Trade and Special Economic Zones

Special Economic Zones (SEZs) are designated and established to encourage foreign direct investment, achieve rapid economic growth, and correct trade imbalances. Typically, these zones are further broken down into free trade zones, enterprise zones, export processing zones, free ports, industrial estates, and the like centered on a myriad of facilities and products and commodities destined for world markets. They tend to be located both in and around coastal cities to facilitate the global shipment and exchange of trade goods to world markets. They generally consist of industrial parks and factories of various kinds (e.g., chemical and auto plants). Policies and legislation enabling the development of SEZs provide investors with tax breaks and incentives while at the same time allowing the SEZs to develop supporting infrastructure in the location without any formal approval or prior assessment in terms of environmental and social impacts. The first such zones were established in the 1950s. Latin America and East Asia established SEZs in the 1970s. For example, in China by 1984 there were fourteen cities designated as SEZs, mostly along the southern coast. Hundreds of thousands of people are economically displaced, if not physically displaced, by SEZs, resulting from losing large portions of their farmlands, pastures, and common property.

Much of the recent research on displacement and resettlement impacts of SEZs focuses on India. Prior to the passage of India's 2013 "Right to

Fair Compensation and Transparency in Land Acquisition, Rehabilitation and Resettlement Act" (commonly referred to as the LARR), land for SEZs and all other purposes was acquired according to the colonial 1894 Land Acquisition Act through eminent domain. India passed an SEZ Act in 2005, which was amended in 2007. Asher and Atmavila (2011, 318) note that there was no provision for the land acquisition process in the legislation.

The land acquired is typically fertile agricultural land and rain-fed, single-cropped land which subsistence farmers lease out to pastoralists in fallow periods, the combination of which constitutes their livelihoods. In addition, state-owned forest land and land perceived to be empty, or "wastelands" are acquired. In actuality, such wastelands most often are the collective, common property of forest-dwelling *adivasis* and the landless, who reside there, cultivate small plots and harvest fuel, fodder, and non-timber forest produce for as much as 12 percent of their household's incomes (Asher and Atmavila 2011, 322). Asher and Atmavila (2011, 319–20) reported that India had "a staggering 513" government- and privately controlled SEZs by the first decade of the twenty-first century, located in nineteen states and territories, established both prior to and since the passage of its SEZ Act of 2005. Levien (2011, 454) reported an approved total of 581. Hundreds more are either in the pipeline or have received "in-principle approval" by central and state governments. For the latter, the land to be acquired totaled 200,000 hectares, greater than the land area of Delhi, which would require the displacement of an estimated 100,140 small farmer households (with an average of 5 persons) and 82,000 farm-worker households. In other instances, agricultural land is converted into "urbanizable" land, which is then used for the construction of upscale housing, resorts, and other real estate ventures.

Civil society resistance has led to the cancellation, withdrawal, or significant slowing of several SEZ projects. Following several violent protests in response to the acquisition of land for conversion to nonagricultural uses, perhaps most infamously the 2007–2008 protests in Singur and Nandigram, the government largely ceded the land acquisition process solely to private developers. They were required to negotiate directly with the landowners for purchase at fair market value, thus increasing the potential for coercion, fraud, and "divide and conquer" strategies for obtaining land without state permission and protections, which violated legal provisions preventing the transfer of agricultural land to private parties (Sharma 2009, 212). For additional case studies, see Sharma (2009) and Guha (2009).

Extractive Industries

Another major driver of involuntary displacement and resettlement is the land-extensive extraction of natural resources harvested for wood, precious minerals, and metals (see Appel 2019; Appel, et al. 2015; Bebbington and Bury 2015; Sawyer and Gomez 2014 for overviews and case studies). These and other megaprojects are usually designed and implemented by large multinational corporations and consortiums with the assistance of national, regional, and local governments, which provide tax breaks and incentives, financial assistance, as well as concession or acquisition of huge amounts of land area that have been targeted as source areas for the resource to be harvested. They are assisted by the MDFIs who provide funding and regulatory guidance in partnership with private sector investors (Hatcher 2014).

Mining

It is generally recognized among specialists that anthropologist Theodore Downing was the first to draw systematic attention to the issue of displacement and resettlement caused by mining (Downing 2002a; Owen and Kemp 2015, 479). Since then, mining-forced displacement and resettlement (MFDR) has become a subspecialty of resettlement scholarship and practice with a burgeoning literature of case studies, policy analysis, and remedial recommendations (see Cochrane 2017; Owen and Kemp 2017; Niederberger, et al. 2016).

Mining proceeds in various ways, with the most common form of mining being open-pit mining, consisting simply of excavating a giant hole in the earth to obtain the subsurface minerals or metals and separating them from the surrounding soil, rock, and processing water using various chemical methods. The backfill is typically dumped at the periphery of the mine itself, as are the multiple chemical solutions used in the process. Liquid wastes are also stored in large tailings dams in proximity to the mine itself. As Owen et al. (2019) point out, "most large-scale mines produce significantly more waste than economic minerals," with an estimated fourteen billion tons of waste generated in 2010. The best case studies, among many, of mining and its environmental and social consequences include the Grande Carajas iron ore mine in Brazil (Treece 1987), the Cerro Colorado copper mine in Panama studied by Gjording (1991), the Ok Tedi and Porgera gold mines in Papua New Guinea studied by Hyndman (1994), Kirsch (1995, 2001a, 2001b, 2006, 2014), and Golub (2014) and Jacka (2015), respectively, the Bibiyana Gas Field in Bangladesh (Gardner 2012) and the Yanacocha and Antamina Mines in Peru. The latter was studied by Szablowski (2007), who explicitly linked the case to World Bank safeguard policies on involuntary resettlement and indigenous peoples. The displacement effects of coal mining in India are covered by Mathur (2008) and Lahiri-Dutt (2014), among others.

Mining presents somewhat unique displacement and resettlement risks to affected communities. Communities displaced and resettled as a result of mining projects face a continuing threat of multiple potential displacements because of the mine's continuously expanding footprint. As veins tap out, the mine needs to expand the area of mineral/metal extraction, which can cause resettled communities to be displaced again and again. Communities displaced by mines and resettled nearby often are left with contaminated surface and groundwater and soils resulting from tailings and other waste disposal methods. An additional risk is displacement caused by tailings dam failures, resulting in massive toxic floods of chemicals, wastewater, backfill rock, and soil, most recently illustrated dramatically and tragically by the 2019 failure at the Corrego do Feijao iron ore mine in Brumadinho, Minas Gerais, Brazil, which killed more than 230 people and contaminated large areas of agricultural land, the Bento Rodrigues tailings dam at the Samarco mine in the same state four years earlier (both owned by the same company), among others (Owen, Kemp, Lebre, Svobodova, and Murillo 2019). These examples point up how development and disaster can be inextricably linked.

Oil and Gas

The MDFIs provide funding support to government, corporate, and consortium-financed oil and natural gas extraction projects. Extraction is carried out via increasingly sophisticated drilling technologies and techniques, as well as more traditional methods, which often result in the physical and economic displacement of communities, leaving in their wake landscapes contaminated due to disposal methods very similar to those of the mining industry or, in the case of pipelines, leaks of various magnitudes that may or may not be repaired. Pipeline projects and their associated infrastructure (roads, pumps, wells, and so forth) frequently require the displacement and resettlement of communities in the right of way along the many kilometers of the pipeline route. Many more others are economically displaced, losing income from access to agricultural land and forest or bush resources.

Perhaps the most visible and internationally known example is the Chevron Texaco case in the Ecuadorian Amazon and its environmental and social impacts on indigenous peoples, which is currently still being litigated in the courts with anthropologists serving as expert witnesses for both plaintiff and defendant. The Amazon case was first brought to the world's attention by Kimmerling (1991) and has since been the subject of numerous studies (e.g., Sawyer 2004 and Cepek 2018). Many such projects have been and remain contentious and controversial. A few examples include the World Bank–supported Chad-Cameroon Pipeline Project, the IDB-supported Camisea Gas Pipeline Project in Peru, the Cuiaba Pipeline Project in Bolivia (Hindery 2013) financed by the World Bank and US Overseas Private Investment

Corporation (OPIC), and the Baku-Tbilisi-Ceylan Pipeline Project in Georgia (Barry 2013), partly financed by the IFC.

Numerous reports indicate that a boom in oil extraction is occurring in African countries such as Uganda, fostering physical and economic displacement, land speculation, restrictions on access to common property resources and ethnic conflict, among other impacts (Ogwang and Vanclay 2019; Ogwang, Vanclay and van den Assem 2018, 2019). The social and environmental impacts of oil in Nigeria have been documented by Watts (2001, 2004, 2012; Watts and Kashi 2008).

Commercial Forestry

The commercial exploitation of forests, particularly in the humid tropics and subtropics, has historically caused the physical and economic displacement of many people, particularly those of indigenous ancestry. Land and forest tenure laws have typically ignored, if not outright excluded, the recognition of the communal tenure systems of forest dwellers by legally categorizing forest land as belonging to the state throughout the world.

The MDFIs have long funded projects in the forest sector, supporting the extraction of valued timber exported for paper, pulpwood, furniture, construction materials, and for domestic fuel in the form of charcoal to meet the ever-increasing demand. To take but one example, the World Bank reports on its website that its portfolio of investment in the forest sector totals $3.05 billion for 2019.

Since the recognition of the reality of climate change, financiers are increasingly cognizant of the value of forests as carbon sinks and have prioritized funding projects that are explicitly dedicated to sustainable forestry, recognize the land tenure rights and forest management systems of indigenous, and other forest-dwelling peoples and include them in the planning design and implementation of community forest initiatives. Some of the most successful of the community forest enterprises have been documented in several Mexican states (Bray et al. 2005).

World Bank and IFC financing of extractive megaprojects, and the severe, adverse environmental and social impacts of such interventions led to massive international civil society backlash in the forms of protest and resistance campaigns coordinated by several environmental groups and NGOs. This backlash led the Bank in 2000 to commission an Extractive Industries Review, which included multi-stakeholder consultations and resulted in the completion of a series of independent reports assessing World Bank Group (WBG) support for extractive industry projects and their environmental and social consequences (World Bank 2003a, b). The review led to new project requirements regarding disclosure, revision of safeguard policies and environmental and social performance standards regarding indigenous peoples and participation, capacity-building for companies, and the establishment of an Advisory Board. The Extractive Industries Review is carried out annually.

Agribusiness

The expansion of agribusiness in the form of plantations for the production of export crops such as palm oil, sugarcane, cotton, soybean, and tropical fruits, as well as beef cattle ranches, displaces tens of thousands of small-holder farmers, farm laborers, and indigenous people. In some instances, such enterprises purchase the land needed for conversion to agribusiness. But in many instances, the land is annexed, claimed, or colonized by politically and economically powerful elites. If the land required for agribusiness is occupied, the elite expel the occupants often through the use or threat of violence. If the land is not occupied, then the elite recruit workers to clear the land and plant pasture for cattle or plantation export crops. The army of laborers clearing forest in the tropics and subtropics are often mistaken by casual observers for small-holder farmer colonists, when in fact they are workers allowed by the elite landowners to clear the land and plant subsistence crops for a few years and then move on to clear more land deeper into the forest (Partridge 1984; Schumann and Partridge 1989).

While the recruitment of colonist farm labor and their migration into the forest might be characterized as voluntary, those involuntarily displaced physically and economically tend to be resident small-holder farmers and indigenous peoples. Most familiar examples are the establishment of banana plantations (Partridge 1979), the 1970s Transamazon Highway (Moran 1981; Smith 1982), Polonoreste (Price 1989), the Indonesian Transmigration Program (Davis and Garrison 1988) and more recently the massive conversion of hectarage from forest to oil palm and soy plantations in Brazil and Southeast Asian countries. These processes have been thoroughly documented by Beckford (1999), Bunker (1983), Davis (1977), Downing, Hecht, Pearson and Garcia-Downing (1992), Halmo and Partridge (1986), Lisansky (1990), and Scudder (1984, 1985).

Biodiversity Conservation and Protected Areas

There are approximately 202,467 protected areas globally, with many more being added every year, primarily in Africa and Asia. Protected areas, originally created to preserve large areas of biological diversity and historical or national and cultural importance, now comprise a significant proportion, up to 15 percent, of the earth's land area and 10 percent of its waters. Large, international conservation organizations have sprung up to lobby and advocate for the preservation of global biodiversity. These include such funding organizations and big international nongovernmental organizations (BINGOS) as the Global Environment Facility (GEF), the World Conservation Union (previously the International Union for the Conservation of Nature, or IUCN), the Nature Conservancy, Conservation International, World Conservation Society, the World Wildlife Fund, Wildlife Conservation Society, World Commission on Parks, and many others. Historically, many, if not most, of these organizations pushed for a conservation agenda based on exclusion, which is to say they worked for the preservation of "pristine" environments or ecosystems untouched by human influence, that is, "nature." We point the reader to numerous collections addressing this topic (Brechin, Wilshusen, Fortwangler, and West 2003; Brockington 2002; Brockington, Duffy and Igoe 2010; Brosius, Tsing, and Zerner 2003; Chatty and Colchester 2002; Redford and Padoch 1992; Stevens 1997, 2014; West and Brechin 1991; Ybarra 2019).

Parks, Reserves, Sanctuaries, and Displacement

As research documented that virtually no ecosystem or environment had not been modified, managed, or altered by human presence, it began to become abundantly clear that an exclusionary "fortress conservation" (Brockington 2002) mindset most often resulted in the physical and economic displacement of resident populations in and around the areas demarcated for protection (Cernea and Schmidt-Soltau 2006). In stark contrast, empirical social and environmental science research has long demonstrated that the subsistence, pastoral, and other management systems of indigenous and traditional peoples actually serve to *increase* biodiversity and sustain ecosystems.

Social scientists, practitioners, and others began to document the magnitude of conservation-related displacements and the compromising of livelihoods of those who resided in and at the margins of all varieties of protected areas. As examples, Chad increased its protected land area from about 1 percent to 9.1 percent, resulting in the displacement of over 600,000 "conservation refugees" (Dowie 2009). One hundred thousand Masaai pastoralists have been displaced from their traditional territories to accommodate parks and reserves in Kenya (Veil and Benson 2004). Geisler (2009) estimated that perhaps fourteen million people were evicted for purposes of conservation since the beginning of the colonial era. India conservatively estimates that 100,000 people have been displaced due to conservation.

Scholars with long experience working with indigenous, tribal, and other traditional peoples began to strongly criticize the large conservation organizations and NGOs as being complicit in the displacement and impoverishment of local communities (e.g., Chapin 2004). This led to an intense debate between conservation scientists (e.g., Agrawal and Redford 2009; Curran et al. 2009; Maisels et al. 2007) and social scientists engaged in field studies of conservation-forced displacement in Central Africa (Cernea and Schmidt-Soltau 2006; Schmidt-Soltau 2003, 2005, 2009; Schmidt-Soltau and Brockington 2007).

It is significant to note here that it was in the context of conservation-forced displacement and resettlement that the very concept of "displacement" was refined and broadened in definition beyond just physical displacement to include those who, while retaining their land and houses, were prohibited from utilizing the varieties of natural resources in their environments to obtain and maintain their livelihoods. In response to the increasing numbers and magnitude of physical and economic displacement of local populations evicted from protected areas, Michael Cernea (2005, 2006) advanced the proposition of "restricted access as displacement" and lobbied for its inclusion in the World Bank safeguard policy on involuntary resettlement. The involuntary restriction of access as a form of displacement was included in the January 2002 revision of Bank Operational Policy (OP) 4.12, and soon replicated by the African Development Bank (2003) and Asian Development Bank (2003), and later by other financial institutions. One outcome of this conceptual and policy advance was the innovation of Integrated Conservation and Development Projects (ICDPs), which began to be funded by the MDFIs and the GEF, with mixed results.

Disasters and Climate Change

Disasters are typically divided into two general types: those that are weather or climate-related and those that are geophysical in nature. They are commonly described as "natural" disasters, owing to their unpredictable and random occurrence. Both types of disasters have historically displaced millions of people and continue to do so. To our knowledge, the earliest social science documentation of a weather-related disaster is Anthony F. C. Wallace's 1954 report of the impacts of a massive tornado on the city of Worcester, Massachusetts, and its residents, and their process of recovery from the event. Although he did not focus on the magnitude of displacement, that engagement led him to formulate a behavioral model of human response to cataclysmic events which he termed "the disaster syndrome."

One of the best systematic investigations of a geophysical disaster is that documented by Oliver-Smith (1986) and Doughty (1999), among others, on the 1970, 7.7 magnitude earthquake in the Peruvian Andes, which resulted overall in the deaths of an estimated 65,000 people and destroyed the community of Yungay, leaving only between 300 and 400 survivors displaced out of a total population of 4,500. Oliver-Smith (1991) subsequently analyzed factors which affect both success and failure in post-disaster resettlement.

In an era of rapid technological innovation associated with the neoliberal quest for expanded growth and increased profits, such technological innovations often become part and parcel of high-risk, high-reward megaprojects, including mining, hydraulic fracturing, and offshore deepwater oil drilling (Sassen 2014; Halmo et al. 2019). In many instances, such megaprojects are implemented using time- and money-saving shortcuts in the use of new technologies. Profit-driven shortcuts, poor planning, siting, and faulty management often lead to catastrophic social, economic, and environmental consequences, including physical and economic displacement of people who live in proximity to these projects and beyond in what have come to be called "anthropogenic disasters." There is a large and rapidly growing literature focused on how development planning, policies, and preferences increase the vulnerability and exposure of human communities to hazards and potential catastrophe (Oliver-Smith and Hoffman 1999, 2020; Hoffman and Oliver-Smith 2002; Hoffman and Barrios 2020; Concha-Holmes and Oliver-Smith 2020). Examples of technological disasters include the tragedies of Bhopal, Deepwater Horizon, and Fukushima. Such catastrophes leave behind in their wake toxic waste dumps, polluted groundwater, and air, which may result in the forced displacement of proximal communities. At the same time, in an era of human-influenced global warming due primarily to carbon emissions, multinational energy companies and consortiums, particularly in the coal industry (the major emitter of carbon into the atmosphere), ironically tend to shun or only reluctantly and occasionally adopt new technologies designed to reduce the emission of carbon because it cuts too deeply into their profit margins.

Climate change and associated extreme weather events and disasters have manifested themselves globally and tend to devastate the lowest income communities (Castro, Taylor, and Brokensha 2012). These communities often occupy areas already prone to flooding, drought, landslides, and other hazards that are particularly hard hit by climate change. Included also are communities destroyed by volcanic eruptions, hurricanes, typhoons, and other calamities. Recent examples include the Asian typhoons, earthquakes in Haiti (Farmer 2011), Japan, and China, the tsunamis devastating Japan, India, Sri Lanka, and Chile, the series of intense hurricanes in the Gulf Coast states of the United States, and the more "slow-onset" disasters (Fiske and Marino 2020) such as the well-documented cases of drought and famine in Africa (Clay and Holcomb 1985; Clay, Steingraber, and Niggli 1988; de Waal 2005; Franke and Chasin 1980; Sen 1981; Watts 2013), and sea level rise affecting coastal areas globally, notably the Pacific Islands and atolls (Lazrus 2012), native Alaskan communities such as Shishmaref (Marino 2015), Kivalina (Shearer 2011), Newtok and others, the US Gulf Coast (Maldonado 2019;

Concha-Holmes and Oliver-Smith 2020), and coral islet dwelling Guna (formerly known as Kuna) indigenous people of the San Blas archipelago on the Caribbean coast of Panama (Displacement Solutions 2014; Lazrus and Arenas 2020), most if not all of whom are seeking assistance for self-resettlement. The most thoroughly documented cases of displacement and resettlement caused by weather-related disasters include Hurricane Katrina on the US Gulf Coast and Hurricane Mitch in Central America (Alaniz 2017; Barrios 2017; Ensor 2009).

While not perpetrated by the state per se, governments have obligations in advance and following disasters to assist those displaced. As climate change deepens in the rest of this century, community displacement and resettlement will intensify in frequency and complexity. Governments have a respon-sibility to ensure resettlement assistance in accordance with international standards and international human rights law. In addition, governments are obligated to prepare and put in place adequate plans to ensure the well-being and livelihoods of residents are safeguarded before, during and after a disas-ter. A number of frameworks for designing and implementing such plans, known as disaster risk reduction (DRR) or disaster risk management (DRM), have been put forward and include the Interagency Standing Committee Operational Guidelines on the Protection of Persons in Situations of Natural Disasters (2011), the 2013 NGO-issued Peninsula Principles (Displacement Solutions 2013), the 2015 Nansen Initiative and Sendai Framework, among others.

Major international efforts have been initiated by UN agencies such as the High Commission for Refugees (UNHCR), MDFIs, private nonprofit research institutions, universities, and other organizations, either individually or in collaboration. Significant among these efforts have been the launch in 2006 of the Global Facility for Disaster Risk Reduction (GFDRR) adminis-tered by the WBG, the cooperative work of the United Nations University Institute on Environment and Human Security and Munich Re Foundation, the collaborative Project on Internal Displacement involving the UNHCR, the UN Organization for Migration (IOM), the Brookings Institution and Georgetown University, and the multicountry project on reducing relocation risk in urban areas carried out by the Bartlett Development Planning Unit (DPU) at University College London (UCL), the Indian Institute for Human Settlements (IIHS) the Latin American Social Science Faculty (Facultad Latinoamericana de Ciencias Sociales, FLACSO), and Makerere University.

The DRR framework includes the planning, design, and implementation of "preventive resettlement" of vulnerable communities increasingly exposed to high levels of risk, hazard, and potential disaster (Oliver-Smith 2020). Guidelines, handbooks, technical reports, and case studies have been writ-ten to inform what is certain to become an increasingly necessary process in the future (Brookings Institution, Georgetown University and UNHCR 2014, 2015; Correa 2011a, b; Ferris 2014; Georgetown University, IOM and UNHCR 2017; Lavell 2016; Oliver-Smith 2009b; Oliver-Smith and Shen 2009). Within the DRR framework, there is a growing conceptual and operational distinction, primarily in the Latin American region, between "resettlement," which alters permanently "the basic structural characteristics of livelihoods, access to resources and social, organizational and environmental relations," and "relocation" for DRR, where resettlement is planned and implemented in an anticipatory or preventive manner, that is, before significant impacts occur (Lavell 2016; Oliver-Smith 2018, 2). Most significantly, all these efforts generally adhere to the provisions and directives entailed within the internationally recognized safeguard policies, standards, and guidelines, as well as international human rights law, including resettlement as a last resort. Anticipatory, preventive resettlement and planned relocations in the context of DRR is discussed in more depth in chapter 5.

Armed Conflict

It goes without saying that, historically, armed conflict is responsible for the involuntary displacement of untold millions. Wars of conquest, wars over land and resources, and civil conflicts, often by proxy, involving ethnic, religious, and political animosities (see below) are inevitably initiated by policies of those in power. The overwhelming majority of those displaced as a result are noncombatants. Major contributions to the analysis of multiple forms of internal displacement include the edited volume by Cernea and McDowell (2000) and Muggah's historical treatment of resettlement in Sri Lanka (2008).

Aside from the Holocaust deeply embedded in national and international memory, many of the recent civil conflicts at the forefront of international consciousness were fostered by racist, ethnic, and religious tensions, often disguised as irreconcilable political or ideological differences. Left unchecked, they resulted in ethnic cleansing and genocide, as in the well-documented cases of Rwanda, Kosovo, Sudan, and Cambodia. To this list, one might add Guatemala and the Democratic Republic of the Congo. A good portion of twentieth-century Latin American history, for example, is dominated by proxy wars involving corporate mercenaries, private armies and paramilitaries and anti-Communist counterinsurgency campaigns masked as drug wars, quashing rebellions, and the like in Chiapas, Mexico (Collier and Quaratiello 2005), Colombia (Partridge 2000, 2001; Tate 2015), El Salvador (Binford 2016; Danner 1994) and Guatemala (Falla 1994; Green 1999; Manz 1988, 2004; Sanford 2003). With specific reference to displacement and resulting resettlement, the best analyses are those of Partridge (2000, 2001) for Colombia and Manz (1988) for Guatemala, who briefly described

conditions in the resettlement camps in Quintana Roo and Campeche occupied by Mayan refugees who were originally relocated to Chiapas.

The growing crisis of internal displacement throughout the 1980s–1990s
led to the adoption by the United Nations of a set of international standards,
the *Guiding Principles on Internal Displacement* in 1998. This achievement
was largely due to the efforts and advocacy of Francis Deng, Roberta Cohen
(Cohen and Deng 1998a, b), Walter Kalin, and others. The process by which
the Guiding Principles came about is concisely summarized by Weiss and
Korn (2006).

It is instructive to note here that, even in contexts of armed conflict, development frequently proceeds unabated. For example, planning commenced
for the development of the Mekong River basin during and immediately
after World War II, culminating with the creation of the Mekong River
Commission (Mekong River Commission Secretariat 2013). The Chad-
Cameroon pipeline project was constructed in the midst of the Chadian civil
conflict; significant loan and oil funds were diverted to purchase arms by the
Chadian government, further fueling the conflict (Horta 2007). In Guatemala,
the IDB and WB-financed Chixoy Hydroelectric Project commenced while
that country's civil war raged. The project area itself was declared a militarized zone in 1978. Affected Mayan communities who opposed the project
and refused to resettle were massacred by the Guatemalan army in a scorched
earth campaign that was later adjudicated as genocide (Johnston 2009).

Racism, Ethnic, and Religious Discrimination

As alluded to in the previous section, much of the recent armed conflict is
fostered by ethnic and/or religious differences and tensions, if not outright
racism. In the wake of 9/11, such xenophobic tendencies have been greatly
exacerbated as part and parcel of resurrected nationalist ideologies. While
genocide is rooted in "annihilating difference" (Hinton 2002), more common
today is the ideology of "excluding difference." Thus, all Muslims are sus-
pect, resulting in visa restrictions and proposed travel bans. Mexican migrants
are collectively branded as drug dealers, rapists, and criminals, resulting in
the militarization of the US southern border.

In China, reports suggest that Uyghur and other Muslim minorities are
being removed from autonomous regions as part of labor resettlement programs with the objective of providing Chinese factories with a cheap labor
force. In the most recent incidence of systematic violence approaching
genocide, Myanmar military forces have engaged in a campaign of ethnic
cleansing in that country's Rakhine state and forced the deportation and displacement of Rohingyas, an ethnic and religious minority, based on a 1982
citizenship law that classified them as stateless and illegal. Over one million

Rohingyas now occupy refugee camps in Bangladesh; the 300,000 Rohingyas still in Myanmar live mostly in concentration camps under heavy security. The International Criminal Court of Justice ruled in February 2020 on a legal case brought by the African nation of Gambia that Myanmar must prevent any further acts of genocide, preserve evidence of atrocities and other crimes against the minority, grant Rohingya full citizenship without discrimination, and repatriate refugees back to their home state in Myanmar (Zaman 2019a, 2020a).

In India, the controversial 2019 Citizenship Law of India and National Registry of Citizens supported by Assam nationalist political interests has put approximately twenty million people, including almost two million Bengali-speaking Muslims, known as Miya, along with Bengali-speaking Hindus at risk of being deported as illegal foreigners, despite a long history of settlement and citizenship in the northeastern state of Assam (Zaman 2019b, 2020b).

Perhaps the most thoroughly documented case of forced resettlement due to xenophobia-driven racism and discrimination from a social science perspective is the forced relocation of Japanese Americans to concentration camps during World War II. Studies include those by Edward Spicer and collaborators (1946), Conrad Arensberg (1942), Solon Kimball (1946) and Alexander Leighton (1945).

Other Drivers of Population Displacement

Just as the MDFIs consider the reduction or alleviation of poverty to be their main objective, nation-states have implemented programs aimed toward achieving the same objective. China, for example, has since at least 2001 engaged in a national program of Poverty Alleviation Resettlement (PAR), which has intensified since 2015. More than twelve million people have been resettled, mostly to urban peripheries from rural and risk-prone, hazardous environments, with ten million more expected to be resettled between 2016 and 2020. The program has been officially described as one of "voluntary resettlement." One empirical study of resettlers in thirty PAR projects in northwestern China concluded, however, that, while the majority of resettlers (those who were younger, wealthier, and with off-farm jobs) responded to surveys that they had voluntarily resettled, there was inadequate consultation in terms of providing detailed information about the resettlement and inadequate time allowed for considering options. The program is purported to be based on voluntarism, such that people have the freedom to remain in their original settlements. Those who remain behind, however, experience abandonment of the area by government and public services, effectively leaving them in isolated ghost towns, which eventually necessitates their *involuntary* migration to better-serviced areas. Those who do resettle voluntarily often find they have to pay higher rents and utility costs (Lo and Wang 2018; Wilmsen and Wang 2015). The contradictions muddle the distinction between "voluntary" and "involuntary" resettlement.

Mega-events like the Olympic Games or football's World Cup have been a significant cause of forced displacement in some cities throughout the world. In preparation for construction of stadiums, sports arenas and facilities, parking areas, and so forth, for such events, mega-events are used by governments as excuses to push through massive land expropriations, infrastructure schemes, and beautification plans that result in evictions of people living in their path. An example is Beijing, China, where massive destruction of communities took place in preparation for the 2008 Summer Olympic Games.

Economic displacement due to the global financial crisis has had a direct and severe impact on low-income households. A number of interdependent factors combined to produce economic displacement. Escalating rental housing costs, in conjunction with increasing levels of poverty, triggered or exacerbated by the recent global financial crisis, have led to an unprecedented increase in forced displacement. Most such economic evictions stem from the nonpayment of rent or mortgage default; nevertheless, governments still have an obligation under international human rights law to ensure such forced displacement does not result in individuals being rendered homeless and impoverished.

SUMMARY

Whatever the cause, if not planned and implemented in such a way as to provide development assistance, forced displacement and involuntary resettlement almost invariably deepen poverty, particularly for those who are already among the most vulnerable. Whatever the cause, involuntary resettlement risks violation of human rights to nutrition, water, sanitation, health, education, and security of person and property. Whatever the cause, the development of policies and legal frameworks to guide and regulate resettlement of displaced population in such a way as to provide development assistance to displaced communities to rebuild their livelihoods and standards of living has lagged behind while the incidence of community displacement has ballooned.

Chapter 2

The Evolution of Involuntary Resettlement Policy

Development projects are almost always successful in terms of engineering or architectural achievement and their intended objectives, whether it be impounding rivers, generating electricity, the extraction of resources, the improvement of communications, public services, and transportation, or the upgrading of urban infrastructure. When evaluated through a social lens, however, the record of development projects involving involuntary displacement and resettlement has been—and for the most part continues to be—one of tragic, costly failure, resulting in the exacerbation of impoverishment for hundreds of millions of affected people.

A series of failed resettlement efforts and the vehement civil society response to these failures between the late 1950s and the late 1970s facilitated the first-ever promulgation of a policy statement which addressed prioritizing social issues in development project investments that entailed the involuntary displacement and resettlement of affected communities. This chapter begins by chronicling the series of failed resettlement programs in early large dam projects financed in part by the multilateral development finance institutions (MDFIs) such as the World Bank and the Inter-American Development Bank, as well as the governments of Mexico, Brazil, Ghana, India, China, and other developing countries.

The growing resistance and international backlash resulting from this series of resettlement failures soon raised the awareness of staff social scientists at the World Bank regarding what was happening on the ground and convinced them that something needed to be done to address the lack of social oversight in project financing. The next section of this chapter thus traces the development of the first social policy on involuntary resettlement, its subsequent international diffusion across the multilateral, bilateral, and private sector levels of financing, and its periodic revision, updating, and refinement as empirical, project-level results and lessons continued to inform the operational knowledge base.

Despite the international acceptance and adoption of the World Bank policy provisions on involuntary resettlement among multilateral, bilateral, and private donors, who incorporated them virtually in their entirety in their own operations along with a suite of other safeguard policies, the record of resettlement throughout the 1980s–1990s continued to be largely one of failure, perhaps more precisely, one of failure to implement the safeguard provisions entailed within the policy on the ground. Periodic portfolio reviews and institutional evaluations of project-level and sector-wide resettlement safeguard implementation throughout this period, both in-house and independent, repeatedly confirmed the record of failure. It was this record in general, and the experiences with high-profile, controversial projects in India and elsewhere, that garnered fierce global opposition and reputational damage for the Bank.

The reader will notice throughout this chapter recurrent references to the World Bank and the hydropower sector. The reasons are threefold. First, most thoroughly documented of the disastrous early resettlement outcomes occurred in projects that were funded in part by the World Bank. Second, it was the first MDFI to innovate and institutionalize a safeguard policy on involuntary resettlement, which was subsequently adopted internationally, and the World Bank has ever since been perceived to be the global leader or model in terms of involuntary resettlement policy by scholars, policymakers, and practitioners alike. Finally, the emphasis on the hydropower sector reflects the fact that many of the failed early efforts at resettlement occurred in the context of large dam projects and have arguably been the most comprehensively studied. However, the emphasis on hydropower should not be taken to mean that there weren't similar resettlement disasters unfolding in other sectors at the same time.

EARLY RESETTLEMENT DISASTERS

Beginning in the mid-1950s and for over a period of roughly twenty-five years, a series of dam projects involving the large-scale removal and resettlement of thousands of people were carried out in Africa, Southeast Asia, and Latin America. These projects and their negative resettlement outcomes became a source of considerable reputational damage for the MDFIs. Their costly resettlement failures set the stage for the emergence of the World Bank´s policy on involuntary resettlement.

Kariba Dam, Northern and Southern Rhodesia, Africa

Efforts to improve involuntary resettlement operations in projects financed by the MDFIs grew directly out of early anthropological research detailing the failure of such operations. One of the most influential works was Elizabeth Colson´s book *The Social Consequences of Resettlement* (1971) on the forced resettlement of 57,000 people in 199 villages of the Gwembe Tonga. It remains one of the best, most comprehensive studies of the social consequences of poor involuntary resettlement up to the present time. Colson drew upon field research conducted jointly with Thayer Scudder in 1956–1957 before the Tonga of the lower elevations of the Gwembe Valley were forcibly relocated in 1957–1958 due to the construction of the Kariba Dam. Resettlement of the Tonga was poorly conceived and crudely implemented as a last-minute scramble and by many measures a disaster for the affected people. Colson documented in classic ethnographic detail the pain and suffering of the families, the increased morbidity and mortality of the elderly and very young, the loss of legitimacy of local leaders, the dismantling of economic production and distribution systems, and the social upheaval and breakdown of social structure. This was followed by systematic studies in 1962–1963 in which changes in the Tonga community organization, social structure, political life, economic system, ecological adaptation, and ritual life as they had to adapt to the disastrous outcomes were documented.

The Kariba case, according to Scudder, is the only case in which the resettlement process has been studied over a two-generation period from a pre-resettlement baseline (Scudder 2009, 25–26). Scudder, Colson, and later colleagues have documented long-term changes in Gwembe Tonga society ever since, both related and unrelated to Kariba Dam, in what has become perhaps a premier example of long-term field-based anthropological fieldwork. The work continues today in the form of the Gwembe Tonga Research Project (GTRP)—education and the formation of an elite (Scudder and Colson 1980), changes in the ritual and secular functions of beer (Colson and Scudder 1988), economic downturn and its impacts (Scudder 1983, 1984), aging, gender and food security (Cliggett 2005), population growth and settlement of new lands (Cliggett 2000, 2014), the failed World Bank-funded Gwembe Tonga Development Project, and recent World Bank and private development interventions in the Gwembe Valley sixty years after Kariba Dam (Harnish, Cliggett, and Scudder 2019).

Kariba Dam was financed in part by the World Bank. At the time, neither the World Bank nor the other multilateral development banks, nor any member government of these institutions, had developed policies on population displacement and involuntary resettlement. In the absence of its own resettlement policy, the Bank tacitly accepted the borrower government´s legal and policy framework, or the lack thereof as in the case of Kariba, for resettlement of the affected people.

Akosombo Dam, Ghana, West Africa

The formulation of World Bank resettlement policy was also influenced by studies of the disastrous impacts of the resettlement at Akosombo Dam in Ghana by David Brokensha (1963; Brokensha and Scudder, 1968), Robert Chambers (1970), David Butcher (1970), and others. Downstream impacts of the dam have been documented by Tsikata (2006). What follows below is based on the summaries of the project and its resettlement impacts by Tamakloe (1994) and Raschid-Sally et al. (2008).

The dam on the White Volta River began construction in 1962, creating a reservoir covering 8,500 square kilometers. The project necessitated the resettlement of between 78,000 and 80,000 people comprising nine ethnic groups inhabiting between 740 and 756 villages and one larger township in an area of nearly 8,000 kilometers. The population of 600 of the 740 villages averaged 100 people. The vast majority were small-scale subsistence farmers, while a minority were river fisherfolk.

The goal of the Ghanaian government was to secure the economic development of the region, and resettlement became part of that effort. To these ends the Volta River Development Act established a semiautonomous body, the Volta River Authority (VRA), to administer the project and the resettlement of the project-affected people (PAP). The original approach was to pay cash compensation for the acquisition of the farmland and pasture, provide public facilities/services, and for the PAPs to build their own houses, open new farmlands, and resettle themselves. Soon it became apparent that this approach was unworkable due to limitations of the amount of land available for traditional subsistence agriculture and inadequate cash compensation being paid. The strategy was changed to "improving" the lives of the PAPs by forcing them onto small, "modern," mechanized, chemically maintained farm plots and "modern" concrete houses with zinc roofs in densely overcrowded settlements, both designed by urban elites with no inputs or participation of the PAPs.

The new resettlement policy and plan consisted of three elements: (i) a cooperative agricultural program centered on the commercialization of agriculture through adoption of modern technology by the PAPs; (ii) the regrouping of resettlement sites into larger communities to more efficiently provide modern infrastructure and services; and (iii) improvement of living conditions by providing modern housing to the resettlers. The original villages were regrouped into fifty-two new settlements consisting of between 2,000 and 5,000 people each. The location and size of the larger new settlements were determined by technical factors of the proposed agricultural program and the density of households and the number of people sufficient to provide other services. New infrastructure included nearly 500 miles of roads, 13,000 houses, 82 schools, 46 markets, 146 public latrines, 52 boreholes, 6 wells, and 162 water standpipes, including 34 mechanical and 23 hand pumps.

Each entitled household was provided with a "core" house according to three design types with concrete floor and aluminum roofing for two rooms, along with two porches. Only one room was completed before housing allocation on the expectation that resettlers would add additional rooms and the porches themselves with materials and assistance provided at the time of their arrival in the new settlement. No separate kitchen, bathroom, or storage was provided as part of the new housing. New housing was planned and only partially constructed without input from the resettlers. It is unclear how the urban elite planners expected the displaced people, who had no income after eviction, to complete construction of the kitchen, bathroom, and expand the number of rooms in the houses, while simultaneously working to cultivate new farms with a foreign, unknown technology, and to feed themselves.

Subsequent surveys showed that 26 percent of the new houses remained in the same unfinished condition they were in prior to removal. In two new settlements, 23 percent of new houses remained unfinished and 42 percent were unoccupied. Only 2 percent were completed and modified. Fifteen years after resettlement, only 34 percent of the houses were occupied. Housing design resulted in overcrowding and conflicted with traditional ethnic cultural norms preventing menstruating women from entering a room with fetishes and/or medicines, revolving use of sleeping rooms among polygamous ethnic groups and the inability of resettlers to complete houses negatively affected their ability to enact the highly valued role as hospitable landlord to visitors. The increased density in the population of the new settlements also led to the erosion of social cohesion, exacerbation of social conflict rooted in prior intra-tribal tensions, outmigration, and a general lack of a collective sense of community.

In terms of land and production systems, initially, each subsistence farmer was to receive a minimum of twelve acres under mechanized cultivation. Tree crop farmers were to be allocated between five and fifteen acres, livestock farmers a minimum of three acres and pastoralists a minimum of thirty acres. The amounts of these allocations were reduced by half, and less than one-third of that reduced acreage was cleared during implementation prior to settler arrival. Mechanized clearing of forest soils resulted in ecological changes such as declining seasonal rainfall and wind erosion of topsoil. These effects, coupled with the new intensive farming system with no fallow period on smaller plots, led to the depletion of soil nutrients, declining yields and thus income. Farmers were unfamiliar with the new cultivation practices, technological inputs were late in arriving, machinery required constant maintenance beyond the capacity of the farmers, and agricultural officers charged with administering or supervising the agricultural program were frequently transferred, resulting in frequent interruptions in the implementation of the program.

Changes in river flow due to the dam altered aquatic and riparian ecosystems. The incidence of schistosomiasis and other ailments increased as a result. The change in flow regime also eliminated seasonal flooding, resulting in the drying up of creeks utilized for fishing and degradation of agricultural land, with negative economic consequences. No fishery program was planned, as it was expected that fishermen would do this themselves. Traditional fishermen largely abandoned the occupation and migrated to work elsewhere. After 1970, however, they were drawn back to the reservoir area and returned to fishing after learning that migrants from other areas of Ghana, attracted by the lake and its fishing potential, established no less than 950 fishing villages around the reservoir margin with a total population of 60,000. Catch returns remained high, providing work for women and an overall increase in relative prosperity. One resettlement area adapted to the new conditions by shifting to drawdown cultivation of vegetables. This system was pioneered by individuals; the high yields resulted in the idea diffusing to others, who petitioned the VRA for licenses to access drawdown land.

Overall, the Akosombo resettlement program was a disaster by any measure. Over twenty-five years after resettlement, many PAPs were still impoverished. Only portions of subsistence plots were actually cultivated; no commercial land was cultivated due to the failure to clear it; promises of subsidized electricity and water were not kept; farming machinery was not maintained; no inheritance of allotment certificates was issued; there was no access to credit; and many settlers still had not received compensation, which prevented their access to allocated land. Rather than reestablishing traditional livelihoods first and then incorporating innovation after food and livelihood security were achieved, the agricultural program was implemented as a social experiment converting a small-scale subsistence agricultural system into one of mechanized commercial farming. Ultimately, the claim to be improving the lives of the displaced was proven to be fiction born of contempt for traditional tribal people. It failed and culminated in a significant number of resettled farmers fleeing the project area.

To address these ongoing issues, in 1996 the Ghanaian Parliament established the VRA Trust Fund, which requires the VRA to provide an annual grant from various sources of revenue to the Fund for community development projects in the fifty-two resettlement localities and improve the living standards of those resettled. The annual grant to the Fund from VRA totals $500,000, an equivalent of only $6 per settler (Raschid-Sally et al. 2008, 10). Although additional revenue from the Ministry of Energy has facilitated the provision of electricity to all new settlements, inadequate financing of the Fund remains a major problem.

Referring to the above-referenced paper, one of the coauthors of which served as the Resettlement Officer for the project between 1962 and 1966 (Chambers 1970, 272), a member of the Ghanaian Parliament in July 2019 reminded that body that the Trust Fund had not fully lived up to its mission of ensuring the well-being and improvement of living standards of those resettled (Dafeamekpor 2019). He cited unpaid compensation, unfinished construction, and a lack of water, sanitation, and electricity in at least two resettlement communities nearly sixty years after resettlement.

Miguel Aleman Dam, Papaloapan River Basin, Oaxaca, Mexico

The reservoir behind the Miguel Aleman Dam on the Tonto River tributary of the Papaloapan, financed by the government of Mexico, began filling in March 1952 and would inundate a total area of 51,000 hectares, requiring the resettlement of 20,000 Mazatec indigenous people. The resettlement operations and outcomes of the project have been systematically documented in the works of Camara Barbachano (1955), Ewell and Poleman (1980), Halmo (1987), McMahon (1973), Nugent, et al. (1978), Partridge (1983), Partridge, Brown and Nugent (1982), Poleman (1964), Schwartz (2016), Stavenhagen, and Villa Rojas (1955). Villa Rojas, Camara Barbachano, and Rodolfo Stavenhagen served as staff of the Office of Population Relocation (OPR) for the Papaloapan Commission, with Villa Rojas as Director. Together they designed and assisted the Commission in carrying out the Mazatec resettlement, under frequent and severe budgetary constraints. The following summary of resettlement operations and outcomes draws for the most part from Partridge, Brown, and Nugent (1982).

As the reservoir began to fill, the OPR had completed a census of the population areas to be flooded, assigned cash compensation values for houses, land, crops and fruit trees, and conducted community studies on Mazatec culture and economy. The plan presented to the Commission recommended that each community be resettled as a unit in order to maintain social cohesion during the move. Ideally, the resettlement sites would be located in areas near the Mazatec homeland to maintain access to markets, reduce transport costs, and avoid relocatee isolation from social networks and institutions with which they were familiar. At the time, funds for only one resettlement community below the dam (called zone 1, the first planned and occupied), consisting of seventy-nine houses, a school, a clinic, potable water, and electricity were disbursed and only 14,000 hectares of land had been obtained. This community was the mestizo town of Nuevo Paso Nacional.

For the Mazatec, 9,000 additional hectares had been acquired in zone 1, which was named Las Margaritas by the OPR. The farmland was fertile and located just off a paved road about five kilometers from the market town of Temascal close to the base of the Aleman Dam. The farmland obtained was sufficient for only 859 of the over 4,000 families to be relocated. The OPR estimated that a total of 60,000 hectares were needed to resettle all the Mazatec; as the flooding of the reservoir commenced, over 40,000 hectares of land still needed to be acquired. Despite efforts, OPR personnel were unable to obtain any additional land below the dam. By November 1952, the original target deadline for resettlement had passed. The reservoir was filling faster than anticipated due to unusually heavy rains.

It was difficult to negotiate the purchase of additional land to resettle the Mazatec due to an inflation of land prices induced by the project itself, which included not only the Aleman Dam but also massive investments in thousands of kilometers of paved roads, electrification of rural towns and villages, construction of sewage systems in larger towns, and building of schools and hospitals throughout the region. Colonists, traders, shopkeepers, and speculators in search of land swarmed into the Papaloapan River Basin served by the new infrastructure. They claimed much of the most fertile tracts, making the resettlement of Mazatec even more difficult.

The Papaloapan Commission was able to overcome the obstacles of limited budget and escalating land values by nationalizing several cattle estates belonging to the Hearst family of San Francisco, California, in four other sites. All the properties were at least 20 kilometers or more from the Mazatec homeland. They included an estate near the town of Los Naranjos in the lowlands of the neighboring state of Veracruz, the estate of La Joya in the eastern Oaxaca foothills, an estate called Yogopi in the Veracruz lowlands, and San Felipe Cihualtepec in the eastern lowlands of Oaxaca. The estates were devoted to extensive cattle ranching, which does not require particularly fertile soils, but despite the fact that they were less than ideal, they were lands to which the displaced Mazatec could be moved on an emergency basis.

Between April and the summer of 1953, Villa Rojas and his OPR staff had to convince the majority of 4,400 Mazatec families to relocate to these unfamiliar areas far removed from the Mazatec area. The OPR staff and the bilingual Mazatec recruited for the mobilization committees and for translation intensified their efforts. These areas still lacked the housing, schools, clinics, potable water, electricity, irrigation, and community centers promised in exchange for resettler cooperation. Those who did cooperate were taken to the resettlement sites to inspect and choose the 10-hectare plots onto which they would move. Others refused to believe that resettlement was necessary; they were taken to the dam site to see the filling of the reservoir. Ultimately, those who refused to move had to be forcibly evacuated by truck and boat, escorted by the police in an emergency evacuation operation.

By the summer and the end of 1953, the originally planned two-to-three phases of resettlement had to be condensed into one. Villa Rojas and the OPR directed the rescue evacuation of about 10,000 people. Only about half of the 4,400 Mazatec families ultimately participated in the resettlement; the rest rejected all five resettlement zones and moved themselves. Around 600 families settled on the margins of the reservoir, while the rest scattered to surrounding towns and Mazatec communities unaffected by inundation. Of those who resettled, approximately 900 families moved to zone 1, about 360 moved to the La Joya zone, some 200 joined the Los Naranjos irrigation experiment, and 800 were split between the distant Yogopi and Cihualtepec zones.

At the end of 1953, the Commission was satisfied that the resettlement had been accomplished, the OPR was abolished and full responsibility for rehabilitation of the resettled communities was turned over to the *Instituto Nacional Indigenista* (INI). A Coordinating Center was opened in 1954 at the base of the dam to handle any completion of resettlement operations and mediate conflicts between people who participated and latecomers moving into established resettlement communities between 1954 and 1959.

The resettlement site at Los Naranjos was designed as a pilot project in pump irrigation to provide capital-intensive agriculture for 1,500 families. The irrigation system largely failed due to budget cuts and a tenfold increase in the 100 pesos per hectare fee to be paid by relocatees in a shortened payment period. Unable to meet the terms, 46 percent of the settlers abandoned their plots. Only 300 of the over 22,000 hectares devoted to the scheme were irrigated, and then for only a few months between 1955 and 1956, and by 1957 the project was terminated.

The La Joya resettlement zone comprised 23,000 hectares, only 7,000 of which were suitable for cultivation, was distributed among 360 families who had chosen it over other resettlement zones. Organized into ejidos, each male of working age received 10 hectares. Originally, the Mazatec were shown already developed and more fertile locations; when they were actually resettled, their lands were located in virgin forest. The site also lacked roads, housing, schools, and other infrastructure, demoralizing and embittering the resettlers. They cleared their own fields and houses and cut an access road into the area, but the Commission judged maintenance of that road to be a low priority, and it became impassable during the rainy season, negating any possibility of the resettlers obtaining income from cash crops because of transport costs. Consequently, they were forced after resettlement to rely on subsistence maize cultivation, the yields of which on poorer soils were very low. As a result, 40 percent of the Mazatec resettled to La Joya left to colonize new land in the vicinity of Cihualtepec.

Approximately 770 Mazatec families were relocated to the Yogopi and Cihualtepec zones. Here as well, housing and infrastructure were not

completed before their arrival. The allocation of individual plots and usufruct rights to land was not completed until 1960, and the entire settlements
were not finished until 1966. Both zones suffered from similar conditions
and circumstances, including failure of cash crops due to poor soils, low
yields, difficult transport and lack of credit, culminating in high rates of
indebtedness. An INI store was established in one of the communities but
was prohibited from selling alcoholic beverages, extending short-term credit
to those faced with emergencies or communal obligations and purchasing
farmer's crops in advance of the harvest, all of which were customary practices among Mazatec shopkeepers. The communities were soon infiltrated
by mestizo shopkeepers who took advantage of defaulting and indebted
Mazatec mixed farmers, bought up the best land and, as prior to resettlement in the lowland zone, came to dominate the ethnic structure of the
communities.

Overall, the resettlement operation throughout 1953 was chaotic and
hastily conducted, due for the most part to Commission inability to provide
suitable farmland serviced by adequate infrastructure, construction and
maintenance of promised access roads, housing and other services (health,
education), as well as indemnification and compensation to relocatees for
lost property in a timely manner. Similarly, the Commission lacked adequate
scientific information on soil quality and studies on irrigation and mechanized
agriculture to help facilitate the development of resettlement communities.
Perhaps most important, the Commission exhibited a paternalistic attitude
toward the people to be resettled (see, e.g., Schwartz 2016). These failures
repeatedly undermined the efforts of the OPR to mobilize people to move
and resulted in bitter resentment on the part of the Mazatec, turning what
was originally planned as a largely culturally sensitive, empirically informed
resettlement into a hectic emergency evacuation operation.

Of the five resettlement zones, only Las Margaritas was relatively more
successful than the other four resettlement zones. This was not only because
it was the first one planned and occupied but also because of its location
just off paved roads, linking the farmers to urban markets. As the resettlement proceeded, however, while officials spent the bulk of their time and
effort dealing with evacuating people to the four other zones and handling
various other crises, Las Margaritas was mostly resettled by early 1953, and
the Mazatec who moved there were then largely left to their own devices in
terms of allocating land, organizing communities, and establishing ejidos
and farming systems. In other words, in effect, they were given *the freedom
to choose among alternative opportunities*. In the aftermath of resettlement
in Las Margaritas, some enterprising households took advantage of those
opportunities while others adopted more risky strategies, resulting in some
families adapting more successfully and others less so. The dynamics of and

reasons for relative success in Las Margaritas are described in more detail in chapter 4.

Chico River Dams, Philippines

A third project that influenced the promulgation of World Bank resettlement policy was a large hydropower project planned for the mountainous uplands of the Philippine island of Luzon in the early 1970s. The project was shelved in the 1980s due to fierce resistance by the indigenous people potentially affected. The circumstances which led to the eventual abandonment of the project are detailed by Drucker (1985) from which the following summary is drawn.

The Philippine government announced in 1973 a plan to develop the mountainous regions of Luzon. The plan called for the construction of five dams in the Chico River basin for the purpose of tripling the country's hydroelectric capacity and was known as the Chico River Basin Development Project. The World Bank funded a feasibility study conducted by Lahmeyer International, a German engineering firm, that identified four gorges in the river valley in Luzon's Central Cordillera range that were suitable for the construction of large dams that, when completed, would be the largest hydropower facility in Southeast Asia. The Bank later provided preliminary funding for dam construction in 1974, which was also contracted to Lahmeyer. The mountain range is drained by the Chico and is home to several indigenous ethnic groups, known collectively as Igorots, with long-established residence and traditions. Intensive cultivation of irrigated rice on terraces carved from the slopes is at the core of Igorot culture and subsistence economy.

The mountain Igorots remained fiercely independent throughout periods of Spanish colonial rule and American economic domination in the decades that followed. The rice terraces, with retaining walls up to some ten meters in height, extend all the way up the Cordillera from the Chico River and have remained sustainably and intensively cultivated without any modern chemical inputs for generation after generation, even under conditions of population pressure. The Chico Dam project threatened this long-established system and the culture of the Igorot people, as it would have created four large reservoirs, inundating 16 villages and 2,753 hectares of rice terraces, forcing the resettlement of approximately 90,000 Igorots from Bontoc and Kalinga ethnolinguistic groups to other areas.

The Bontoc and Kalinga were not unfamiliar with the government's poor record in keeping promises of compensation for lost properties in earlier failed resettlements. Staunchly opposed to the project and resettlement, they made repeated appeals to halt the project. When these went unheeded, Bontoc villagers then began to harass survey teams and destroying their equipment. Ultimately, they began violently attacking National Power Corporation (NPC) crews. The then-president Marcos ordered the NPC to stop work in the basin as a result. The head of the department of the Presidential Assistant on National Minorities (PANAMIN), however, traveled to Kalinga and persuaded villagers well outside of the project area to endorse the agency as their representative in any future dam project negotiations. Through the use of bribes and other promises, other villages also aligned themselves with PANAMIN, in a classic divide-and-conquer strategy. (The Bontoc and Kalinga later ceremonially sealed a peace pact which prohibited cooperating with the NPC.) PANAMIN arranged for a delegation of Kalinga representatives to meet with the president. Prior to the meeting, they were required to sign blank sheets of paper, which became, when the meeting occurred, statements of consent for the construction of one of the Chico dams. PANAMIN also organized an intimidation campaign by recruiting, enlisting, and arming Kalinga traditional enemies with high-powered rifles, escalating old feuds in which many people were killed or injured. The Chico IV dam site was militarized by battalions of armed forces and civilian militias of PANAMIN comprising 850 men. The Kalinga potentially affected by the Chico II and III dams, in turn, formed their own militia units, which were armed and trained by the New People's Army (NPA), a national revolutionary movement. Attacks and reprisals turned the area by 1980 into a war zone, making it unsafe for the NPC to proceed with the Chico IV dam.

Due to the conflict and growing opposition to the project, which now included peasant groups, labor unions, and the Catholic Church, the government in 1981 "postponed" the Chico Dams project, according to official government reports. There were still plans, however, to build and implement a scaled-down version of the Chico River Irrigation Project (CRIP), located 40 kilometers downstream from the Chico IV dam site, with World Bank funding totaling $50 million. By the 1980s, some of the supporting infrastructure (powerlines, canals) has been put in place. The project was appraised by the Bank in 1976, evaluated in 1989 and, according to the project page on the Bank's website, was given an "unsatisfactory" outcome rating.

Sobradinho Dam, Brazil

Beginning in the 1960s, the Brazilian energy agency Centrais Eletricas Brasileiras, S. A. (ELETROBRAS) drew up plans for the Sobradinho Dam and reservoir, designed to meet growing industrial and power demand in the northeastern part of the country. The project and its resettlement impacts are concisely summarized by Hall (1994) and Serra (1993), and we draw upon those summaries here in what follows below.

Construction on the Sobradinho dam began in the early 1970s by the *Companhia Hidreletrica do Valle do Sao Francisco* (CHESF), the northeast regional utility company, with a combination of financial assistance totaling $85 million from the Inter-American Development Bank (IDB), $81 million from the World Bank, $72 million in bilateral loans and domestic funding. When filled, the reservoir would flood an area of 4,150 square kilometers, making it the second-largest inland water body in Latin America. An appraisal of the project conducted by Robert Goodland for the World Bank (Goodland 1973, cited in Hall 1994, 1795) identified several potential adverse social and environmental impacts, not the least of which would be the involuntary displacement of 70,000 people and the economic displacement of 50,000 farmers and their dependents downstream, whose riverine rice fields comprising 9,000 hectares would be completely inundated by the increased flow of the Sao Francisco river. To counteract the adverse impact on downstream cultivators, the government expropriated 25,000 hectares for "emergency" polder irrigation schemes. Ultimately, there was no coherent plan for resettling those to be displaced. As the reservoir began to fill, people refused to move, and eventually the military was called in to forcibly evict them (Mathur 2011, 1–2; Wade 2011, 47).

Among those to be physically displaced, 25 percent lived in four small towns and were to be resettled to new urban centers lakeside with the same names. Based on what Hall (1994, 1795) describes as a "very selective and flawed sample survey," the company predicted that 50 percent of 50,000 rural people displaced would move to a new resettlement project upstream, known as Serra do Ramalho. An additional 30 percent were expected to move to thirteen planned *agrovilas* surrounding the reservoir. Another 10 percent were said to find local jobs associated with the construction boom, and the remaining 10 percent were predicted to resettle themselves out of the project area. The basis upon which the company calculated or assumed these responses to forced resettlement is not clear. What is certain is that the vast majority of those to be displaced were not consulted about resettlement options.

Compensation for lost land and assets was to be paid in cash; those displaced had to either accept the compensation offer or leave with nothing. This resettlement "plan" was, at best, woefully inadequate (Serra 1993, 71) and, at worst, nonexistent (Mohan 2011, 1). Serra (1993, 71) describes the handling of resettlement operations as "an instance of reactive intervention, where measures were taken by the utility in response to social problems as they emerged in the course of project implementation, with little or no prior programming."

The dam was completed in 1978. On the ground, what actually happened was that 70 percent of those displaced remained in the area around and near the reservoir, 19 percent accepted cash compensation and resettled themselves elsewhere, and a mere 8 percent moved to the new colonization scheme.

The Serra do Ramalho colonization scheme was "an unmitigated disaster." It was located 1,000 kilometers from the dam in an area of poor soils. There were no irrigation facilities, agricultural support, and inadequate supporting infrastructure for the resettlers. Of the 4,500 families expected to resettle there, only 1,000 actually traveled upstream to the site. The decline in rainfall caused by deforestation resulted in lower crop yields, impoverishing farmers, and resulting in high turnover. Complaints and protests failed to bring any improvements, as government cuts in spending largely eliminated any further support for the scheme.

In the area around the reservoir, 22,000 people decided to remain, well above the 14,000 projected by the utility. Consequently, the number of planned *agrovilas* had to be increased from 13 to 25. To this lakeside population was added numbers of disillusioned colonists from Serra do Ramalho and in-migrants drawn to the area by road construction, land speculation and irrigated farming. The replacement of inundated riverine rice cultivation consisted of undersized plots with infertile sandy soils in sites that were poorly selected. The lack of paid compensation to people with informal tenure—that is, no legal title which was required as proof of ownership and eligibility for indemnification, post-resettlement support and unemployment—instilled a great deal of psychological stress among hungry and malnourished resettlers who had no choice but to move due to the coercive tactics used by the utility company. Consequently, many abandoned their plots or sold out to commercial farmers, leaving largely empty *agrovilas*.

The downstream polder irrigation projects, funded partly by the World Bank to the tune of $75 million, necessitated the eviction of 50,000 people comprising 10,000 families from the lower valley to make way for the five schemes. Only 2,500 families were incorporated into the schemes, leaving 37,000 people (7,500 families) largely without livelihoods.

The major factors contributing to the resettlement failure at Sobradinho included poor planning and implementation, lack or absence of consultation with those to be displaced, failure to pay what were, at best, inadequate compensation amounts which only covered improvements because most of the displaced lacked legal title and coercive tactics of eviction. The opposition to the project and high levels of stress generated by forcible eviction fomented bitter resentment. The protest campaigns they and their supporters (i.e., the Church) launched were quickly repressed. The four municipalities in the project area directly affected were declared national security zones in 1974, replacing elections with appointments to office by state governors (Serra 1993, 73).

A 2019 study interviewed residents in one of the new urban centers at the reservoir margin, *Nova Sento Se*, named after the original town (*Sento Se*, now known as *Velho Sento Se*). After four decades, they still have vivid memories of the old town and the move to the new lakeside settlement. They also continue to voice persistent complaints regarding land allocation and engage in efforts to obtain fair and just compensation for the properties submerged by the dam and its reservoir (Amaral and dos Santos 2019).

THE DEVELOPMENT OF INVOLUNTARY RESETTLEMENT SAFEGUARD POLICIES

By the late 1970s, the recognition that, more often than not, involuntary resettlement by development projects resulted in the impoverishment of the affected people—the opposite of what was supposed to be the purpose of development investment in the first instance—was firmly established in the international development community. The World Bank had already suffered reputational damage due to its involvement in the resettlement disasters summarized above, which continued into the 1980s with its financing of the Polonoroeste project in the Brazilian Amazon (Wade 2016a, b) and the Narmada projects in India (see below). It was in the World Bank, however, that social scientists both within and outside the institution were compelled to act.

According to his own recollection, it was the resettlement disaster at Sobradinho, and also the conflict and resistance surrounding the four dams planned for the Chico River in the Philippines that became the tipping points which convinced Michael Cernea, a sociologist and himself an involuntarily displaced refugee from his native Romania in 1944—and the first noneconomist social scientist hired by the World Bank in 1974 as Adviser for Social Policy and Sociology—that something needed to be done. Cernea took on the task of researching Bank files and past projects over several months, which would inform the drafting of guidelines for including social issues in involuntary resettlement projects (Cernea 1993a, 19–21; Cernea and Freidenberg 2007, 345, 349–50; Mathur 2011b, 1–2; Oliver-Smith 2010, 221).

Cernea enlisted the assistance of Thayer Scudder, a California Institute of Technology anthropologist, who had worked with Colson in the study of the Kariba Dam resettlement, and David Butcher, an Edinburgh University anthropologist who had studied the equally disastrous consequences of the Akosombo Dam resettlement (Cernea and Freidenberg 2007, 349). Together they drafted the World Bank's first operational guidelines on involuntary resettlement in 1979, which were ultimately approved by both Bank management and the then Bank president Robert McNamara and formally issued by the Bank´s board of executive directors representing all member countries as Operational Manual Statement (OMS) 2.33, *Social Issues Associated with Involuntary Resettlement in Bank-Financed Projects,* in February 1980.

It is important to emphasize here, however, as Cernea has pointed out, that this was no easy task. Once the guidelines were drafted, standard Bank procedure was that they be presented to the management and technical staff of divisions, departments, and sector offices up the "chain of command" for review and comment prior to being submitted to the board and the president. Bank management and technical staff were (and still are) dominated by economists and engineers, many with comparatively little social and cultural knowledge of people affected by projects. Moreover, they may not be overly concerned with such matters as their jobs are to plan, design, and implement physical projects and, as has been often stated, to "move money." By and large, those opposed to the guidelines perceived resettlement to be a local or country issue, a side effect, an externality not within the purview of the Bank. Others, including Cernea's supervisor, the director of the Agricultural and Rural Development Department where Cernea was housed at the time, did not share that view.

It can be argued, as noted by Oliver-Smith (2010), that international civil society and affected people's resistance movements, protests, and unrelenting pressure on donors might have had an important impact in persuading World Bank management to take action to address the impoverishment consequences of poorly conceived and implemented involuntary resettlement operations. The argument goes that while the World Bank is given credit for developing the world's first involuntary resettlement policy, the credit may actually belong to civil society organizations and affected people whose constant pressure account for the policy. This view begs the question of why no concerned nation-state government faced with identical pressure from their own citizens failed to respond constructively to civil society demands, even to the point of unleashing unspeakable violent repression on the victims.

In point of fact, the Bank´s policy was the product of a conscious effort on the part of social scientists within the Bank, together with key consultants from outside the Bank, who were unconstrained by nation-state politics, who felt the need for a peaceful solution to a festering dilemma, and who could see no reason that would justify forcing people into poverty as a necessary cost of much-needed development investment. Moreover, these social scientists had actually researched why and how involuntary resettlement operations so often harmed displaced people. Like civil society activists, they called attention to the irrationality and injustice of the situation. Equally important, however, these social scientists had the professional skills not just to point to the problem but to design concrete, practical, and actionable measures that the Bank management and staff could act upon to address it. Such measures took the form of proposed development policy directives to avoid impoverishment of the displaced, resulting in the issuance of OMS 2.33 by the Bank's board of executive directors. The process by which this was achieved was complex and difficult, but it is instructive to examine it to see how changes in the culture of institutions like the MDFIs actually take place.

THE EMERGENCE OF A WORLD BANK INVOLUNTARY RESETTLEMENT SAFEGUARD POLICY

Cernea (1993a, 20–26; 2005b, 78–84) has outlined the history and process by which the initial guidelines moved through the institution,+ were "tested" on the ground, evaluated as to their effect on project performance, and eventually evolved into a formal safeguard policy.

The OMS 2.33 guidelines he and others prepared were the subject of numerous seminars for Bank staff, often chaired by Bank managers, and continuous lobbying efforts throughout the Bank. The case for a more socially informed approach to resettlement was bolstered by empirical evidence from past project cases, mostly comprised of the disasters discussed above, along with the recognition that mounting pressure from outside the Bank necessitated an internal change in the approach to dealing with involuntary resettlement. Along the way, discussions and consultations within the Bank engendered a range of responses, including support, inertia, "sharp disagreements openly aired" (Mathur 2011, 2), intense debate, diplomacy, "'bargaining' facts" (Cernea 1993a, 21), and resistance on the part of many mid-level managers and staff. On the part of borrowing agencies, there was shock at the prospect that they would have to change their standard procedures for expropriation and handling displacement (Cernea 1993a, 22). As pointed out by the former vice president and general counsel of the World Bank, loan agreements with the Bank signed by member governments are *governed by public international law and consequently the member concerned is under obligation to adapt its domestic law to the agreement with the Bank* (Shihata 2001, our emphasis). All such loan agreements automatically incorporate the Bank´s policies such as OMS 2.33. Of course, this obligation to adapt domestic law applies only to Bank-financed projects, not to domestic law more generally. Such a legal injunction, however correct, did not prevent some borrower country politicians from complaining that the Bank was intervening in their sovereignty, ignoring the fact that their governments that sat on the Bank's board of executive directors had approved OMS 2.33. It was, in fact, binding on all member countries.

OMS 2.33 represented a paradigm shift in development policy and its approval by the board and the president conferred upon it the weight of formal policy. It required that planning and financing of resettlement be included as "an integral part of the project . . . clarified before, and agreed upon during, loan negotiations" (World Bank 1980, 1). Referring to past failures, the OMS, for the first time, required the preparation and financing of a resettlement plan as an integral part of the project. It brought attention to the need to prioritize community infrastructure and social services, avoiding the fostering of dependence, planning land allotments ahead of time to accommodate the natural growth of resettled communities and their needs into the second generation, engaging in effective communication, consultation and facilitating the participation of affected people and their leaders in the planning of resettlement, accounting for host populations and mitigating potential social conflict, taking into account resettler cultural values and preferences regarding housing and land so as to not restrict their farming practices, the extension of houses and building shrines, the special issues involved in urban resettlement, and promoting the transfer or handing over of community management responsibilities from borrower government administrative agencies to the resettled people themselves (World Bank 1980, 1–3). The 1980 OMS 2.33 presented for the first time the three major pillars of resettlement standards that still apply today. First, to avoid or minimize resettlement whenever feasible. When resettlement was unavoidable, Bank staff should determine during identification and appraisal whether displacement could be reduced "to a minimum compatible with the purpose of the project." Second, when avoidance or minimizing displacement was not feasible, "relocation of those affected should be undertaken in conjunction with a well-prepared resettlement plan," the details of which would vary on a case-by-case basis (World Bank 1980, 3). And third, the core requirement of such a plan was reestablishing or rebuilding the livelihoods and socioeconomic productivity of the displaced people which has been destroyed by the loss of farmland, orchards, wells, pastures, fisheries, workshops, businesses, or employment.

Compensation, over and above existing borrower country laws emphasizing supposed market values, should reflect replacement costs of houses, including improvements to houses and land, including field crops, gardens, tree crops, and livestock pens and other infrastructure. Similarly, assets such as access to kin, social, and economic networks, shrines and other culturally important locations, as well as common property resources such as pastures, fishing grounds, and forest resources, were to be replaced at resettlement sites. Finally, the policy document recognized that cash compensation alone is insufficient for resettlers to reestablish livelihoods and thus required that resettlement assistance to build new livelihoods be included in resettlement component budgets (World Bank 1980, 4).

Resettlement operations were explicitly linked to the project cycle in the OMS, placing primary responsibility for carrying out the resettlement on borrower governments. The document required planning resettlement at the earliest possible stage to avoid project delays and cost overruns. The magnitude of the resettlement should be determined, and the preparation of the resettlement component should begin during the project identification phase. The borrower government should be prepared to discuss its policies and plans for acquiring resettlement sites and the institutional and legal arrangements for conducting the resettlement. The document recommended that the preparation of the resettlement component involve an expert in resettlement social science, preferably from the host country, on the ground in the field.

Project design and the schedule for resettlement operations should be complete prior to project appraisal so that an accurate assessment of feasibility could be made, including the adequacy of asset inventories and valuation, whether adequate land was available in the resettlement sites and the legal and policy framework within which the resettlement operation would be carried out and by whom (World Bank 1980, 4–5). It advocated that the cost of the resettlement component of a project be included in the cost of the total project. The borrower should be able to satisfy the Bank that it had a resettlement plan that could be effectively implemented in accordance with the criteria put forth in the OMS and that it accepted the obligation to carry out the resettlement component (World Bank 1980, 5).

APPLYING OMS 2.33 TO BANK-FINANCED PROJECTS

Between 1982 and 1983, OMS 2.33 was put to the test on the ground for the first time. The policy statement became the standard by which resettlement operations related to the construction of the Bank-financed Sardar Sarovar Dam on the Narmada River in India were to be evaluated. The dam and its canals were the first of a planned complex on the river to generate electricity, deliver irrigation, and improve domestic water supply. A coordinating body, the Narmada Control Authority, was established by the Government of India to coordinate and oversee the project. An interstate Tribunal Award in 1979 legislatively determined that Sardar Sarovar would entail differential impacts unequally distributed across three states. The state of Gujarat, where the dam was located, would largely benefit from the irrigation component. The reservoir would mostly submerge land in Madhya Pradesh, requiring the displacement and resettlement of 80 percent of the 245 villages to be inundated, in exchange for relatively little project benefit. Maharashtra would share some of the costs and benefits. Differences in political power and culture within and between the states facilitated frequent conflict between government authorities throughout the project cycle. Except for Gujarat, which had long prioritized irrigation development, the other states had no substantial interest in the project. All three of the states placed a very low priority on resettlement and consistently resisted efforts on the part of the Bank to implement the resettlement provisions in OMS 2.33.

From the outset, the guidelines and their intent were subverted and undermined, when not outright ignored, by powerful individuals and units within the Bank. Cernea (2005b, 79) recounts that the Regional Division in charge of the project "deliberately bypassed the policy" in the preparation and appraisal report. No resettlement plan was included. When this omission was brought to his attention, Cernea rejected the appraisal and refused to give it clearance because the absence of a resettlement plan contravened Bank policy in the form of OMS 2.33. Cernea was backed up by the director of the Department of Agriculture and Rural Development, and they, in turn, were backed up by the vice president for operations. They unanimously demanded that the resettlement component be appraised. This set off a long, intense in-house debate between divisional staff and managers, one that would plague the rest of the Bank's involvement with the project. (For a riveting, detailed insider account of the internal social and political dynamics surrounding the Bank's experience with this project, based on a years' work inside the Bank involving researching the project files and interviews with staff, managers and consultants, see Wade 2011). Despite the appraisal mission already being underway, the Country Department staff were instructed to reappraise the project, despite their request for a "policy dispensation."

Two additional reappraisal missions were sent to India with the objective of including a resettlement component and plan as part of the project. Thayer Scudder was recommended by Cernea to serve as the resettlement social scientist for the missions, a recommendation accepted by the responsible Country Department. The approval of the project was delayed by six months. The failure to include an adequate resettlement plan during appraisal set the stage for polarization within the Bank and between the Bank and the Government of India, with adverse ramifications throughout the implementation of resettlement operations. Scudder recommended a compromise, rolling annual resettlement plan to culminate in an overall, comprehensive plan, as a way of empowering those concerned with resettlement in Indian government ministries responsible for the project as well as ensuring that his report was not simply cast aside and ignored. The Country Department responsible accepted the recommendation and the project was ultimately approved by the board (Wade 2011, 48).

A full-fledged, comprehensive plan was never completed by the Indian officials in charge. Throughout the late 1980s and early 1990s, resettlement operations were an abject failure, resulting in growing opposition and resistance both within India and internationally, despite the Bank's continuing public positive spin campaign. The resettlement operations were highly unsatisfactory and conflict-ridden, negative findings of resettlement expert reports were altered (Wade 2011, 49), and thousands of those displaced were never resettled and/or rehabilitated (this remains the case today). The unfolding disaster culminated in the appointment by the then Bank president Lewis Preston of an independent review panel to evaluate the project. The 1992 report (Morse and Berger 1992) was scathingly critical of both the Bank and the Indian government regarding the implementation and outcome of resettlement operations and the failure to meet the standards set by OMS 2.33 and other safeguard directives, severely damaging the Bank's reputation. The Bank Country Department and Indian authorities were infuriated by the independent review's findings and recommendations, and the Bank decided to continue its involvement with the project, setting new benchmarks for resettlement. But by early 1993, it became clear that benchmarks set for resettlement and other components of the project would not be met. By mutual agreement between the Bank and the Indian government, the Bank ceased any additional loan disbursements, effectively canceling its financial support of the project.

Thereafter, and throughout the 1990s, the Bank reduced its funding for large dam projects to around four per year (Piccioto 2013, 248). Two of these were the Bujagali Dam in Uganda and the Lao PDR's Nam Theun 2 (NT2). The latter was the first instance of the Bank's renewed commitment to financing "high-risk, high-reward" large dam projects in the wake of rejecting most of the recommendations of the World Commission on Dams (WCD 2000), a major international body it had taken the lead in forming with the IUCN—The World Conservation Union and the World Bank Group 1997; Scudder 2005) in the aftermath of the Sardar Sarovar travesty. NT2 was touted as "sustainable hydropower," coupling the dam project with funding the creation and management of a large national reserve on the Nakai Plateau adjacent to the dam site and reservoir, thereby marrying large infrastructure and conservation (Goldman 2005, Rich 2013, 125–28; Shoemaker and Robichaud 2018). The Bank engaged in a public relations campaign to rebrand itself as a financier of "green" development that had learned its lessons, taking advantage of the ascension of climate change and biodiversity conservation as priority issues to promote its participation in the financing of large and controversial projects. Following long delays and fourteen independent reviews (Piccioto 2013, 248, n.13), World Bank support, in the form of loan investment guarantees and risk insurance, was approved and a concession agreement signed in 2005 for NT2 as a "build-own-operate-transfer" (BOOT) project.

Despite international opposition to the NT2 project due to its devastating social and environmental impacts, many of which were predicted both by preconstruction independent and project-contracted field research and assessment—especially for the over 100,000 villagers living downstream—and actual results on the ground between 1997 and 2010, the Bank continued to project a narrative of NT2 as a signature example of success, both on its website and in publications (Porter and Shivakumar 2011). Independent researchers, as well as the Bank's own International Panel of Experts (POE, which included Thayer Scudder as a member), contracted to oversee project implementation and monitoring, documented empirical evidence of a different outcome, reaffirming the negative conclusions of preconstruction assessments (Scudder 2017, 2019b; Shoemaker and Robichaud 2018).

The contentious and failed experience of Sardar Sarovar did, however, subsequently lead to the Bank formulating new policies on information disclosure and transparency, along with the establishment of the Inspection Panel, an independent investigative unit serving as a grievance mechanism for handling complaints of harm by project-affected people due to Bank failure to abide by its own safeguard policies.

The extended discussion above regarding the first field test of OMS 2.33 is meant to emphasize several points. First, Sardar Sarovar was the first major field test of the first-ever set of resettlement guidelines. Second, this initial experience illustrates that, no matter how comprehensive social safeguard policies, standards, and directives might be, there is a continual challenge and struggle entailed in their (i) gaining acceptance in massive bureaucracies dominated by economists, engineers, and others with technocratic and economythic biases (Cernea 1993b, 2005b, 72); and (ii) remaining constantly vigilant that the policy proscriptions in those safeguards are actually *implemented* on the ground. It is only half-jokingly (if that) that Cernea refers to development social science as a "contact sport" (Cernea and Freidenberg 2007). Third, the example points to the fact of differential power and influence, both within MDFI central, regional, sectoral, or country offices and borrower government agencies, of elite or privileged units or individuals, that can make the difference between success and failure, compliance or noncompliance. It could be argued that it takes only the decision of a single person in a position of power and influence (e.g., task manager) to determine whether certain policy directives are implemented or not (Kabra 2018, 275–76; Murray 1997, 249; Partridge 1995, 206–07, 2013). The need—indeed, the ethical obligation—for sustained and militant advocacy based on empirical facts obtained on the ground by resettlement social scientists is addressed more fully in chapters 3 and 10.

OMS 2.33 underwent its second major field test in the mid-1980s as China became a member government of the Bank. China had a record of disastrous resettlement outcomes associated with large dams throughout the 1960s–1970s, so the question naturally was raised as to whether the Chinese government would accept and abide by the provisions set forth in OMS 2.33.

When a Bank appraisal mission presented the government with the policy document for incorporation into the Shuikou Dam project, which was in the pre-appraisal stage, authorities included its provisions and agreed to comply with its requirements (Cernea 2005b, 80).

OPN 10.08

As the resettlement fiasco of Sardar Sarovar continued to play out, Cernea undertook the first portfolio review of Bank-financed projects involving involuntary resettlement in 1985 (Cernea 1986, 2005b, 79). The findings revealed that most projects with an involuntary resettlement component financed by the Bank between 1979 and 1985 were out of compliance with the Bank policy directives contained in OMS 2.33. Seventy-five percent of project appraisals were conducted without the input of a resettlement specialist. Presented with the review findings, a furious vice president of operations demanded to know who wasn't doing their job. The regional vice presidents all indicated that it was Cernea, who responded by producing a stack of memos from his files, demonstrating that his and others' efforts at ensuring that resettlement issues were addressed were repeatedly ignored (Wade 2011, 63, n.18). Over the objections of regional administrators, the senior management of the Bank adopted all the review's recommendations and, on Cernea's advice, approved the issuance of a follow-on policy note to OMS 2.33. Operations Policy Note (OPN) 10.08, "Operations Policy Issues in the Treatment of Involuntary Resettlement in Bank-Financed Projects," issued in October 1986, reaffirmed and expanded the OMS policy, strengthening procedures for planning and implementation both within the Bank and on the part of borrowers by including the input of social specialists, and further insisted on the borrower's adherence to the policy included in loan agreements and reiterated the objective of providing those displaced and resettled with a sound productive basis and a share in project benefits, along with host populations (Cernea 1993a, 23, 2005b, 80).

The OMS and OPN were synthesized into a technical paper, *Involuntary Resettlement in Development Projects: Policy Guidelines in World Bank-Financed Projects*, published in 1988 (Cernea 1988). The landmark document was the first time an internal Bank policy had been published for public distribution. The technical paper combined the provisions in the two prior policy statements and clarified each of their key points, as well as more specifically detailing operational procedures. The paper also contained three new annexes centered on a guide for the preparation of resettlement operations, a set of indicators to be utilized during monitoring and evaluation of resettlement operations and a "how to" guide for conducting financial and economic analyses of resettlement costs and expenditures (Cernea 1993a, 24, 2005b,

80–81). The first author of the present volume, who had at the time been hired by the Bank, authored the annex of guidelines on preparing a workable resettlement plan and the necessary steps to be taken to achieve the policy objectives and overall compliance (Partridge 2013, 155).

The technical paper was distributed widely and subsequently translated into many languages, either through the efforts of NGOs (e.g., India, Indonesia) or authorized by government officials (e.g., China). It is safe to say that the translation and wide distribution of World Bank Technical Paper Number 80 brought international attention to resettlement and resettlement policy for the first time.

OD 4.30

Following the 1989 completion of the internal reorganization of the Bank spearheaded by the then-president Barber Conable, all prior policies and guidelines were reissued in an updated and new format. The resettlement policy was revised, enhanced, and reissued as Operational Directive (OD) 4.30 "Involuntary Resettlement," in June 1990. Among its revisions, OD 4.30 expanded the policy's applicability to all relevant sectors beyond just hydropower and irrigation (Cernea 2005b, 81) on the recommendations of a March 1990 review (Butcher 1990). Most significantly, the OD coalesced the preceding decades of knowledge and experience with resettlement into the strongest series yet of coherent policy provisions. The basic message of the policy was as follows: because forced resettlement destroys a previous way of life, all resettlement operations must be designed, appraised, and implemented as development investments to rebuild livelihoods. When the World Bank was asked to support development investments that required physical or economic displacement of people, its Operational Directive 4.30 on *Involuntary Resettlement* was to be complied with by the member-borrower government.

OD 4.30's provisions specifically required that involuntary resettlement should be avoided or minimized wherever feasible. All viable alternative project designs, such as realignment of roads or reducing dam heights for the purpose of reducing the number of people potentially displaced and resettled, should be explored. When resettlement was unavoidable, "resettlement plans should be developed. All involuntary resettlement components should be conceived and executed as *development programs*, with resettlers provided sufficient investment resources and opportunities to *share in project benefits*" (World Bank 1990, 1, emphasis in original). Those displaced should be compensated for their losses at full replacement value prior to removal, assisted with relocation, and supported throughout the transition period in the new resettlement site, and assisted in their efforts to *improve* their former living standards, income earning capacity, and production levels, or at least to restore them (World Bank 1990, 1, our emphasis), with the needs of the poorest groups displaced and resettled receiving adequate attention.

Moreover, OD 4.30 required that, to the extent desired by the affected people, those displaced should be assisted in moving as groups to preserve existing social and economic networks and units of social organization. The distance between original and resettlement sites should be minimized whenever possible, while considering costs and benefits of tradeoffs between geographic place and potential economic opportunities elsewhere. Community participation in the planning and implementation of resettlement should be encouraged, including the transfer and reestablishment of social and cultural institutions in the new location. Consultation with and provision of information to the displaced regarding entitlements, options, relocation timetables, and the like should be ensured throughout resettlement planning, preparation, and implementation. New settlements should be designed as viable communities with adequate infrastructure and services, including land and housing. Customary and usufruct rights to land and the absence of legal title should not disqualify certain groups (indigenous, ethnic or pastoralists) from receiving compensation and rehabilitation. Procedural requirements were attached to each of the policy provisions, the most significant being the requirement that a comprehensive resettlement plan, budget, and timeline be submitted for review prior to appraisal and approval for financing (Cernea 1993b, 24–26; World Bank 1990).

The Bank-Wide Review on Resettlement

In the wake of the earlier portfolio review findings and based on the accumulating experience with OMS 2.33, OPN 10.08, and OD 4.30, Bank management approved the proposed appointment of a Resettlement Task Force to conduct a full review of the entire portfolio of projects approved since 1985. The review was published in 1994 and reissued in March 1996 as Environment Department Paper Number 032. *Resettlement and Development: The Bankwide Review of Projects Involving Involuntary Resettlement, 1986-1993* (World Bank 1996) was written by Task Force members Cernea and Scott Guggenheim, a fellow Bank anthropologist, with support from the other Task Force members.

Among its many findings, which showed some improvements in the Bank's handling of resettlement issues in its projects, one glaring conclusion was that "projects appear often not to have succeeded in reestablishing resettlers at a better or equal living standard and that unsatisfactory performance still persists on a wide scale" (World Bank 1996, 9). While the number of projects with appraised resettlement plans rose from 50 percent between 1986 and 1991, 70 percent in 1992, 93 percent in 1993, and 100 percent in 1994, nearly half of all the active projects approved during the review period were submitted to the board without a resettlement plan prepared by the borrower and appraised by the Bank, directly counter to Bank policy. The numbers of people to be displaced continued to be underestimated by borrowers. Such failures in planning and appraisal were seen to be the root causes of problematic resettlement operations (World Bank 1996, 129). The Task Force's recommendations for improved performance moving forward essentially reiterated the policy provisions set forth in OD 4.30, but with an emphasis on ensuring borrower commitment to implementing their own legal and policy frameworks concerning resettlement and restoration, with a commitment on the part of the Bank to assist them in building country capacity (World Bank 1996, 183). Another significant recommendation focused on remedial and retrofitting actions for projects not in compliance with Bank resettlement policy. Field missions were conducted to assess such cases and take the necessary corrective measures (Cernea 2005b, 82). The results of regional remedial action planning were documented in a one-year follow-up report to the *Bankwide Review* (Cernea 2005b, 82; World Bank 1995a).

OP/BP 4.12

Cernea and his now substantial cadre of resettlement and social development specialists in the newly created Social Development Department continued to confront ongoing attempts within the Bank to restrict the resettlement policy's provisions and application. One such attempt included the commissioning of a "policy creep" review, based on the argument that compliance with the resettlement policy "increased the costs of doing Bank business" (Cernea 2005b, 82; World Bank 2001b). The argument ran counter to the fact, based on evidence from a series of 1998 evaluations conducted by the Bank's Operations Evaluation Department (OED; see Piccioto, van Wicklin and Rice 2001), that more, not less, staff and other resources were needed for improving resettlement operations. It is Cernea's judgment that the ongoing attempts at undermining the policy fostered an atmosphere of "considerable turmoil and confusion in the Bank" (Cernea 2005b, 82) and made "consistency more difficult for the Bank's resettlement policy" (Cernea 2005b, 83). It might be noted here that another factor contributing to the inconsistency in the application and enforcement of the resettlement policy was inertia on the part of many borrowing country governments in implementing national-level legal and policy frameworks regarding land acquisition, compensation, and resettlement operations as stipulated in the Bank policy. The stronger the Bank policy became, the more borrower governments became resistant to complying with the policy and its provisions, partly due to a lack of sufficient staff and institutional capacity to handle the many and complex issues involved, and partly because some perceived the strict requirements as an affront to their sovereignty.

By the late 1990s, the resettlement policy, along with the other safeguards, was slated to be converted to a new format. OD 4.30 would become a three-document set: Operational Policy 4.12, the policy itself, Bank Procedures (BP) 4.12, laying out the processing requirements for projects, and Good Practices (GP). Both OP/BP 4.12 were binding on both the Bank and borrowers; GPs were not (Clark, 2009, 203).

The conversion process entailed a protracted, five-year review and revision of OD. 4.30, which had remained the standard for nearly a decade. The review and revision process, headed up by an appointed Resettlement Thematic Group working in collaboration with an Operations Policy Committee, involved consultations in fourteen countries and was opened to the public for comment in 1999, likely in accordance with Bank policies on transparency and accountability, in what to our knowledge may be the first-ever instance of an MDFI engaging in a public consultation on its review and revision of policy. The inclusion of nongovernmental, civil society, corporate and financial institutions, organizations, and interested individuals further intensified the already polarized atmosphere in the Bank and added to the number of issue-oriented collisions between those in favor of strengthening the policy and those in favor of diluting it (Cernea 2005b, 83). For the first time, the policy was formally subjected to intense scrutiny and criticism from organizations and individuals outside the Bank, including resettlement experts who had served at various times as consultants on Bank-financed projects with resettlement components.

To take but a few examples from among the voluminous comments on numerous policy issues received, we focus here on those most relevant to the present volume. Some external commentators claimed the proposed draft revision weakened the Bank's policy. Thayer Scudder, a frequent Bank consultant and internationally recognized expert on involuntary resettlement, provided extensive comments on the proposed policy revision (Cernea 2005b, 83; Scudder 1999, cited in Clark 2009, 207, 222). He considered OD 4.30, though flawed, to be the strongest policy statement on resettlement by the Bank (Scudder 2005, 278). Scudder felt the "restoration" clause was the main flaw which, he believed, undercut the objective of development benefits being shared with displaced people, allowing the option of merely restoring prior standards of living. He advocated adopting "improve" liveli-hoods, rather than at least restore, as the more development-focused wording (Scudder 2005, 278–81; 2019a, 244) and Downing (2002), Clark (2009) and others echoed Scudder´s recommendation.

This argument, however, ignored well-documented negative consequences of imposing the top-down notions of "improvement" often promulgated by university-educated planners, administrators, bureaucrats, and politicians. Too often displaced people are perceived as backward, ignorant, traditional folk that need to be told what to do and to be dragged into what bureaucrats think are "modern" production systems, jobs or occupations, and houses. In other words, at the very moment when stress on displaced people is highest, when they are most frightened about the future, when they are facing disappearing incomes, dismantled social support networks, collapsing production systems, and have no idea how they will feed themselves tomorrow, too often overzealous planners advocate treating them as guinea pigs, foisting upon them what university-educated professionals perceived as "improvements."

As we saw in Ghana in the case of the resettlement at Akosombo (see above), overzealous resettlement planners forced farmers into precarious reliance upon a new, foreign agricultural technology, confined to farm plots too small for the technology they understood, depending upon machines they could not maintain, victims of changed financial priorities of the authorities resulting in broken promises for missing infrastructure, fertilizer subsidies, agricultural extension services, access to markets, and so on. We noted also the effort in Mexico´s Papaloapan Project to modernize displaced Mazatec people in Los Naranjos by forcing them to be dependent on an irrigated agriculture experiment, which was a failure resulting in the abandonment of the experiment and flight from Los Naranjos (see above). We could add the "improved" houses for the resettled Mazatec in zone 1 with concrete slab floors, zinc roofs, and milled timber prone to termite infestation, which the Mazatec promptly tore down, preserving the (much appreciated) slab for (i) drying corn and chiles, rebuilding houses alongside the slabs using local wood impervious to insects and palm-thatched roofs to permit circulation of air rather than sweltering under the heat of zinc roofs, which were sold in town to mestizos, or (ii) using the slab as the house floor but replacing the milled timber walls and zinc roofs with walls of local wood and thatched roofs. We could add the example of resettlement of displaced Maya people in Guatemala´s Chixoy Project, who had, of course, built their own homes for centuries on packed-mud floors, out of timber, with palm-thatched roofs, with kitchens, latrines, and livestock pens, gardens, fruit trees, and corn-fields out the back door. Their lives were "improved" by urban architects from Guatemala City who designed their concrete block, cement-floored, zinc-roofed resettlement houses in a grid-pattern resembling a suburb of Austin, Texas, composed of plots too small for gardens and livestock, with no latrines, no kitchen, no trees, and no farmland to plant corn. The Quiche Maya resettlers refused to live in the buildings and instead built their own housing around the edge of the reservoir (Partridge 1995, 206–07, 2006). Similarly, we can cite the case of displaced Maasai pastoralists in Kenya resettled by the Olkaria Project on to house plots too small for their milk cows and calves, which the Maasai always kept by the house. But on the tiny plots, they were given concrete block, cement-floored, zinc-roofed houses of the kind the dominant Swahili government officials in charge of the resettlement considered an improvement (Partridge 2015).

For these reasons, we see the wisdom of the wording of virtually all MDFI involuntary resettlement policy: displaced people should be assisted in their effort to improve their livelihoods and standards of living or at least restore them. Recognizing that it is impossible to fully restore that which has been destroyed, it is equally impossible to fully change everything. Along that spectrum between restoration and improvement, the choice belongs to the displaced persons themselves. In our view, the wording in the original OMS 2.33 remains valid: to encourage *"government policies that both permit individuals and household heads to choose their future from a number of acceptable alternatives and assist them to rebuild their lives through their own efforts"* (World Bank 1980, 4, our emphasis). This should be considered the central message of the widely accepted Bank policy that emerged and is the central message of the present volume.

It was a long, intense, and demanding internal struggle within the Bank to establish the legal and policy frameworks together with the instruments, process, and procedures to improve the survival chances of people swept up in the path of development projects, displaced from their homes and livelihoods, and for the vast majority unprotected by nation-state statutes on the exercise of eminent domain. That struggle initiated by Michael Cernea was quickly joined by Gloria Davis, William Partridge, Shelton Davis, Cynthia Cook, Maritta Koch-Weser, Dan Aronson, Augusta Molnar, Ashraf Ghani, and Scott Guggenheim, to take on the burgeoning workload of projects entailing involuntary resettlement that required the support of social scientists. In the following decade, this small cadre of anthropologists and sociologists working on involuntary resettlement swelled to scores of social science professionals within the Bank and hundreds of consultants outside. Around the same time, the other MDFIs following the World Bank lead began to develop their own policy frameworks, instruments, processes, and procedures to better deal with population displacement.

THE WORLD BANK SHIFT TO AN ENVIRONMENTAL AND SOCIAL FRAMEWORK AND STANDARDS

Although most of the other MDFIs had already done so previously (see chapter 3), in 2012 the World Bank, considered by many to be the global pioneer and leader in the promulgation of involuntary resettlement policy, initiated a process which would convert its suite of safeguard policies into a set of Environmental and Social Standards (ESS) subsumed under an overarching Environmental and Social Framework (ESF). It is for this reason that we treat the process separately here. The safeguards review was opened to public consultation and, according to the Bank, constituted the largest consultation it had ever undertaken. It involved governments, civil society groups, development experts, and others in over sixty countries. The review solicited comments on at least two drafts of the proposed ESF, its newly crafted "Environmental and Social Policy for Investment Project Financing," and/or its component ESS and accompanying Guidance Notes (GN) during three phases of external consultations. Bank president Jim Yong Kim publicly stated at the time that there was no intent on the part of the Bank to dilute the existing safeguards (Bugalski 2016, 10).

While developing country governments expressed support for the revision, and even lobbied for further simplification, the flood of civil society and professional comments received on the ESF drafts and the consultation process was sharply critical, including from the US Treasury Department, UN Special Rapporteurs and the Independent Evaluation Department (IED) of the ADB, which advocated in a press release for "'the continued use of a requirements-based safeguards system . . . rather than a switch to an aspirational one' as proposed by the World Bank" (ADB 2014; Bugalski 2016, 32). The ADB IEG suggested that the Bank's "'more flexible approach to its safeguard policy . . . could dilute the strength of social and environmental protections'" (ADB 2014; Bugalski 2016, 32). Even some WB Vice Presidents criticized what they viewed as a dilution, according to leaked internal memos (Ulu Foundation, Friends of the Earth-US and Ecological Justice Indonesia 2014). Among those most critical of the proposed ESF and ESS was Michael Cernea, the former Senior Adviser for Social Policy and architect of the first WB resettlement policy (Cernea 2016; Cernea, Thomas, and van den Berg 2016; Cernea and Maldonado 2018).

Cernea and Maldonado saw the conversion and revision as a "de-ranking" and "replacement" of the prior safeguard policies with standards "binding for the borrowers but not binding on the Bank itself" (Cernea and Maldonado 2018, 4). In their view, it represents a discontinuing of the Bank's safeguard policies as mandatory for the Bank in terms of its exercising its responsibilities and shifts what had been mandatory policies for the Bank into recommendations to the borrowers (Cernea 2016a, xix; Cernea and Maldonado 2018, 23). In this view, operationally, the ESF transfers to the borrowers the prior Bank responsibilities for protecting the populations impacted negatively. But in point of fact, it has always been the borrower's responsibility to implement OD 4.30 and later iterations of WB resettlement policy and thereby hopefully protect displaced populations from negative impacts. Bank staff and management cannot execute development projects financed by the Bank, and they have no real power to protect displaced populations from negative impacts, apart perhaps from withholding loan disbursements, unless the borrower agreed to be guided by the Bank's resettlement policy. It is and has always been the responsibility of the borrower to define the legal and policy framework for involuntary resettlement, to establish compensation and livelihood improvement or restoration measures, and to staff and finance the implementation of these.

To some critics, the conversion to a new ESF indicates the Bank has moved "away from a policy compliance approach—specifically by relying instead on 'project commitments' agreed to by the Bank and the Borrower on a project-by-project basis" (Bugalski 2016, 11). Instead of ensuring borrower compliance with previous safeguard policy requirements, the ESF allows broad discretion to negotiate and agree on certain measures in any given project rather than insisting on policy compliance across the board. In the new framework, there would be "less front-loading" during project preparation which, Bugalski asserts, seems to imply that detailed plans and budgets addressing social and environmental risks of projects would not necessarily have to be prepared prior to consideration and approval of a project by the Bank's Board of Directors (Bugalski 2016, 11–12). Instead, on a project-specific basis, the Bank and borrower agree on an Environmental and Social Commitment Plan (ESCP), which becomes part of the loan agreement, and specifies what steps and plans are required within a given timeframe. Ostensibly in some cases, an ESCP would permit borrower plans, including a resettlement action plan, to be prepared at a future date (Bugalski 2016, 26), a drastic departure from the earlier requirement of a fully appraised and approved resettlement plan being a condition for overall project approval. She argues (Bugalski 2016, 19) that the ESCP promotes use of borrower country legal and policy frameworks for management of social issues provided these are consistent with the ESS. Where there are gaps, the Bank and the borrower negotiate measures to fill them, although Bugalski points out that the policy clearly indicates that this will be done on a project-specific basis, rather than as an attempt to strengthen the borrower framework in a comprehensive manner (Bugalski 2016, 19).

Bugalski´s critique would be valid only if one believes that the Bank´s policy objective was to comprehensively transform a country´s entire legal and policy framework regulating land tenure rights, land acquisition, eligibility for compensation, and the like through its financing of a single development project. In fact, as Ibrahim F. I. Shihata, former vice president and chief legal counsel of the World Bank has pointed out, member countries are obligated under public international law to adapt their domestic law to the agreement with the Bank in the case of Bank-financed projects, but not "across the board" to all instances of application of said domestic law in the country (Shihata 2001). The purpose of previous Bank policy and present ESS 5 on involuntary resettlement, which retains most if not all of the major provisions and directives of OD 4.30 and OP/BP 4.12, albeit in revised language, is clearly to safeguard the well-being of people affected by a project it is financing, to ensure no harm is done in its name, and to delimit its ethical and moral liability, not to reform a country's entire legal system. Were the latter the real objective it would be a case of a very small tail wagging a very large dog!

Many critics concluded that, with the conversion of its safeguard policies into standards folded into an umbrella framework, the World Bank lost its leadership role in social and environmental safeguard policy. Writing before the ESF process began, former director general of the Bank's Independent Evaluation Group (IEG) Robert Piccioto had reached the same conclusion but for different reasons entirely. He points out that what he perceived as the Bank's "unrealistic goal of 100 percent compliance and its vision of resettlement as a 'development opportunity'" ultimately prevented any consistent achievement given the conflict between and constant collision with country systems, within which civil servants "cannot realistically be expected to ignore or flagrantly circumvent the rules and edicts of their own government. Nor can they single-handedly overcome the enormous handicaps created by large regulatory gaps or deeply rooted governance weaknesses" (Piccioto 2013, 243). He argues it was the Bank's unwillingness to "integrate its multiple safeguard policies under a single umbrella, that it would not relax its standards to accommodate borrowers' systems, and that it would not relinquish its rigid approach and process-ridden controls" that caused country interest to evaporate in the Bank's pilot attempts to use country legal and regulatory frameworks for the implementation of its safeguard policies (Piccioto 2013, 254–55; see also Humphrey 2016).

The World Bank's board approved the ESF in August 2016, and it was released in 2017 (World Bank 2017a, b, c). The ESF went into effect on October 1, 2018, for new projects. Projects operational prior to that date continue in accordance with the previous safeguard policy regime.

What emerged from the World Bank experience with resettlement policy was a new series of resettlement policies promulgated by the Inter-American Development Bank, the Asian Development Bank, the African Development Bank, the International Finance Corporation, the Organization for Economic Cooperation and Development, and the European Bank for Reconstruction and Development and others. These policies, despite containing subtle differences in context and wording, are essentially the same as that of World Bank policy discussed above. Taken together, they can be considered the *International Standard for Involuntary Resettlement.* In conjunction with the emergence of that international standard, pressure mounted for the nation-states that make up the membership of these multilateral institutions to follow suit and promulgate their own domestic statutes to manage population displacement and resettlement. It is to these developments that we turn in chapter 3.

Chapter 3

The International Standard for Involuntary Resettlement and Country Legal Systems

The involuntary resettlement policy of the World Bank, beginning with the issuance of OMS 2.33 in 1980 and subsequently OD 4.30 in 1990, became, during the remainder of the decade, a widely accepted international standard in terms of resettlement policy, as it was adopted by all the other MDFIs. The standard represented a sea change in thinking about the management of the social consequences and opportunities presented in the economic development process. Population displacement and involuntary resettlement that had heretofore been accepted as an unfortunate but inevitable cost of the development of highways, airports, dams, cities, and other large-scale infrastructure projects was henceforth to be conceptualized, designed, and implemented as development investment. The emergence of a consensus international standard held out the hope that impoverishment need not be the fate of displaced people if they were incorporated into the development process as full participants in the design and implementation of their own resettlement.

The impacts of what began as a policy innovation in the World Bank and soon spread to all the international development finance organizations are still unfolding. Those impacts include the crafting of new policies and practices not only in the MDFIs but also in key nation-state governments. Diffusion across the world's governments is uneven, in some cases halting, partial, and piecemeal, and in others, not even begun. It is a process of cultural change in development thinking that is still evolving, with a few countries advancing more surely and creatively than others, but it is a process that is inexorable. There is no turning back the tide of civil society and displaced people's demands for justice and equitable access to the benefits of economic development. Here we will first trace the emergence of that consensus international standard among the international development finance institutions and then examine the enormous challenges being faced in its diffusion to nation-state governments.

DIFFUSION OF RESETTLEMENT POLICY ACROSS DEVELOPMENT FINANCE INSTITUTIONS

The 1988 technical policy paper, with its worldwide public distribution, and the 1990 issuance of OD 4.30, the strongest policy statement to date, facilitated a ripple effect by which other development finance institutions, both public and private, multilateral and bilateral, promulgated their own resettlement safeguard policy modeled after that of the World Bank (Cernea 2005b, 84–96; Mathur 2011b, 3). This diffusion process occurred along several "tracks" in addition to the internal one inside the Bank: an international track, encompassing the other MDFIs and international public financial institutions, a national track involving the adoption of some or all of the policy by national governments, and a private sector track composed of investment banks and transnational corporations culminating in the Equator Principles and including adoption by Export Credit Agencies (ECAs) of the industrial countries.

It is not our intent here to dissect every policy directive or provision contained within each of the policies. Suffice it to say that the involuntary resettlement policies issued by the other multilateral development banks and international development financial institutions are broadly similar in terms of the major policy objectives which concern us here, to the World Bank policy.

International Finance Corporation

The International Finance Corporation (IFC), established in 1956, is the private sector financing arm of the World Bank Group. From 1990 until 2006, all IFC projects were processed with reference to the World Bank's OD 4.30 (International Finance Corporation 2002, v). Yet its systematic application in practice was lacking. Many in the IFC claimed that the differences between public and private sector projects made such policies inapplicable to private sector project investments. The ensuing battle triggered a firestorm within the Bank group, involving not only staff and managers but also lawyers, senior management, and the respective boards. What changed the IFC's position was the IFC's damaging experience with the Pangue hydroelectric project in Chile that it had financed and the project's negative impacts on the indigenous Pehuenche communities in the project area. The negative impacts were exposed by a consultant's evaluation report (Downing 1996; Johnston and Turner 1998; Johnston and Garcia-Downing 2004; Simon and

Gonzalez Parra 2019), confirmed by an independent review of the project commissioned by the then World Bank president (Hair, Dysart and Danielson 1997), and a "devastating self-analysis" conducted by the IFC's Compliance Advisor Ombudsman's (CAO) office between 2001 and 2002 (Cernea 2005, 93; International Finance Corporation 2008).

Following the CAO review of IFC safeguard policies in 2003, which cited confusion and problems among private sector clients having to comply with a public sector resettlement policy and recommending an "overhaul" of IFC safeguards (Compliance Advisor Ombudsman 2003, 33–34, 52), the IFC developed resettlement guidelines, published a handbook on preparing a resettlement action plan (IFC 2002) and undertook between 2004 and 2005 a public consultation on its proposed conversion of the safeguards into what it called a "Sustainability Framework" which included a suite of performance standards and guidance notes. The IFC replaced its nominal reliance on OD 4.30 with "Performance Standard (PS) 5, Land Acquisition and Involuntary Resettlement" (International Finance Corporation 2006). Virtually identical to World Bank OP 4.12, the objectives of PS5 are to "avoid or at least minimize involuntary resettlement wherever feasible by exploring alternative project designs," "providing compensation for loss of assets at replacement cost," "ensuring that resettlement activities are implemented with appropriate disclosure of information, consultation and the informed participation of those affected," "to improve or at least restore the livelihoods and standards of living of displaced persons," and "improve the living conditions among displaced persons through provision of adequate housing with security of tenure at resettlement sites" (International Finance Corporation 2006, 18). One innovation in PS5 entailed encouraging clients to acquire land through negotiated settlements with affected persons or communities, even if the client has the legal means to obtain the land without the seller's consent, to eliminate the need for forced evictions by government authorities (International Finance Corporation 2006, 18). The final Sustainability Framework and Performance Standards were issued in April 2006.

In 2010, the IFC again opened its framework and standards to public consultation for the purpose of revision. Following receipt of public comments, the revised framework and standards were issued on January 1, 2012. The objectives of PS5 remain unchanged from the 2006 version. It retains the recommendation that borrowers seek "negotiated settlements" in accordance with the standard even when they have the authority to acquire land without consent (IFC 2012, 1). Negotiation of land purchases, or "willing buyer-willing seller" transactions, are encouraged to eliminate or avoid the need for eminent domain expropriation and forced evictions. While perhaps preferable, the notion of negotiated settlements raises potential issues in terms of power asymmetries, legal representation for PAPs, good faith, and the probability that those who refuse to sell will be subject to eminent domain takings and forced eviction as the final result (Price 2015, 2017, 283–84). However, it is a clear recognition by the IFC and a clear signal to private sector actors that people threatened with displacement have the right to negotiate the terms of that displacement and satisfactory compensation and mitigation measures such as resettlement and reestablishment of livelihoods.

Organization for Economic Cooperation and Development

Between 1990 and 1991, Michael Cernea was invited by the Development Assistance Committee of the Organization for Economic Cooperation and Development (OECD) to draft resettlement policy guidelines on the recommendation of the UK's development agency and Oxfam. The guidelines were endorsed by the Ministers of Development Cooperation of all OECD countries in 1991, and the *Guidelines for Aid Agencies on Involuntary Displacement and Resettlement in Development Projects* was formally issued in 1992 (OECD 1992). The policy objectives of the OECD guidelines mimic those of OD 4.30.

Inter-American Development Bank

The process by which an involuntary resettlement policy was adopted by the Inter-American Development Bank (IDB) was very similar to that which occurred within the World Bank. With the World Bank's support, the IDB began in the late 1980s to consider involuntary displacement and resettlement and other social issues in its projects. Like in the World Bank, this effort was led by anthropologists Anne Deruyterre and John Renshaw and, again, like in the World Bank, the policy emerged through a series of internal dialogues, revisions, strengthening, and drafts, culminating in the board-approved issuance of the IDB's OP-710 on Involuntary Resettlement in 1997 (IDB 1997a). The policy and accompanying background paper (IDB 1997b) were supplemented in 1999 by the publication of a "principles and guidelines" document (IDB 1999) and a 2001 private sector "Guideline for Resettlement Plans" (IDB 2001). The policy's objective is

> to minimize the disruption of the livelihood of people living in the projects area of influence, by avoiding or minimizing the need for physical displacement, ensuring that when people must be displaced they are treated equitably and, where, feasible, can share in the benefits of the project that requires their resettlement. (IDB 1997a, 1)

The policy objective is to be achieved by following principles which are nearly identical to provisions in World Bank policy: "avoid or minimize resettlement and, when unavoidable, a resettlement plan must be prepared that ensures affected people receive fair and adequate compensation and reha- bilitation," including "achieving a minimum standard of living and access to land, natural resources and services at least equivalent to pre-resettlement levels, recovering all losses caused by" displacement and resettlement, "expe- rience as little disruption as possible to their social networks, opportunities for employment or production" and "access to opportunities for social and economic development" (IDB 1997a, 1). Because the Latin American region is heavily populated by indigenous and tribal people, the IDB policy pays special attention to the rights and to the protection of ancestral territories and traditional cultures of those groups.

Asian Development Bank

The promulgation of the Asian Development Bank (ADB) resettlement policy paralleled that of the WB and the IDB. The initiative was taken on by staff after instructions from the ADB president in 1994 to staff to utilize WB OD. 4.30 as a guide in the preparation of ADB policy (ADB 1995, 9). The policy also drew upon previous guideline documents on social issues (ADB 1994). The final policy was approved by the ADB Board and issued in April 1995. Its objectives, not surprisingly, are virtually identical to those in WB OD.4.30 (ADB 1995, 9–11). It also issued a separate policy on social protection in 2001 (ADB 2001). The ADB subsequently published a guide to good practice in resettlement (ADB 1998) to better inform resettlement operations.

The ADB then embarked on a program, as the World Bank had attempted earlier (Piccioto 2013, 254–55), of regional technical assistance to borrowing countries to build capacity and enhance country legal and policy frameworks. The first effort involved seven countries and was followed up by a similar effort in six countries (Cernea 2005b, 90; Price 2011, 5).

The ADB replaced its safeguard policies in 2009 with a Safeguard Policy Statement (SPS, ADB 2009), merging all of its prior policies under one umbrella, after what Price described as "a lengthy and spirited process of public consultation" in which civil society groups expressed concern that "precision in the essential resettlement principles might be lost in the conver- sion" and that ADB ignored "new research findings on resettlement impacts," including "the need to go beyond mere restoration of incomes to achieve 'resettlement with development'" (Price 2011, 5). The ADB continued its efforts to improve borrower country legal and regulatory frameworks regard- ing involuntary resettlement and other issues in 2010 (Price 2011, 5). In 2012, it issued a draft working document on *Involuntary Resettlement Safeguards: A Planning and Implementation Good Practice Sourcebook* (ADB 2012).

African Development Bank

The African Development Bank (AfDB) was established in 1964 and began operations in 1966. It was not until 2003, however, that the AfDB issued a board-approved resettlement policy, despite the large-scale displacements experienced in the Kariba, Akosombo, and Aswan Dam projects and the social science knowledge generated by those resettlements.

The goal and objectives of the AfDB resettlement policy are largely similar to those of the other MDFI policies. One significant difference, however, is that the AfDB policy does not include the "at least restore" option. Instead, the policy strictly requires the improvement of living standards, income earning capacity and production levels (AfDB 2003, 9).

Like the IFC and ADB, the AfDB subsumed all its safeguard policies under a single "Integrated Safeguard System" in 2013 (AfDB 2013). The 2003 resettlement policy was incorporated into that integrated document. The AfDB published an implementation review of the policy in 2015 (AfDB 2015).

European Bank for Reconstruction and Development

Like the other MDFIs, the European Bank for Reconstruction and Development (EBRD) had an integrated "Environmental and Social Policy" issued in 2014, which included a series of what it calls "Performance Requirements" (PRs). Among these was PR5 on "Land Acquisition, Involuntary Resettlement and Economic Displacement." PR5 appeared to mimic IFC PS5, except for one significant difference in the wording of its objectives: PR5 required borrowers to "restore or, where possible, improve the livelihoods and standards of living of displaced persons" (EBRD 2014, 30). When the Environmental and Social Policy was updated and reissued in 2019, the language of PR5 was changed to require borrowers to "improve, or as a minimum restore the livelihoods and standards of living of affected persons" (EBRD 2019, 41). A *Resettlement Guidance and Good Practice* handbook was issued by the EBRD in 2017.

United Nations Development Programme

The United Nations Development Programme (UNDP) adopted its Social and Environmental Standards in 2014, which became official UNDP policy on January 1, 2015. Among the policy standards is one that addresses displacement and resettlement (Cernea 2016a, xxi).

New Development Bank

The New Development Bank (NDB) was established in 2014 by the BRICS countries (Brazil, Russia, India, China, and South Africa). It is headquartered in Shanghai, China. It issued its Environmental and Social Framework, entailing a series of Environmental and Social Standards (ESS), in 2016. ESS2 addresses involuntary resettlement. ESS2's objectives and requirements mirror the policies and standards of the other MDFIs.

Asian Infrastructure Investment Bank

The Asian Infrastructure Investment Bank (AIIB), based in Beijing, China, is a relatively new MDFI, having begun operations in 2016. Like other MDFIs, it has an Environmental and Social Framework which consists of ESS. The initial 2016 framework and standards were opened to public consultation. Environmental and Social Standard 2 deals with involuntary resettlement. The objectives and requirements are virtually identical to the policies and performance standards of the other MDFIs. As of this writing, the revised 2019 framework and standards have been opened to public consultation and review, with the presentation of a final revised framework and standards to the Board anticipated by September 2020.

One significant innovative development throughout the course of policy development and adoption was the increasing establishment of independent advisory panels and/or Panels of Experts (POE). Several MDFI-financed projects beginning in the 1990s contracted such panels and international advisory groups to oversee, monitor, and evaluate projects, with frequent field visits, throughout the design, planning, loan negotiation, implementation, and monitoring and evaluation stages of their respective projects. Such panels submitted periodic reports, usually twice a year, if not more often, detailing progress and problems with the project and/or its resettlement component.

A number of public and private international agencies issued various guidelines addressing involuntary displacement and resettlement. It should be noted, however, that, while valuable, these are guidelines and, hence, voluntary, not binding on any agency, financial institution, or country.

United Nations Guidelines on Development-Based Evictions and Displacement

Prior to the issuance of its Guidelines on Internally Displaced Persons in 1998, the UN issued "Comprehensive Human Rights Guidelines on Development-Based Displacement" (UN 1997). This was followed up in 2006 with "Basic Principles and Guidelines on Development-Based Evictions and Displacement" as Annex 1 of the report of the Special Rapporteur on Adequate Housing as a Component of the Right to an Adequate Standard of Living (UN 2006).

UNCHR Guiding Principles on Business and Human Rights

Following the Equator Principles, the United Nations Commission for Human Rights (UNCHR), through the office of the Commissioner, issued its *Guiding Principles on Business and Human Rights* in 2011. They are intended to provide business enterprises with guidance on avoiding adverse human rights impacts and remedying any potential violations.

PRIVATE SECTOR LENDERS

The private sector, as Cernea points out (2005b, 91), remained uninfluenced by public agency safeguard policy development. Involuntary displacement and resettlement occurred in privately financed projects, such as the Camisea gas pipeline project in Peru, without virtually any regulatory framework. NGO pressure on and criticism of the private sector eventually drew the attention of some corporations and investment banks, who began conditioning their loans for large projects on there being a resettlement action plan in place. In 2003, the situation changed.

Equator Principles

In 2002, the IFC and ABN Ambro, a major European private bank, organized a meeting of private sector banks to discuss social and environmental risks in their projects, discrepancies in social standards among and between them, the pressure being placed on them by NGOs, and the need for a common and standardized approach. After several months of negotiations, a set of principles, which came to be named the Equator Principles (EPs), were drafted (Cernea 2005b, 92–93). They are intended to serve as a framework and minimum standard for assessing the social and environmental risks of private sector projects to inform individual institutional safeguard frameworks. The principles lay down social and environmental safeguards, including a resettlement policy modeled after IFC PS5. By 2003, private sector lenders adopted them voluntarily, first by ten major transnational banks, with the number of signatories increasing significantly in the first year. Export Credit Agencies (ECAs) soon followed suit, issuing a "Common Approaches on the Environment" document in 2007, which was updated in 2012 (OECD 2007, 2012). By 2019, a total of ninety-four financial institutions in thirty-seven countries had formally adopted the Principles. The third iteration of the Principles was issued in 2013, and the fourth, in July 2020.

There have been cases in which multinationals have addressed displacement and resettlement impacts of their projects independent of the EPs. Cernea (2005b, 95–96) cited two: the British Petroleum-financed Tangguh

LNG project in Papua, Indonesia, in which senior management committed to achieving, if not surpassing, the World Bank standards on the project's resettlement component. Based on first-hand observations during his three-year involvement with the project, Cernea stated that the resettlement of the community principally affected by the project took two years of preparation on the ground and was carried out in June 2004. BP's organizational, technical and financial inputs in his judgment met, and in several aspects, surpassed World Bank standards (Cernea, 2005b, 95).

Similarly, Shell Corporation committed to following an international standard such as the World Bank's, which would require compensation exceeding that provided for in national legislation and ensure benefits and entitlements required to meet international standards in cases where national laws on land acquisition do not provide them (Cernea 2005b, 96, citing Fossgard-Moser 2004).

BILATERAL AGENCIES

All twenty-four bilateral development aid agencies of OECD countries adopted policies similar to the International Standard on Involuntary Resettlement in the course of time. These included the US Agency for International Development (USAID), which issued its *Guidelines on Compulsory Displacement and Resettlement in USAID Programming* in May 2016, the German Technical Cooperation Agency (GTZ), and the Japan International Cooperation Agency (JICA), which issued its *Guidelines for Environmental and Social Considerations* in 2010, and *Requirements for Resettlement Action Plans* in 2012. Australia's Department of Foreign Assistance and Trade (DFAT) issued *Displacement and Resettlement of People in Development Activities*, its resettlement policy, in April 2015, an updated and revised version of its earlier policy issued in May 2014. Its policy objectives mirror those of the MDFIs. A more recently revised and updated version of its *Environmental and Social Safeguard Policy* was issued in March 2019, with accompanying guidance notes.

THE INTERNATIONAL STANDARD FOR INVOLUNTARY RESETTLEMENT

Taken together, these policy principles, provisions, and directives require, first, that population displacement and forced resettlement should be avoided or minimized whenever possible. Second, where involuntary resettlement is unavoidable, international standards require that the inherent risks of impoverishment induced by involuntary resettlement should be mitigated by providing project resources to displaced people that enable them to reconstruct their livelihoods and standards of living.

Taken together, we argue that the principles, provisions, and directives contained in the collective past policies and current performance standards comprise what we define here as the *International Standard for Involuntary Resettlement*. The International Standard for Involuntary Resettlement is defined as *that body of provisions and directives, derived from decades of empirical observation and results on the ground, comprised of and subsumed within both prior safeguard policies and current performance standards of development finance institutions, both multilateral and bilateral, public and private*. The logic of our argument in defining an International Standard for Involuntary Resettlement is as follows: all MDFI, bilateral, and private sector policies are modeled after the WB policy and all their major provisions are virtually the same. By extension, then, the International Standard for Involuntary Resettlement is comprised of that body of provisions and directives contained in all of those policies.

While the concept of the International Standard for Involuntary Resettlement is inclusive of all prior policy provisions and current standards of the MDFIs, we argue that the concept is best exemplified by WB OD 4.30 of 1990, which we, along with Scudder (2005, 278), believe to be the strongest policy statement to date on involuntary resettlement. The concept necessarily excludes various sets of guidelines set forth by international agencies, research institutions, nongovernmental organizations, and think tanks. As immensely important, valuable, and worthy of application as they are, they are guidelines, and thus voluntary, not binding on any public financial institution, private bank, implementing organization, corporation, bilateral agency, or country.

MDFI experience with involuntary resettlement operations over the last three decades has been mixed. That the World Bank tends most visibly and often to be the target of the bulk of public criticism regarding failure is attributable in part to the "unusual transparency of its processes" (Picciotto 2013, 243) relative to the other MDFIs (e.g., Cernea and Maldonado 2018, 38, n.3). This has resulted in protest campaigns focused on the Bank, excluding borrower countries. In other words, if any blame for failure is to be placed, it must be placed firmly at the feet of *both* the MDFIs and, *as importantly*, borrower governments.

In many instances, MDFI management and staff were successful in persuading borrower governments to build upon the accumulating scientific knowledge of what works and adopt relevant MDFI policy to prevent the impoverishment of displaced people. In the chapters that follow in this book, we will analyze a great number of cases in which the directives of OD 4.30, subsequent OP/BP 4.12 and other MDFI resettlement policies, all constituent elements of the International Standard for Involuntary Resettlement, contributed to successful involuntary resettlement operations. But it is important to emphasize here that there are many more cases in which MDFI management and staff did not comply with the involuntary resettlement policy or failed to convince borrowers to implement its policy. Too many times, resettlement operations in the MDFI projects were a failure, leaving the displaced people impoverished, due to violations of that policy that went unchecked and uncorrected—failure to inform and consult PAPs in resettlement planning; absence of a viable resettlement plan to be agreed at the time of appraisal; underestimation of project impacts causing population displacement and number of PAPs; forcing resettlement alternatives favored by authorities instead of providing PAPs the right to choose among alternatives; absence of socioeconomic and cultural analysis of the sustainability of livelihood restoration measures; racist and discriminatory perceptions of PAPs as culturally backward, ignorant, undeserving of respect, and incapable of intelligent decision-making; a lack of transition support and follow through in the provision of technical assistance; treating PAPs like guinea pigs for risky experiments that planners considered improvements; compensation for lost assets paid below replacement value, if paid at all; assignment of implementation responsibility to unqualified political appointees without the suitable language and technical skills required; budgetary shortfalls reneging on promised financial commitments to implement agreed upon programs; and of course corruption and more corruption.

One can conclude from this mixed record of success and failure that implementation of the International Standard for Involuntary Resettlement to a very large measure depends on the professionalism and integrity of individual MDFI managers and staff. Just as in nation-state government bureaucracies, there are many honest, dedicated professionals willing to apply MDFI policies and lessons learned, in the MDFIs there are also many honest, dedicated professionals who do their best to guide borrowers to implement the directives of resettlement policy. Yet there are just as many managers and staff in the MDFIs and in borrower governments perfectly willing to subvert or disregard resettlement policy, who could care less what happens to the displaced people, and whose idea of professionalism is to move the money to build the dam, construct the highway, excavate the mine, or carry out the urban gentrification plan. Put in another way, this mixed record of some positive results and many abject failures shows that the MDFIs never have any real power to compel or enforce compliance (other than perhaps to withhold loan disbursements), only to persuade and convince. For example, for over thirty years, the World Bank and its Executive Board never disciplined, punished, or fired a single staff member for violation of Bank policy; it was obvious to everyone there were no consequences for ignoring the policy. Resettlement performance, then, clearly depends entirely on the professionalism and integrity of MDFI management and staff coupled with the professionalism and integrity of their counterparts in borrower governments.

Current MDFI frameworks permit more or less considerable leeway and negotiation of alternatives between the MDFI and borrowers, including on land acquisition, involuntary resettlement, compensation and other entitlements, and protections for project-affected people. Negotiated agreements on the application of the International Standard on Involuntary Resettlement will clearly henceforth take place on a project-by-project basis. This has always been the case, but now without the pretense of leveraging a project to reform the entire legal and policy framework of a country. Consequently, the focus of policy execution must, first and foremost, to a greater extent shift from persuading MDFI staff and managers to compel borrower compliance toward persuading borrower country government officials, administrators, ministers, and other civil servants what must be done in order to achieve successful resettlement outcomes. Like the process of getting the first resettlement policy through and approved by the World Bank in the 1980s, this will not be an easy task (e.g., Humphrey 2016, 6).

It means working directly with engineers, lawyers, and other government civil servants—ministries of public works, secretariats of agriculture, electricity companies and energy corporations, departments of irrigation, housing, and urban development officials—to correct past errors and avoid future ones. It means recruiting host-country anthropologists and other social scientists with linguistic and cultural knowledge gained through in-depth fieldwork. It means confronting frequent opposition, whether in the form of polite indifference or outright hostility. It means contending with a mindset that views involuntary resettlement as "collateral damage," an unavoidable cost of development and even the exclusive prerogative of government. It means having to become a reasonably competent legal researcher, especially in the areas of land, expropriation and compensation law. It means challenging and correcting the institutionalized social exclusion that perpetuates persistent poverty. It means going well beyond Picciotto's (2013, 243) recommendation of learning to exercise the "art of the possible." It means, finally, insisting on the application of the historically long and empirically based funds of knowledge regarding what must be done to achieve the improvement of livelihoods, living standards, and social development of displaced and resettled communities in accordance with the most stringent policy proscriptions entailed within both previous and present safeguard policies and performance requirements, what we have called the International Standard on Involuntary Resettlement. Rebuilding livelihoods is at the core of involuntary resettlement plans that meet the International Standard for Involuntary Resettlement.

For any resettlement operation to be viable, it must fit a country's legal, regulatory, and policy framework, specifically, the statutes governing land acquisition, compensation, and resettlement. Most such frameworks are woefully inadequate and in need of major improvement. It is to country frameworks that we now turn.

BORROWER COUNTRY LEGAL FRAMEWORKS FOR LAND ACQUISITION AND RESETTLEMENT

MDFI efforts to improve country-level legal, regulatory, and policy frameworks pertaining to involuntary resettlement have been ongoing since the first involuntary resettlement policy was promulgated by the World Bank in 1980. Initiatives of the ADB and WB were mentioned briefly earlier. The results have been, at best, mixed.

There appears to be a consensus among former World Bank staff, external resettlement experts, evaluators, legal analysts, and CSOs that a significantly more substantial amount of responsibility and obligation has been transferred to borrowing countries for planning, designing, implementing, and overseeing resettlement operations (see, e.g., Cernea 2016; Cernea and Maldonado 2018a, b; Price 2019a, 2, 2019b; Price and Singer 2019; Tagliarino 2016, 2017, 2018a, b, 2019). Borrower governments must now, at least in theory, ensure that they have the capacity, skills and legal, regulatory and policy architecture in place to plan and carry out resettlement operations that satisfy or meet the requirements of the International Standard for Involuntary Resettlement. Countries such as China, India, Bangladesh, Laos, Vietnam, and other Asian, Pacific, and African states have made important strides toward improving their national legal, regulatory, and policy frameworks on displacement and resettlement (see, e.g., Cernea 2016b; Cernea and Maldonado 2018; Padovani 2016; Price 2019; Price and Singer 2019; Shi 2018; Zaman and Khatun 2019, among others). Still, huge gaps remain, potentially placing millions of displaced people at risk of increased impoverishment.

Loan agreements signed by member governments of multilateral organizations like the World Bank are "governed by public international law and consequently the member concerned is under obligation to adapt its domestic law to the agreement with the Bank" (Shihata 2001). Therefore, when gaps exist between a country's domestic legal framework and the current international standards on involuntary resettlement agreed with the member countries of MDFIs, project-specific measures, including, for example, depending on the financing institution, an Environmental and Social Commitment Plan (ESCP) and Resettlement Action Plan (RAP), are to be negotiated and agreed that fill the gaps and bring the former more into alignment with the latter.

This section of this chapter summarizes the state of country systems or frameworks for conducting resettlement operations. We focus on land acquisition and issues surrounding compensation, based on the findings of several recent legal and social science analyses.

Land Acquisition and Expropriation

The principal cause of population displacement and resettlement in development projects is the expropriation of land and other property or restrictions on access or use of resources such as forests, fisheries, and grasslands upon which people depend for survival. Ideally, the key policies and principles governing involuntary resettlement would be spelled out in the legal statutes for the taking of land or other resources of any given country. In most countries, however, legal frameworks for land acquisition are "entirely silent on resettlement and re-establishment of people displaced" by expropriation of properties upon which they depend (Shihata 2000; see also Shihata 1993). Indeed, a recent analysis of national laws and policies regarding land acquisition in fifty countries found that, while some countries may have nonbinding policy statements, "hardly any of the 50 countries (with the exception of China, India, Laos, the Philippines and Vietnam) have enacted binding laws with provisions for resettling and reconstructing the livelihoods of displaced people" (Tagliarino 2018a, 273). An earlier analysis of the national laws regarding expropriation and compensation in thirty African and Asian countries found that in only four was the concept of "public purpose" clearly defined legally; two limit the amount and types of land that the government and/or partner entities could acquire; only three required surveys and consultation with affected people; in only six were people with customary tenure rights and usufruct rights to undeveloped lands entitled to receive compensation; none of them required gender-sensitive valuation and calculation of compensation; only eight required prompt payment of compensation, and recognized the right of PAPs to negotiate and challenge compensation determinations before courts and other tribunals; and only one (India) had a national law that required stringent resettlement and rehabilitation measures (Tagliarino 2016, 3). That is to say that, in the majority of countries whose frameworks were assessed, displaced people do not have any formal legal guarantees regarding resettlement and rehabilitation.

Using WB OP/BP 4.12 and 2017 ESF, IFC PS5 and several voluntary guidelines including the United Nations *Voluntary Guidelines on Responsible Governance of Tenure* (VGGT, UN 2012) as international standards, the frameworks (constitutions, regulations, statutes and legislation) for twenty-one countries in Asia, twenty in Africa, and nine in Latin America, low- and medium-income countries with significant amounts of land held under customary tenure or occupied by informal settlers (see Tagliarino 2018a, 2019 for details), were assessed as to whether "content indicators" were present in their legal, policy, and regulatory frameworks. These indicators included (i) the existence of a national-level law with legally binding procedures for (ii) resettling and rehabilitating the displaced, (iii) provision of relocation assistance, (iv) provision of suitable replacement land and housing, (v) prior and informed consultation with the displaced, (vi) a requirement to avoid or minimize resettlement and (vii) a requirement to provide sufficient funding for implementing resettlement operations.

The legal analysis found that only three of the fifty countries assessed (India, Laos, and Vietnam) have statutes or regulations regarding resettlement procedures that are legally binding on all projects which require the expropriation of land (Tagliarino 2018a, 280). While China has made significant progress in legislating a series of laws, policies, and regulations, they are mostly applicable to the hydropower sector. It has no overarching law which applies to *all* expropriation projects and thus does not provide *all* displaced persons with resettlement and rehabilitation procedures. Forty-four of the fifty assessed countries have no legally binding resettlement procedures for projects entailing land expropriation. Twelve countries have drafted or adopted resettlement policies, but the policies are not legally binding (Tagliarino 2018a, 281).

Four of the fifty countries legally provide a relocation allowance to cover the costs of resettling on alternative land. Seventeen provide such an allowance as part of the compensation package to eligible landholders, those with registered or legally recognized land rights, but do not ensure all displaced persons will receive such an allowance. Twenty-eight of the fifty countries have no explicit or implicit provision in their laws regarding a relocation allowance (Tagliarino 2018a, 282).

In terms of providing the displaced with alternative land and/or housing, only three of the fifty countries have laws with such a provision. Twenty-six provide alternative land as a compensation option, but only at the discretion of the government. Twenty countries do not legally provide displaced people with any right to alternative land; the majority of displaced people thus have no guarantee of obtaining alternative land. As an example, in Bangladesh prior to 2017, a survey of those displaced found that 77 percent viewed their overall compensation as insufficient, while 90 percent reported that they were unable to purchase the same amount of land with the compensation payment that was provided. Moreover, only one country out of the fifty assessed explicitly included in law the provision of *productive* alternative land and/or *suitable* alternative housing. Four countries include such provisions in some cases but provide no guarantee. The laws of forty-four of the fifty countries contain no requirement regarding the provision of productive replacement land or suitable replacement housing (Tagliarino 2018a, 284).

Only five of the fifty countries assessed explicitly require consultation with PAPs throughout the resettlement process. In forty-three of the fifty countries, neither the government nor the acquiring entities are legally required to consult with PAPs (Tagliarino 2018a, 286).

In terms of avoiding or minimizing displacement and resettlement, only one country—India, in its LARR of 2013 explicitly requires avoidance and/ or minimization of displacement and resettlement. Two countries require minimization or avoidance in some cases, while in forty-six of the fifty there is no legal obligation or avoid or minimize displacement and resettlement in the policy framework (Tagliarino 2018a, 286–87).

Ensuring that there is sufficient funding for the implementation of resettlement operations is legally mandated in only three of the fifty countries assessed. Forty-six do not have a law that requires the government or acquiring entities to provide sufficient financial resources for resettlement and reconstruction operations (Tagliarino 2018a, 287).

Valuation and Compensation for Expropriated Land

National legal and policy frameworks for the expropriation of property usually call for cash compensation to be paid to the property owners. The practice of compulsory land acquisition varies among governments, with some states making relatively minimal use of the process and relying more heavily on market-based transactions to acquire land. Where markets exist for land, houses, and other properties, governments may utilize market-based, voluntary transactions by paying cash compensation at replacement value. Compensation paid at replacement value is required by the International Standard for Involuntary Resettlement to ensure that property owners are able to use property markets, where they function, to replace lost assets and to resettle themselves.

Unfortunately, most country legal frameworks do not require compensation at replacement value. This leaves property owners with insufficient resources to compete in the property market, particularly when prices are inflated by the impacts of the very large-scale public works projects that are displacing them. For this reason, the International Standard for Involuntary Resettlement requires the design and financing of a RAP to assist displaced property owners to relocate and reestablish their livelihoods and, where possible, improve their living standards.

Tagliarino (2017) identified ten "content" or "legal" indicators in the legal frameworks of the fifty countries regarding the valuation of compensation for expropriated land. These included (i) alternative approaches to compensation based on "fair market value"; (ii) compensation for people with unregistered customary tenure; (iii) ensuring female landholders receive fair compensation; (iv) compensation for loss of economic activities; (v) compensation for land improvements; (vi) compensation for intangible land values (cultural, spiritual, and/or historical); (vii) a right to replacement land as a compensation option, (viii) the right of PAPs to negotiate compensation amounts, (ix) timely payment of compensation; and (x) the right of PAPs to challenge compensation decisions in courts of law or in tribunals. Each of these indicators is summarized in turn.

Only eight of the fifty countries have legislatively established alternative approaches to the fair market value method of calculating compensation. Five have established such alternatives only in certain circumstances (Tagliarino 2017, 10).

Noting that both WB and IFC standards do not distinguish between customary and statutory land rights for purposes of compensation, such that all PAPs are entitled to receive compensation, Tagliarino (2017, 11) found that only seven of the fifty countries assessed provide for compensation of PAPs regardless of tenure status. Eight of the fifty provide compensation to those with customary tenure only in some cases. Thirty-five of the fifty countries do not grant communities with customary tenure the right to compensation. The significance of denying the right to compensation of PAPs with customary tenure is dramatically illustrated by the following facts: 70 percent of the world's land is unregistered, and 2.5 billion people currently hold land under customary tenure. Many countries require that indigenous people and local communities with customary tenure (IPLCs) must register their land in order to be eligible and qualify for compensation. This can be an extremely lengthy and burdensome process. For example, in Peru indigenous forest communities must navigate their way through and satisfy no less than twenty-seven legal and bureaucratic hurdles in order to achieve official recognition of their lands and obtain legal title, a process that can take well over a decade (Tagliarino 2017, 10).

Only two of the fifty countries include consideration of female landholders' rights to receive fair compensation, including widows and divorcees. However, the laws of these countries do not ensure women's rights to compensation will be protected in every instance (Tagliarino 2017, 12).

Twenty-seven of the fifty countries have legislated that compensation is to be paid for loss of economic activities. In ten of the fifty countries, laws provide for such compensation in some cases, but not all. Thirteen of the fifty do not explicitly or implicitly provide compensation for loss of economic activities; that is, their laws provide for the calculation of compensation according to fair market value without any additional provisions for such losses. In terms of compensation for land improvements, thirty-two of the fifty countries provide such compensation, eleven provide such compensation in some but not all cases, and the laws of seven countries contain no requirement to assess the value of improvements or provide compensation for them (Tagliarino 2017, 13).

Only two of the fifty countries consider the cultural, spiritual, and/or historical value of land and provide compensation for such losses. Seven provide compensation to some extent, while in forty-one of the fifty countries, laws do not include the assessment of intangible land values in calculating compensation (Tagliarino 2017, 14–15).

Of the fifty countries assessed, nineteen provided alternative land as a compensation option, whether instead of or in addition to cash payments. Seven provide for such an option only in some cases. Twenty-four of thirty countries have laws in which there is no provision regarding alternative land as an option (Tagliarino 2017, 15).

The right of PAPs to negotiate, on an equal footing and level playing field, fair and just compensation for lost lands, houses, and other assets has become a major topic of discussion and debate in recent years. As mentioned previously, IFC PS5 emphasizes negotiated settlements between project proponents and PAPs over eminent domain expropriation and acquisition, even if governments and acquiring entities have such legal power. Thus, it is significant, indeed surprising, that only twenty-seven of the fifty countries assessed by Tagliarino legally provide PAPs with the right to negotiate compensation amounts. Eight provide this right "if necessary," meaning that it is not guaranteed. Astonishingly, fifteen of the fifty countries' laws do not provide PAPs with the right to negotiate the amount of compensation to be paid (Tagliarino 2017, 16–17).

In terms of timely compensation payments to PAPs, twenty-one of the fifty countries' laws require payment of compensation either before the actual acquisition of land or within a specific timeframe thereafter. In thirteen countries, laws establish deadlines for payment but include exceptions in the form of extensions to those deadlines. Sixteen of the fifty countries do not require the payment of compensation either before land acquisition or within any legally specified timeframe (Tagliarino 2017, 18).

The right of PAPs to challenge compensation decisions in courts of law or before tribunals is recognized in the laws of twenty-five of the fifty countries assessed. These rights are recognized with limitations in eight countries, while in seven the laws do not provide PAPs with the right to challenge decisions regarding compensation amounts. In these seven countries, compensation is a "take it or leave it" proposition, and PAPs are left with no legal redress or remedy (Tagliarino 2017, 18–19).

Tagliarino's legal analysis showed that none of the fifty countries assessed achieved a perfect "score" for all ten legal indicators pertaining to valuation and compensation. Latin American countries (see, e.g., Nahmad 2019 for Mexico) lagged far behind Asian and African countries in adopting legal mechanisms in the forms of laws, statutes, regulations, or policies approaching the International Standard for Involuntary Resettlement on valuation of compensation for land, houses, and other assets lost by affected communities to project-related expropriation (Tagliarino 2017, 19). Kamakia, Shi, and Zaman (2017) identified significant gaps in Kenya's national resettlement policy. Rhoads and Mugyenyi (2019) analyzed progress and pitfalls in Uganda.

Land Tenure and Eligibility for Compensation

National legal and policy frameworks for the expropriation of property almost invariably fail to cover the poorest and most vulnerable persons displaced by the land acquisition. These include landless laborers, renters, employees, sharecroppers, and many small farmers lacking title to their farms. It also includes most hunters-and-gatherers, pastoralists, fisherfolk, indigenous people, or ethnic minorities who do not have title to the resources or lands they have traditionally occupied. Colonial governments systematically refused to regularize or legalize the ancestral rights to the lands of indigenous peoples of Africa, Asia, and the Americas.

The categories of people mentioned above almost invariably do not receive any compensation to enable them to be resettled because they are not considered as legal owners of the resource upon which they depend for their livelihood. This is always because the state has failed to provide them legal titles or other protection of their rights. Since these categories of displaced people do not receive compensation, their resettlement and reestablishment must be based on and financed by other legal mechanisms.

Building on an earlier legal analysis of the national frameworks of thirty African and Asian countries (Tagliarino 2016, 2018b, 2019) assessed whether land rights of indigenous people and local communities with customary tenure (IPLCs) were recognized to the extent that customary systems of land ownership qualified or made them eligible for compensation in the context of land acquisition and expropriation. Countries and their legal systems were "scored" or assessed on whether laws allowed for compensation to be paid to communities with (i) formally recognized tenure rights; (ii) unregistered or unrecognized land rights; and (iii) formally recognized land rights regardless of whether such land was developed, cultivated, or otherwise improved, that is, access and use rights to common property forests, grasslands, pasturelands, woodlands, wetlands, and the like. The assessment of fifty country frameworks, including Latin American countries, on this issue was briefly summarized above.

The laws of twenty-two of the thirty countries assessed provide for the payment of compensation to communities with formally recognized land tenure rights; five of those twenty-two explicitly entitle IPLCs with customary tenure rights to receive compensation. The laws of seven of the thirty countries do not provide a right to compensation to communities upon the expropriation of their land (Tagliarino 2019, 64–65).

Regarding IPLCs with unregistered land, seven of the thirty countries' laws (six in Africa) grant communities a right to compensation regardless of whether their land rights are formally registered or not. In five countries, the rights of some IPLCs to compensation are legislated, but not all. Eighteen of the thirty countries do not have laws that provide compensation for formally recognized IPLC tenure rights, regardless of whether such rights are registered or not (Tagliarino 2019, 68–70).

In fifteen (eight in Africa, seven in Asia) of the thirty countries assessed, the rights of IPLCs to compensation for loss of access and use of common property lands and resources is granted. Thirteen (five in Africa, eight in Asia) of the thirty countries' laws do not provide IPLCs with the right to compensation for common property, regardless of whether their commons have been cultivated, improved, or otherwise developed. For example, China, Cambodia, Ethiopia, Namibia, Nigeria, and Zimbabwe all require that communities cultivate, improve, or otherwise develop land in order to be eligible for and receive compensation (Tagliarino 2019, 71–72).

Much of the problem regarding IPLCs with customary tenure revolves around issues such as the legal definition of "community land," including the length of time the land has been occupied and/or the number of people occupying that land. In many countries, communities must prove they have occupied and used the land for a legally determined time period. In India, for example, Tagliarino notes that the LARR of 2013 explicitly states that the land must have served as a primary source of livelihood for a period of three years prior to the expropriation. Even more stringent, India's Forest Rights Act of 2006 specifies that, in order to qualify for compensation, communities must prove that the land has served as the primary residence and provided a legitimate livelihood *for at least three generations* prior to December 13, 2005, Tagliarino 2019, 72–75, emphasis added).

In a parallel analysis, Price (2019b) examined the legal frameworks of forty Asia-Pacific countries. One presumes there is some overlap in terms of countries with the assessments made by Tagliarino. She found that in only four of the forty frameworks she examined were there any measures legislated to avoid or minimize displacement in laws and/or regulations regarding land expropriation (Price 2019b, 194).

Only "a few" of the forty require detailed social risk and impact analysis, including census and surveys of project-affected communities. Only one requires gender-sensitive analyses (Price 2019, 196). In only one country of the forty does the law contain "firm legal arrangements for replacement land"; three "spell out replacement principles," three "provided explicit transitional support," and three "required specific livelihood strategies." She found that few laws even mention the term "livelihood," "very few frameworks guaranteed people without formal title benefits or other forms of assistance" other than land compensation payments, and "few articulated a livelihood enhancements objective" (Price 2019b, 198).

Only 25 percent of the forty countries require any "meaningful" or "systematic" consultation with PAPs. Twelve of fourteen Pacific states are "innovating new approaches to negotiated short- and long-term leases and land swaps with customary landowner groups," but one assumes that these are in various stages of development and/or implementation and "the impacts have yet to be assessed." One-third of twenty-six Asian countries "are increasing opportunities for negotiation instead of or as part of eminent domain procedures," and only two "use a legal framework with negotiation to ensure . . . negotiation practices do not leave people worse off" (Price 2019b, 199). Only eight of the forty countries examined have "instituted formal project-based grievance procedures," while "others have in place procedures for legal appeals under pre-existing laws" (Price 2019b, 200).

Wilmsen and colleagues (2020) have recently analyzed the social and environmental safeguard policies of the Belt Road Initiative (BRI). The BRI is a massive program of both multilateral and bilateral infrastructure investment and projects led by the Chinese government and its national partner construction firms, national and private banks, and other financial institutions, a growing list of partner countries and MDFIs including the WB, ADB, NDB, and AIIB, which have agreed to or are considering cofinancing BRI projects. Additional countries are being invited to join, and the list of participants continues to grow (Wilmsen et al. 2020, 115). In the first eight months of 2016 alone, for example, Chinese companies signed a total of 3,912 project contracts involving sixty-one countries. Many projects touted as "new" BRI projects are old, stalled projects which are being resurrected under the BRI banner (FOE 2016, iii).

This enormously complex multilateral and bilateral conglomeration of countries, sectors, public and private banks, companies, and financial institutions complicates the issue of exactly what set of social and environmental safeguard standards and guidelines will apply to BRI projects. In other words, there will be collisions of global, MDFI, country-level, and private sector standards. China has both a set of evolving domestic safeguard standards and policies and an evolving set for overseas investment and operations (Wilmsen et al. 2020, 121), while its banks, firms, and other financial institutions have overseas operations policies and guidelines, some binding and some voluntary, of their own (Wilmsen et al. 2020, 123–24). Recipient countries each have their own legal and policy frameworks. The MDFIs each have their own frameworks and standards on social and environmental risks. China's policy on development assistance and foreign investment is one of "non-interference," preferring to not involve itself in the internal affairs of other countries. Many developing countries prefer this policy approach; "it comes without Western lectures about governance and human rights" and does not necessarily entail the perceived burdensome "social, environmental and accountability standards of Western donors." In cases where BRI projects are solely funded by Chinese banks and implemented by Chinese construction firms (who have received the majority of project contracts), the management and mitigation of social and environmental risks will be the responsibility of recipient countries (Wilmsen et al. 2020, 117, 120).

Focusing on the social risk of involuntary displacement and resettlement, Wilmsen et al. (2020, 118, Figure 6.1) assessed the national frameworks of laws and regulations of countries participating in the BRI. They found that many of the 17 BRI countries to date, "particularly those in Central and South East Asia, are noncompliant with a majority" of the involuntary resettlement guidelines of the ADB. "Indeed, no country, apart from India, is compliant with more than a small fraction of the ADB guidelines. Importantly, China's own resettlement standards are mostly noncompliant with the ADB standards, although significant progress has been made in the area in recent years" (Wilmsen et al. 2020, 119). In contrast, Shi (2018) and others (Cernea 2008, 2016b; Downing 2016) have argued that China's legal and policy framework for involuntary resettlement surpass the MDFIs in terms of safeguarding and providing sufficient financial resources for the economic reconstruction of displaced people.

Given the consensus alluded to in chapter 2 and above that the 2017 WB ESF and its ESS shifts most of the responsibility for planning, designing and implementing environmental and social programs, including involuntary resettlement operations, to borrower countries, along with the dismal picture painted above regarding the state of country legal systems around the issues of expropriation, compensation, and resettlement, the risks of impoverishment of people affected by BRI projects, failed resettlement outcomes, and corruption would seem to be significantly elevated.

National and State Government Dilution of Law

Finally, it is important to note here that Tagliarino points out that he did not assess "subnational laws" as part of his assessments. This leads, perhaps, to an even more important point: *even in cases where national governments have formally legislated legally binding, comprehensive national laws on expropriation, compensation, and resettlement, the real issue is how such legislation is interpreted, translated, and implemented at governmental levels below that of the nation.* To take but one example, India's LARR of 2013 has been amended twice since, in 2014 and 2015. According to Saxena (2015), the 2014 amendment diluted or nullified several provisions of the Principal Act. Section 109 of India's LARR of 2013 permits "appropriate governments," meaning state governments, to "make rules for carrying out the provisions of this Act" upon notification. Kohli and Gupta (2016) have documented how some Indian states, taking advantage of this clause, have legislated rules that, for example, shorten the time frame for conducting SIAs mandated by the national law, even eliminating the SIA process altogether, make reductions in compensation awards, modify the retrospective clause in the Act, and include provisions to remove the requirement of consent from the land acquisition procedure (see also Kabra and Das 2019). In effect, state rule-making efforts result in "dilutions" of the national law at the state level, with serious consequences for people threatened with involuntary displacement and resettlement in those states.

Changes and repeals to parts of new legislation do not necessarily negate the overall progress some countries have made to date in their legal and policy frameworks. But, as Downing points out, such political dynamics "demand constant vigilance lest they be reversed" (Downing 2016, xii).

STANDARDS, FRAMEWORKS, AND ACHIEVING SUCCESSFUL RESETTLEMENT

As briefly alluded to in chapter 2, it is our view that academic and semantic debates over "improve" versus "restore," "policy" versus "standard," "safeguards" versus "frameworks," and so on mean very little, if anything, to people facing involuntary displacement and resettlement. Frankly, such debates do nothing to inform the practice required on the ground to achieve "resettlement with development" such that the latter transcends being just another development slogan or mantra.

The "safeguard policies" which have been replaced by environmental and social frameworks and variously labeled "performance standards" generally retain much of the same directives and provisions. A "standard" is something by which something else is to be measured, for example, "did Y meet the standard(s) set forth in X?" As illustrated in chapter 2, OMS 2.33 was the standard by which resettlement operations in the Sardar Sarovar Project in India were judged or evaluated. Each of the current MDFI frameworks and associated performance requirements provides a standard by which the success of resettlement operations will (or should) be measured. Each is an important and valuable guide for the planning, design, financing, and implementation of resettlement operations. The issue is not whether guidance is in the form of a "framework," "policy," or "performance requirement," but rather how such guidance, whatever its form on paper, is translated into effective practice on the ground. The failure of many resettlement operations has little or nothing to do with a specific clause in any resettlement policy or performance requirement. The bulk of such failures are due to many other more determinant factors, including derision of and contempt for displaced people by dominant groups, failure of implementing agencies to allocate promised budget amounts to resettlement operations, the assignment of unqualified personnel like engineers to direct resettlement, top-down planning, and execution of resettlement with no meaningful participation of those displaced, imposition of "social experiments" rooted in planners', architects', and others' ideas of "improvement" based on racist and discriminatory stereotypes of poor, rural and indigenous people and practices as "backward," rather than listening to what displaced people want and can manage, forcing the displaced into debt to finance resettlement, failure to allocate adequate land to replace that which was expropriated, breaking up communities and social networks vital to the poor, lack of continuity in both MDFI and borrower teams such that support and supervision changes hands continually, and rampant corruption in local and state governments. Those who blame the failure of resettlement operations on a clause in a policy simplify a complex, multifaceted set of conditions that contribute to failure.

Our focus is on how resettlement operations and outcomes can be made successful, whether they be guided by "policies," "standards," or whatever "frameworks," such that displaced and resettled people are enabled to achieve sustainable social, economic, and human development, better living standards, and well-being *as defined by them*. This is the reason we have argued for and conceptualized the International Standard for Involuntary Resettlement. This requires adhering to the frameworks, performance requirements, and country legal systems where they are helpful, but also the ethical commitment to go beyond applicable frameworks and performance requirements, as legally allowed by borrower country legal systems, to fill the gaps that exist on a case-by-case, project-by-project basis. As Ravindran and Kumar have noted, "laws and policies can only make generic provisions which are common for all communities affected by projects. Inferences made from one project may not be equally applicable to all projects. Real solutions are project-specific, as there can be no one-size-that-fits-all kind of solutions" (Ravindran and Kumar 2019, 272). In a very real sense, *the project thus becomes the unit of analysis*.

As stated previously in the Introduction to this book, we extrapolate from Sen (1999, 2009) the argument that country governments and their constituent ministries, financing institutions, including managers and staffs, specialists, and consultants, as well as nongovernmental organizations, and any others responsible have a moral responsibility and obligation to conduct resettlement operations, where they cannot be avoided or when they are necessary to save lives, in a socially and culturally appropriate manner in close and constant collaboration with the affected people as full partners and fellow citizens. In accordance with the International Standard for Involuntary Resettlement, project-affected people must be fairly and justly compensated for *all* their losses, both material and economic, at replacement value, provided with adequate, productive replacement land and security of tenure, suitable (to the displaced) housing, infrastructure, and public services to reconstitute their communities, and the necessary training, education, and other assistance to enhance successful adaptation and rebuilding their livelihoods in the new environment and conditions. Wherever possible, they must be entitled *with priority*, over and above compensation and other forms of restitution, to receive a fair proportion of project revenues as full beneficiaries (Cernea, 2007, 2008, his emphasis). Most importantly, resettled people must be given the *freedom to choose* among alternative opportunities which may arise in the aftermath of resettlement. The ultimate objectives of resettling forcibly displaced communities must be their *sustainable social, economic, and human development, better standards of living*, and *achieving well-being as defined by them*. Resettlement operations should be carried out *in accordance with the strongest directives and provisions of both prior safeguard policies and current standards*; that is to say, the International Standard for Involuntary Resettlement. The challenge will be working with borrower country governments to ensure that the most stringent resettlement standards are met in their legal and policy systems.

Achieving real resettlement with development will require a praxis of ethical commitment to taking politically effective actions to empower displaced communities, accepting the challenge of designing and negotiating project-specific resettlement policy, planning and implementation together with all stakeholders in community, organizational, and institutional contexts. Such praxis is required to achieve successful resettlement, whether those responsible be national or international nongovernmental organizations, administrative and service agencies of government at all levels, private and public sector business firms, or transnational and multilateral institutions, to confront and correct policy and legal frameworks that deepen exclusion, oppression, poverty, and other forms of exploitation. Such praxis requires dealing with the powerful as well as the powerless in working toward leveling the playing field to permit the active, direct participation of displaced people in the design and execution of their own resettlement, which is the only way to achieve sustainable social, economic, and human development.

The first, and arguably most important, task for those involved in resettlement operations is to acquire as deep an understanding as possible of the *in vivo* structure, organization, production and exchange systems, land and resource base, livelihood strategies, and other dynamics of communities that are faced with involuntary displacement and resettlement. It is crucial that this understanding be based on more than the simple "development tourism" of missions and site visits conducted by bureaucrats and technicians wherever and whenever possible. Understanding communities and their dynamics requires empirical facts gathered on the ground. The following chapter presents our understanding of communities and their social, cultural, and economic dynamics, obtained from the empirical field work of social anthropologists that can inform appropriate planning, design, and implementation of resettlement with the participation of affected communities.

Part II

APPLYING THE INTERNATIONAL STANDARD FOR INVOLUNTARY RESETTLEMENT IN CONTEMPORARY RESETTLEMENT OPERATIONS

Chapter 4

The Nature of Human Communities Facing Displacement and Resettlement

As one team of development analysts eloquently put it over forty years ago, "culture change is still not seen as a transgenerational process of adaptation, but as a one-shot transformation. Tradition, poorly understood and still not the subject of systematic inquiry, continues to be the enemy" (Nugent et al. 1978, 61). Unfortunately, this assumption remains, to a large extent, firmly entrenched in development thinking.

As social scientists have long known, the rural and urban poor, indigenous and tribal peoples, and peasant small farm holders have been consistently characterized as homogenous, static, conservative, backward, passive, apathetic, illiterate, inarticulate, and marginal in terms of national societal and development interests (see Mathur 2019, 49–55; Alcorn 1984, 392; Arensberg 1978, 61; Clawson 1978, 324–25, 336; Denevan 1983; Johnson 1972; Pitt 1976, 14; Salisbury 1970, 2–4; Scudder 1980, 395–96; 1985, 149–50). Those who hold this notion continue to assert that development occurs (or should) in a quantum leap from traditional to modern (Pitt 1976, 10; Warren 1979). The myth of conservatism continues to lead development planners to believe that there is a need to integrate "marginal" peoples into the national mainstream society and economy through the introduction of technological packages, chemical inputs, cash crops, and the like. As Scudder put it, developers generally believe that poor peoples' "interests are best served by transformational approaches superimposed upon them by government planners" (1980, 395–96). The idea here is that total transformation is desirable and beneficial (Pitt 1976, 10). The results in practice are projects which are originated, administered, and managed exclusively from project center headquarters to peripheral communities in a blueprint fashion (Korten 1980), what has long been known as paternalistic, top-down development. River basin development schemes are a "classic example" (Scudder 1980, 395).

89

Moreover, development interventions are most often designed and planned by males and oriented toward males. In many societies, however, kin relations are reckoned through the female line; women own and/or have primary responsibilities for managing land, planting, weeding, and harvesting crops from fields and home gardens, collecting fuelwood and wild food and medicinal resources from forest, bush and other common or communally held property, preparing meals, performing domestic chores, instructing both male and female children on proper role behavior and the like. Women may even own parcels of land or inherit it on the death of their spouse. These facts are often overlooked, neglected, or ignored by male development "experts" and technocrats.

This all too common paternalistic, assimilative objective of development was illustrated dramatically and literally in the case of the Aleman Dam project that resulted in the resettlement of 20,000 Mazatec indigenous people (see chapter 2 and below). The major objective of the Papaloapan Project was, in ideological terms, the incorporation of affected indigenous communities into the national economy and society. That objective was explicitly stated in official documents of the Papaloapan Commission itself (Nugent et al. 1978, 52). Administrative commitment to assimilation was further symbolized by a large mural at the top of the Aleman Dam, depicting the transformation of the Mazatec from impoverished, "primitive" digging-stick cultivators into healthy and wealthy commercial farmers utilizing modern science and technology (Nugent et al. 1978, 51–52). As we saw in chapter 2, transformational and assimilative development, rooted in racist notions of primitivism and backwardness, where resettlement programs are designed as technological and social experiments geared toward "improvement" without any input by affected communities, invariably result in social and cultural failure.

This chapter sets out our understanding of the nature, characteristics, and complexity of human communities and their cultural dynamics, grounded in empirical social anthropological research. It takes as its point of departure an empirically grounded example, based on long-term field study, of differential adaptations to resettlement among a community of Mazatec indigenous people resettled in zone 1 to make way for the construction of the Aleman Dam. The chapter concludes by teasing out the theoretical and conceptual issues and implications derived from the Mazatec example, emphasizing those elements that are critical to sound planning, design, and implementation of resettlement operations for achieving successful community resettlement.

DIFFERENTIAL ADAPTATIONS TO RESETTLEMENT IN THE MAZATEC COMMUNITY OF LAS MARGARITAS

The resettled Mazatec community of Las Margaritas has been intensively studied (Nugent, et al. 1978; Partridge and Brown 1982, 1983; Partridge,

Brown, and Nugent 1982), perhaps more so than any community resettled to zone 1 to make way for the construction of the Aleman Dam. Substantial data has been marshaled on the human ecology, health, and economic adaptations of this community since resettlement in 1952–1953. It is one of the few cases of relative success intensively analyzed and documented in zone 1.

Las Margaritas was the largest of all resettlement communities in zone 1, with a land base of 2,300 hectares (Villa Rojas 1955, 146). It was composed largely of more progressive *ejidatarios*, their families and dependents from the villages of El Crucero, Boca Tilpan, and La Guadalupe in the municipality of Soyaltepec, who arrived in the early years of resettlement, 1952–1953 (Villa Rojas 1955, 146; Partridge and Brown 1982, 6). Only 22 percent of *ejidatario* families resettled in Las Margaritas; the other 78 percent chose other sites (Partridge, Brown, and Nugent 1982, 251). Such socio-demographic dynamics altered the social structure of the new community.

Because the more conservative private property owners and *ejidatarios* rejected Las Margaritas as an alternative, more progressive individuals took advantage of the opportunity to assume positions of authority and leadership. These were the individuals who assisted resettlement authorities in mobilization and educational campaigns prior to the move. A small-scale shopkeeper, artisan *ejidatario* and their brothers, families, and relatives assembled networks of kin and allies and, once in Las Margaritas, divided the best alluvial soils and other resources among themselves and defended their group interests from others outside the network. In other words, these individuals formed new corporate groups (Smith 1974) which gained control of the best land in the new *ejidos* of La Guadalupe and El Crucero. Eventually, these families came to control local commerce and the ferry (*panga*) which provided transportation across the Tonto River to the dirt road leading to nearby market towns. These corporate group leaders also lobbied successfully for building materials for school rooms, a church, tubed water, electricity, and agricultural credit, thus solidifying the loyalty of their corporate allies (Partridge, Brown, and Nugent 1982, 251–52.

As corporate lines were defined and households shifted into clusters of "patrilineally related extended family compounds" (Partridge, Brown, and Nugent 1982, 251), the task of clearing and planting fields and gardens commenced. The first ten years of transition were characterized largely by slash and burn cultivation of subsistence maize, beans, chilis, fruit trees, tubers of manioc and sweet potato, gourds, and squashes. Women planted spices, condiments, and vegetables in the home gardens (Partridge and Brown 1982, 6). Those families who took the nutrient-rich alluvial soils soon obtained maize yields of 1,200 to 1,500 kilograms per hectare, while those with poorer rocky soils managed to get only 800–1,000 kilograms per hectare. At first, only traditional digging stick and machete were used for clearing and planting, but as wealthier families generated more income, they began to rent tractors for field preparation (Nugent et al. 1978, 186; Partridge, Brown, and Nugent 1982, 253). When not in the fields, communal labor parties were involved in building schools, a community center, and a clinic with materials provided by the Papaloapan Commission and Instituto Nacional Indigenista (INI; Villa Rojas 1955, 150). Soon after the move, residents of Las Margaritas were also active in promoting and participating in health education and anti-malaria campaigns in their community. Villa Rojas noted that Las Margaritas was the most active of all communities in these efforts (1955, 152).

As a result of INI assistance in arranging bank loans, Mazatec *ejidatarios* who farmed the better soils were able to market substantial portions of their maize harvests and still retain enough to provision the household. Those with poorer soils remained subsistence-oriented farmers (Nugent et al. 1978, 186–87; Partridge, Brown, and Nugent 1982, 253).

The trend of socioeconomic stratification continued during the ten-year transition period, as wealthier families sought out and forged fictive kin networks far beyond the community. Kin ties were also maintained with relatives in other resettlement communities. Alliances were struck with mestizo merchants, government authorities, and technical personnel as well (Nugent et al. 1978, 188). Less affluent families continued to rely exclusively on ties to ethnic kinfolk or attempted to establish links with the more powerful extended families and corporate groups (Partridge, Brown, and Nugent 1982, 253).

Socioeconomic stratification intensified following the end of the transition period. In 1963, the *ejidatarios* of Las Margaritas were granted formal legal title to their lands in the form of a presidential decree documenting community boundaries and *ejido* rosters naming individual plot owners and listing no less than five heirs in succession (Partridge and Brown 1982, 6). Thus, having replicated a safe level of subsistence and assured at last of land security, the Mazatec successfully passed through transition and entered a stage of social and economic development.

The period of experimentation and innovation began for the Mazatec after 1963. In 1964, a group of *ejidatarios* entered into a contractual arrangement with a local mill for the production of sugar cane. They consolidated portions of their *ejido* plots and devoted them to the production of cane. Most of these farmers cautiously committed only 2 to 3 hectares of their fields to sugar cane and retained the remaining nine to eleven hectares for subsistence and commercial maize production. Others took a greater risk and devoted between 9 and 11 hectares of the 12- to 15-hectare plots to sugar cane cultivation.

Under the contractual agreement, Mazatec farmers simply grew sugar cane on their land in exchange for cash advances from the mill to purchase fertilizer at lower than market prices and other inputs entailed in cane production.

Cane farmers were paid two or more times throughout the year for their harvests (cane was harvested for up to six months, from December to May). The mill then processed the cane and generated its own profits from the sale of raw sugar and aguardiente, a rum-like cane alcohol.

Some of the more innovative Mazatec farmers ingeniously diverted inexpensive fertilizer purchased with cash advances to their maize crop. This had the positive effect of enhancing already higher than average maize yields (up to 2,000 kg/ha), and effectively ended the slash and burn method of cultivation, for, now, fields could be more intensively cultivated and fallow periods shortened without exhausting soil nutrients, which were maintained through the application of fertilizer (Partridge and Brown 1982, 6–7).

Cultivation of small parcels of sugar cane had a number of benefits aside from those already mentioned. Cane production added a measure of security in terms of income, for in the event other crops were damaged by pests, excessive rainfall, and fluctuations in market prices, income (though small as it was at about 1,200–2,000 pesos/ha) generated from cane enabled these farmer households to purchase needed food or other necessary household items (meat, cooking oil, fuel). Moreover, cash advances permitted the rental of tractors for the preparation of fields, thus lowering labor costs (Partridge and Brown 1982, 7).

At about the same time, buyers from outside the community offered Mazatec who cultivated a variety of fruit trees high prices for their produce, especially mango. The INI had provided up to sixty seedlings per family (Villa Rojas 1955, 150), and those who saved and planted them received additional income as truckloads of pickers arrived in May and June to harvest the fruits. Other commercial fruit trees included avocado, orange, lime, and *guanabana*, among others (Partridge and Brown 1982, 7). Additional cash crops with which they experimented included rice and sesame. In all these instances, the wiser among Mazatec farmers devoted only small portions of their fields and gardens to the production of these items. Over the years, these fruit tree enterprises grew to be successful endeavors.

In 1969, the Mazatec got word of a program for beef cattle production that entailed the conversion of fields to pasture. Some fifty farmers decided to form a cattle association and each consolidated ten hectares into a common pasture. The land was then leveled and planted to Estrella de Africa grass, an excellent pasture forage, free of charge. The farmers received a loan of two million pesos from a private bank in Veracruz, and by 1970 six hundred head of Zebu-Swiss cattle roamed the pasture (Partridge and Brown 1982, 7).

Unfortunately, the terms of the loan did not stipulate funds for the annual replanting of the artificial grass, as must be done with Estrella de Africa. All profits generated from yearling sales went solely to repay the loan according to its terms, and cattle buyers handed over the money directly to bank representatives at the pasture gate. Consequently, the pasture could not be maintained in artificial grass and reverted to native species and weeds. Cattlemen expended additional labor and expenses to cut out invading weeds, as native grass could not be burned over without destroying it, to be replaced by weeds only. The endeavor thus generated little if any profit for the Mazatec who participated in the scheme because of high calf mortality during dry seasons and lower calf birth rates due to less nutritious forage. Cattle raisers had to seek supplemental wage labor in order to provide food for their families. With most of their land in pasture instead of food crops, these farmers spent what little income they obtained on expensive processed food items from stores.

With little hope of viability beyond repayment of the loan, cattle raisers began withdrawing themselves and their 10-hectare plots from the association. By 1982, twenty-five participants (half of those who were originally involved) tended to 147 cattle which grazed "a field of weeds higher than a man's head" (Partridge and Brown 1982, 7). By 1984, the loan had apparently been paid off and the cattle experiment had been virtually abandoned. *Ejido* plots were then turned entirely over to sugar cane.

One *ejido* agreed to a contractual arrangement for rubber production in 1982 (Partridge and Brown 1982, 8), and as of 1985, the small, plantation-like parcels planted in rubber trees were still being tapped. Other experiments included beekeeping and citrus fruit (primarily orange) groves, and these experiments continued. Successful Mazatec shopkeepers were able to purchase trucks which they rented to farmers throughout the agricultural year (Partridge and Brown 1982, 8).

As successful experiments were incorporated into the farming systems of enterprising Mazatec families, their annual incomes increased. Aside from economic and dietary benefits, cash donations from wealthier families enabled the Mazatec to make improvements in the community through communal labor provided by the traditional *faena* work party. A new Catholic church began construction and was near completion by the mid-1980s. Cash pledges enabled the purchase of a new bell to be placed in the church tower. Additions were built onto houses, schools, and other public buildings. Cement floors and latrines were added by several families. In 1980, the community built its own secondary school to go along with its kindergarten and primary schools. Pledges and voluntary communal labor were also used to maintain village roads, the community plaza/park, electricity, and other needed repairs.

Economic experimentation initiated the evolution of two disparate corporate groups in terms of farming systems employed. Those farmers who added sugar cane and mango production to subsistence and commercial maize, bean and chili production in the fields, as well as maintaining mixed gardens and orchards of fruits, vegetables, tubers, spices, and medicinal plants as a single farming enterprise constituted "complex farmers" (Partridge and Brown 1982, 8). This system of diversified field and garden production for both household consumption and commercial profit, combined with small-scale animal husbandry of chickens, ducks, turkeys, and pigs, enabled families involved to produce sufficient food throughout the year as well as generate an annual income of between 50,000 and 80, 000 pesos (Partridge and Brown 1982, 7).

The profits derived from complex enterprises permitted household purchases of meat, fish, cooking oil, store-bought processed foods (cookies, pasta, canned goods, bread, and the like), kitchen utensils, furniture, radios, televisions, refrigerators, stoves, and other household improvements. This income also allowed the financing of continued education for offspring. Ritual, fictive, consanguineal, and affinal kin obligations could also be met by providing gifts, food and fiestas for birth, baptisms, graduations, marriage, and funeral ceremonies as these rites of passage throughout life cycles of relatives, *compadres, padrinos,* and godchildren occurred. Not all successful families invested in every item, only those which were perceived to be essential to maintaining household needs and social networks. In fact, most of the wealthiest families continued to live in traditional pole and palm thatch dwellings. This preference exemplifies Robert Chambers' (1985, 406) observation that first impressions of "rural development tourists," derived from socioeconomic "indicators" such as housing style, often reveal little about the people who reside in them.

In contrast to the complex system described above, those farmers who took land out of mixed production and converted it either to pasture or to sugar cane monoculture constituted "simple" farmers. Their radical departure from traditional farming practice began to evolve in 1969 with the cattle experiment. When that failed, farmers turned exclusively to sugar cane production in the hope of generating sufficient income. Long-term studies have shown this to have been too big a gamble.

Simple farming families lacked the diversity of staple foods, supplementary garden fruits and vegetables, and sufficient income which could be generated from mixed production. Consequently, meager incomes of 20,000 pesos per year, less than half of that generated by complex farmers, had to be spent almost entirely on expensive market and store-bought foods, many of which were lower in nutritional quality. Little savings were left to purchase additional household needs.

It must be emphasized at this point that development "experts," agricultural economists and extension workers would have us believe that conversion to cattle ranching and commercial monoculture sugar cane production represents agricultural "modernization," a transition from "simple" primitive mixed production to a more "complex" system of production for the market. In fact, the evidence marshaled above demonstrates beyond doubt that *it is precisely the smaller-scale innovations added or incorporated into the well-established traditional, indigenous system of mixed subsistence production in fields and gardens that is the more "complex" system*, a process Arensberg (1978) called "reciprocal accommodation." Netting (1993), for example, marshaled abundant cross-cultural empirical evidence of the economic, social, and eco-logical sustainability of such complex, diversified mixed production systems among smallholder households that unquestionably supports this assertion.

Trapping of wild animals was reported long after resettlement, and in at least one instance, evidence indicated that such hunting or trapping of wild animals was practiced by the more destitute of simple farming families, based on ethnographic observation of the roasting of an unfamiliar and unidentified animal carcass that was prepared for a meal. Such an observation illustrates the tenuous situation experienced by some simple farming families during hard times.

The collection of wild plants also continued to occur among the Mazatec of Las Margaritas following resettlement. Whether foraging was more prevalent among simple farming families than among complex farming families was never conclusively determined. While one might quickly assume that gather-ing of wild plants was more prevalent among simple farming families, it may have actually been the case that they foraged less than their complex farm-ing counterparts. The inference is drawn from observations which suggest that some simple farming families perceived themselves as "modernizing" (though they were, in fact, less well off) and therefore may have rejected several aspects of traditional economic activities and practices in favor of novel ones. Gathering of wild plants may well have been one such activity rejected by these families because it was perceived to be associated with being a "backward Indian."

Among complex farmers, gathering wild resources, and dooryard hor-ticulture were related or complementary activities. Wild plants were col-lected not only for immediate household consumption alone but also for trial experimentation in the household garden. In other words, gathering was employed with the purpose of facilitating expanded horticultural production. In contrast, when (and if) collecting of wild plants occurred among simple farming families, it was more likely to have been for immediate household consumption as a short-term subsistence strategy, rather than as a long-term production strategy.

The two divergent farming systems in Las Margaritas also had signifi-cant consequences for offspring generations. Children of complex farming families generally performed agricultural and household chores according to traditional gender roles. Partly because of better nutrition, however, these children attained a higher degree of education (including postsecondary schooling) and eventually sought further training outside of the community. Many returned after technical and professional training to become resident teachers, technical experts, small business operators, and farm managers (Partridge and Brown 1982, 8).

Children of simple farming families, on the other hand, shouldered much more of the domestic burden than their complex farming family counterparts. Because the head of the household frequently left in search of wage labor, male and female children performed much of the agricultural and household tasks. Such labor commitments made attendance in school very irregular and frequently resulted in either longer or terminated educational careers. Inadequate nutrition is linked to poorer performance and extended time in school. Nutritional assessments demonstrated that children of simple farming families were more severely malnourished than those of complex farming families (Partridge, Brown, and Nugent 1982, 254–55). Moreover, young adult males frequently sought wage labor throughout the year as well to supplement household income, and thus many of the agricultural tasks, in addition to domestic chores, fell to female children.

Traditional elements of the indigenous knowledge system were differentially transmitted to the offspring generations. That this was so was evidenced in a panel-like discussion forum in 1982 in which Mazatec elders and younger adults from both corporate groups identified key aspects of traditional knowledge which they deemed would be important for young people to know. Among several areas singled out by the elders were: a familiarity with types of wood used for construction purposes, medicinal plants, and their uses in preparing remedies for illness, recipes for preparing traditional foods and meals and useful wild plants found in *milpas* (maize fields) and surrounding areas. Having elicited what may be termed culturally defined "domains of priority," samples of children aged four to nineteen years from both farming system groups were then interviewed to ascertain the range and extent of knowledge acquired and retained concerning these resource areas. Results showed significant differences between children of complex farming system families and those of simple farming system families. The former demonstrated, for example, a more comprehensive knowledge of food preparation methods, wild plants and their edible parts, useful tree species and where such resources could be located. The latter group of children, on the other hand, lacked detailed knowledge beyond the ability to name certain resources (Partridge 1983b, 8–10).

The disparity in traditional resource knowledge might very well stem from two things. First, labor requirements of the simple farming system necessitated frequent familial separation, as males continually searched for wage work opportunities. This prevented, or at best limited, parent-offspring (father-son) interaction and thus the extent of socialization and transmission of knowledge in the context of cooperative farm labor. In contrast, complex farmers were almost always accompanied by one or more of their younger sons to the fields on a daily basis, especially during peak labor periods. Close interaction in cooperative work provided an important setting for imparting wisdom and transmitting information about agronomic methods and principles, natural ecological conditions, and zones of useful resources, as well as instruction in novel technical knowledge (e.g., application of herbicides). Likewise, mother-daughter interaction among simple farming families may have been hampered in that female children would likely have spent much time away from the household doing agricultural chores while their mothers remained to complete daily household tasks or vice versa.

Second, the simple farming system was centered largely around sugar cane monoculture. Cane is planted in neat rows and uniform stands in the fields, and its propagation is dependent on constant clearing and weeding between rows. All intrusive plants may thus have been categorized as weedy pests and slashed out in order to give the cane a competitive advantage in absorbing soil nutrients. In this context of monocultural production, complex, detailed knowledge of interplanting techniques, individual soil, shade and moisture requirements of various crops and the role of multiple crops in reducing insect pests may have become unimportant, unnecessary, and therefore not transmitted. In other words, the simple system relied on a single management strategy as opposed to many.

By 1985, then, more than thirty years after resettlement, Las Margaritas was characterized largely by two corporate factions embedded in the farming systems employed, as well as their inclusive social networks and structures of ritual and political authority. In many instances, however, these distinct corporate factions merged together in order to accomplish the larger corporate goals of the community as a whole. Yet, while there was much cooperation in the community and respect for village leaders, there was also a silent, underlying tension and mistrust (see Mathur 2019, 50) of more powerful extended family units on the part of poorer families. As Las Margaritas continued to develop in the aftermath of resettlement, the disparities in social, economic, educational, dietary, nutritional, and other indicators were easily discerned in offspring generations (Partridge, Brown, and Nugent 1982).

By the mid-1980s, Mazatec culture consisted of much that was traditional and much that was novel. Many of these elements, however, cross-cut corporate lines. For example, Mazatec was the primary language of domestic, social, and commercial interaction, unless such interaction was conducted with outsiders. Preferences for traditional foods and delicacies were still common among many elders. Methods of meal preparation over the traditional hearth continued. Reciprocal labor exchange among allied households continued, and day laborer relatives were even granted use rights to small parcels of *ejido* plots for a small fee. Sons and brothers worked each other's fields in extended families which together controlled well over 100 hectares of land in some cases, and *compadres* were allowed to graze their animals in fallow portions of *milpas*. The *faena*, or communal work party, still engaged in community labor projects each weekend. Repairing electrical wiring, doing construction, setting up facilities for community-wide events such as graduations (in which families contribute tables, chairs, food, and personal time), and maintaining the village plaza were just some of the tasks performed by the *faena.*

Traditional birth, funeral, and other religious ceremonies continued to be carried out (Partridge, Brown, and Nugent 1982, 253). Transfer of statues depicting Christ and the Virgin from church to church was still conducted by procession through community streets. Traditional folk healing ceremonies continued to be held by some older shamans and curers. Finally, emotions still ran high regarding the lost lands in Soyaltepec, which became an island in the middle of the Aleman reservoir. Community members visited the *isla* long after resettlement and, while still emotional, the Mazatec grieved much less for lost homes (Fried 1963).

Las Margaritas was in the mid-1980s a conglomeration of tradition and change, exhibited in dress, infrastructure, material goods, economics, social status, and ritual culture. In only a short time, one could observe first-hand virtually the entire spectrum of tradition and modernization. Houses of sun-dried brick and stucco with zinc roofs stood alongside modern school buildings, which in turn stood amid traditional pole and palm thatch houses. Gravel roads were offset by networks of footpaths and trails throughout village compounds and surrounding areas. On these roads could be seen trucks, buses, tractors, and cars moving people every day, while other men and women still traveled by horse, mule, and foot on the trails, hauling sacks of corn, loads of firewood, and other goods. One could pass chemically fertilized, mechanically prepared, plantation-like fields and, short distances away, encounter swidden *milpas* extending up the steepest of rocky foothill slopes.

Within households could be seen almost infinite combinations of indigenous and modern technology, from fire-hardened clay *comales* to ceramic dishes, cups, pots, and silverware; sun-dried foods to packaged items, refrigerators, and stoves; wooden chairs and jute cots to cushioned sofas and beds; earthen floors to carpeted concrete ones; oral passing of folk songs and stories to TVs, radios and tape players; traditional *huipiles* to the finest dresses and suits; and "peasant" swidden cultivators to professional teachers and owner/operators of cottage industry bakeries, soon to become mechanized, furniture shops, and stores.

Mazatec culture was not destroyed by resettlement; it was transformed to be sure, but merely as a means to survival (Kottak 1985, 332), encompassing the maintenance of traditions (rite of passage ceremonies, social obligations, and interaction networks) and social and human development (financing children's secondary and postsecondary education). Resettlement did not foster differentiation but did exacerbate it (Partridge, Brown, and Nugent 1982). Many of these changes represent significant adaptive strategies in the aftermath of resettlement. The Mazatec of Las Margaritas were allowed, whether by accident or design, to rehabilitate and change or develop themselves at their own pace and on their own terms as a community in a context of *semiautonomy*. As we have previously mentioned, they were allowed the freedom to choose. Phrased in terms of the World Bank OMS 2.33, individuals and household heads were permitted to choose their future from a number of acceptable alternatives and to rebuild their lives through their own efforts.

IMPLICATIONS FOR COMMUNITY RESETTLEMENT

Through long-term, microlevel case study investigations, social anthropologists have long known that communities are stratified and hierarchical below the abstract, mythical level of traditional culture (Pitt 1976, 14), wherein individuals and groups display a differential willingness and capacity to challenge that tradition at the pragmatic level of social activity by innovating and taking risks in adapting to novel conditions (Barnett 1952; Cancian 1972; Partridge and Brown 1983; Scudder 1985, 130). In this perspective, change and development can occur not only from above or below but, perhaps most significantly, from *within*. By what mechanisms, then, do change and development from within communities take place?

Culture and Community

There are myriad definitions and theories of culture, which are well beyond the scope of the present analysis (but see, e.g., Mathur 2019, 149–52). Culture is generally understood as a set of conventional understandings among groups in society. These understandings, in turn, derive from a set of "primary questions" such as, among others, "Who are we?" "Where did we come from?" "What are our responsibilities to others and to ourselves?" (Downing and Garcia-Downing 2009, 228). They are the "rules," invariably unwritten, which govern proper or moral behavior, gender and age-grade roles, and social interaction. They are "codified in language, symbols, places endowed with meaning, kinship categories, ritual, dance, humor, public works, access rights to certain areas and resources, titles and job descriptions, and other socio-cultural expressions" (Downing and Garcia-Downing 2009, 228, 230).

As we saw in chapter 2 in the Ghana Akosombo case, as well as the other examples briefly described, there were common understandings, for example, of what an appropriate community size should be, what an appropriate house should consist of, an appropriate number of people who should reasonably and comfortably reside in that house, an appropriate spatial patterning of distance between houses, and what appropriate conduct in terms of hosting and hospitality toward visitors should entail. All these specific, culturally defined understandings of what was considered "appropriate" were severely disrupted by resettlement to externally designed and constructed resettlement sites and houses.

The primary questions and rules form the warp and weft of the social fabric that constitutes a community, what social anthropologists have variously called "social structure," the "structural order," or the "symbolic-structural order," those systems of symbolic logic by which "legitimacy is established, claims are justified, identities are secured, and boundaries asserted" (Partridge 1985, 146). In other words, culture and its structure are social constructions of objective reality, a theory or way of knowing about the world and how people should behave in it; in every society, the transmission of this knowledge is controlled by certain individuals and groups who resolve challenges and contending assertions in conflict with the established order through the exercise of social power. Social life and cultural reproduction are invariably "carefully circumscribed by public and private ritual enactments that are designed to reinforce conviction in cohesive, enduring unquestionable cultural truths," thereby making such codified, objective knowledge powerful for social actors; they only need be convinced once more of the "obvious" (Partridge 1985, 147).

In this sense, culture is understood as "routine," as heritage or tradition, and generally assumed to be equally subscribed to by all members. But as Downing and Garcia-Downing point out, the patterns of routine behavior are continually navigated, adjusted, negotiated, redefined, and grappled with as *"individuals and groups judge certain constructs to be more desirable or undesirable than others . . . Not everyone understands, agrees with, or accepts his or her place with the constructs, nor the constructs themselves"* (Downing and Garcia-Downing 2009, 228, our emphasis). In short, culture is constantly negotiated and renegotiated (Downing and Garcia-Downing 2009, 229). This process of navigating, negotiating, and challenging the rules occurs at the level of social organization, the "informal, inarticulate and perhaps subconscious behavioral patterns" as distinguished from the more formal social structure (Partridge, 1985, 152; Firth 1951).

We would argue that culture is both more and less than heritage and tradition. It is less because in no sense does the totality of a culture's experience continue into the present. It is more because it is continually being reinvented to serve the needs of the present. Culture, in other words, is constructed daily and continually by social groups that are interacting, sometimes in conflict and sometimes in agreement.

Our view of culture largely follows that of M. G. Smith (1974) and others who view culture as social life shaped by such factors as labor, money, land, and language through the functioning of corporate groupings (e.g., households, kindred, clans, villages, communities, unions, and occupational associations). Through leadership hierarchies, laws, procedures, and sanctions, human corporate groups organize personnel, marshal resources, and channel energies into practical activities. Groups and the structure of incentives and constraints that they enforce determine in large part the response of their constituent members to development opportunities. In this definition, the key questions concern how people are organized into groups—that is, leadership hierarchies, how followers respond to leadership, how leaders are made accountable to followers, and so on (Partridge 1995, 207–08).

From our perspective, culture is seen not as determining a uniform set of responses and patterns among all individuals and groups, but as the ever-changing product of practical activities and subjective experiences of contending social units involving manipulation, barter, negotiation, conflict, cooperation, improvisation, and adaptation in social and environmental interactions (Partridge 1985, 152–53). It is through the community and its organizational patterns, uniting and distinguishing individuals and larger behavioral units from each other that cultural traditions—the symbolic logic or structural order—are generated, maintained, and transformed (Kimball and Partridge 1979, 2–3; Partridge 1985, 152).

Downing and Garcia-Downings's description of what they call routine culture—and, just as importantly, its underlying dynamics—is the most recent articulation of what social and cultural anthropologists have long known. A number of ethnographic studies have documented these dynamic processes of social interaction that challenge received wisdom and social order. Bateson (1935 a, b), Bailey (1969), and Parkin (1972), for example, similarly viewed culture as a product of social forces involving manipulation, negotiation, barter, cooptation, dispute, and conflict between dynamic social groups with differential social power regarding varying constructions of genealogical rights to land and labor resources, "correct" construction of past relationships based on the number of one's descendants and dependents, resulting in a pragmatic organizational rationale that created "a set of competing constraints and incentives to those embedded in the symbolic/structural order." As organizational patterns changed, social actors felt no particular need to retain intact a symbolic/structural order ill-suited to the new conditions, and they experimented freely with little regard for the integrity of the old order. As a result of these conflicts, the symbolic/structural was transformed and reinterpreted to fit the needs of the factions with little regard to the integrity of the established order (Partridge 1985, 147–53).

The collective activities and subjective experiences of corporate groups, and the collaborations and conflicts which result shape the conception of the new order (Smith 1974). It is an order which emerges as neither new nor old, but some combination of both to which these corporate groups differentially subscribe. In other words, "culture is a resource, but only one, upon which actors draw in an ever present process of recasting, reinterpreting, reinventing and revising culture so that it conforms to the needs of the social practice then emerging" (Partridge 1985, 147). The subjective experience, practical activities, and collective interactions among contending corporate groups are the generative forces by which culture persists or changes (Partridge 1985, 154).

Moore's (1975) treatment of "uncertainty in situations" and "indeterminacies in culture" postulate much the same kinds of processes surrounding social relations among members of communities. In her model, individuals and groups operate under a system of rules (the symbolic-structural order) which is open to manipulation and reinterpretation in situations of uncertainty (Moore 1975, 220). Rules are continually exploited, sometimes through the calling up of their timeless fixity; in others they are manipulated, redefined, and recanted to fit a particular situation. "Despite all attempts to crystallize the rules, there invariably remains a certain range of maneuver, of openness, of choice, of interpretation, of tampering, of reversing, of transforming" (Moore 1975, 222).

Situational adjustments are "the means by which people arrange their immediate situations by exploiting indeterminacies in situations, by reinterpreting or redefining rules and relationships" (Moore 1975, 235). Situational adjustments can be likened to adaptive strategies, "the patterns formed by the many separate adjustments that people devise in order to obtain and use resources and to solve the immediate problems confronting them" (Bennett 1969, 14), action-oriented decisions which are differentially employed by individuals and group members (Denevan 1983). Similarly, Johnson (1972) argued that behavior cannot always be explained by the symbolic-structural system of culturally transmitted rules and traditions which program a limited number of responses among individuals. While culture provides at least "some security in the face of uncertainty through ritual and time honored . . . .practices," attention should be paid to the degree to which some individuals and groups "reject the somewhat illusory security of conformity to prescribed rules in favor of active, although cautious, confrontation with the uncertainties" (Johnson 1972, 153). His examination of ethnographic cases clearly indicates that while traditions are largely forceful, they do not "imply uniformity of behavior and an unwillingness to innovate" (Johnson 1972, 156). The high degree of individual variation and diversity of practices exists through the mechanism of constant experimentation; other researchers have argued that experimentation is the primary vehicle by which indigenous and local knowledge systems and economies change (Howe and Chambers 1980, 331; Salisbury 1970, 2–6). This continual experimentation with new ideas and resources "is probably as natural as conformity in traditional communities" (Johnson 1972, 156). Such a degree of variation, diversity, and experimentation leads to a view of adaptation as a *creative* process by which communities "transform" and enhance their physical and social environments "in the process of adapting" to them (Johnson 1972, 154; Richards 1985, 1986).

A misguided goal of development has thus been "to convert everyone . . . to a single adaptive strategy" (DeWalt 1979, 261). Development recommendations have often been based on the inaccurate assumption that everyone is and has been doing the same things (Belshaw 1976, 236). In any culture or community, not all individuals or groups are involved in doing the same kinds of things, despite the tendency to categorize them uniformly as farmers, fishers, herders, foragers, or wage laborers. In most cultures and communities, people engage in multiple livelihood activities, employing a suite of strategies, some of them primary and some secondary or complementary, some seasonal or depending on circumstances.

Persons or groups may have differential knowledge, economic and social capacities, or the political power to perform these behaviors. For example, Cancian (1972) demonstrated the differential willingness and capacities of Mayan farmers to cultivate new fields in lowland Chiapas to produce corn for newly established markets in the area. He found that groups of lower middle economic standing were more aggressive in taking advantage of the uncertain situation, while both wealthy and poor farmers declined, and the upper-middle-class groups hesitated and gauged the success of the experiment before making a commitment.

Moone (1981), utilizing concepts drawn from earlier treatments of acculturation (e.g., Spicer 1961) and long since neglected by anthropologists and other social scientists, outlined the mechanisms by which relationships are confirmed, resources and innovations adopted, and change takes place. Symbolic forms, functions, and meanings, both old and new, are fused, incorporated, compartmentalized, added, deleted, and replaced to produce a cultural order that is neither wholly traditional nor modern, but a completely unique product. Cultural maintenance is thus possible even in situations of disruptive change and transformation; conversely, change and transformation are common even in the most staunchly "traditional" systems (Moone 1981, 240, 242).

Spicer (1971) and others since (Castile and Kushner 1981) likewise described several examples of how "persistent cultural systems" endure and change simultaneously. Individuals, as members of groups, form a collective identity, the affirmation of which results from the selection, display, manipulation, and interpretation of symbols. These symbols serve to stimulate or renew long-held sentiments associated with them. The meaning, form, and historical dimensions entailed within these symbols recall "historical events in the experience of the people through generations" which are "shared with and through ancestors." These events, however, are "not objectively organized historic facts, but history as people believe it to have taken place" (Spicer 1971, 796). That is to say, the beliefs stem from individual and collective subjective experiences through time (Partridge 1985, 146–50).

Culture or identity, however, in no way implies a notion of static human groups. Such systems may endure over the long term despite changing structural environments and severe pressures for assimilation into such structures which members continually resist. They operate within a context of an "oppositional process" (Spicer 1971, 797) and are, in fact, frequently a product of conflict situations. Differences between "traditional" peoples and the larger society are either imposed by the latter or maintained by the former through the use of identity symbols. Although exploited economically, denigrated socially and culturally and politically powerless to a large extent, they continually resist total assimilation into the larger national structure. Their local communities are usually enclaves (Castile and Kushner 1981) in what have been called "refuge regions" (Aguirre Beltran 1973) which are increasingly coming under the purview of development initiatives in attempts to integrate communities into the national mainstream society and economy by expropriating land and exploiting the resources such communities rely upon for their livelihoods.

Internal processes of culture building, razing, and recasting by contending social interactions among groups are exclusive of how group members identify themselves. While there is overall common participation, individuals and groups are constantly recycled in and out of the system and decreases and increases in sentiment toward symbols vary between actors at any given point in time. Even so, core individuals, families, and corporate groups of a given community may maintain their culture and identity by (i) communication through language, whether indigenous or not; (ii) conventional understandings concerning proper or moral behavior; and (iii) some kind of organization for achieving group goals as a whole (Spicer 1971, 799). This implies at least semiautonomy in interactional spheres of activity, be they social, economic, or political in nature. It is through these interactional spheres of activity that corporate groups comprising communities survive and persist (Smith 1974).

Integrationist development programs and policies often function, however unintentionally, to heighten consciousness of cultural differences between rural and urban poor, indigenous and tribal peoples, and the national society. For our purposes, the symbol of territory serves as a prime example. In terms of involuntary displacement and resettlement, it is thus significant here that "displacement most often has the effect of *reinforcing* identity, provided certain structural conditions can be maintained within the group. Sentiments regarding the land become intensified . . . names of selected places may become very sacred symbols in terms of lost territory" (Spicer 1971, 798, emphasis added). This was the case, in a well-known example, soon after the announcement that the Aswan Dam would necessitate the relocation of Egyptian Nubians (Fahim 1983; Scudder 1973, 707). The cultural significance of places was also documented in the cases of Bujagali Falls in Uganda for Busoga people (Downing 2008) and Ol Njorowa Gorge for Maasai people in Kenya (Inspection Panel 2015). Resettlement communities or places associated with those communities are often named after the original settlements that were lost to inundation. It was no accident that those resettled by the Zimapan Dam in Mexico, who were relocated on top of a plateau from their fertile river valley homes, named the new community *Bella Vista del Rio* even though the river could no longer be seen, and their principal community street River Street (Aronsson 2002; Downing and Garcia-Downing 2009, 251). Likewise, Mazatec resettled to Las Margaritas named their new *ejidos* La Guadalupe and El Crucero, after the villages submerged by the Aleman reservoir. The enduring fond remembrances of people for their original town of *Sento Se* forty years after relocation to *Novo Sento Se* by the Sobradinho Dam was mentioned in chapter 2. Whether ancestral territory, specific sites within that territory, or simply "home," a great deal of cultural value and significance is ascribed to places that people inhabit.

As Downing and Garcia-Downing argue, while "routine culture imparts a degree of order, stability, security and predictability in daily life, a sense of health and well-being" (2009, 230), even the imminent threat of involuntary displacement and resettlement "drastically destabilizes routine culture by threatening it or rendering it meaningless," replacing it with a "dissonant culture," forcing a re-ordering of "space, time, relationships"—indeed the very constructs—that make up the structural order, in an atmosphere of chaos and uncertainty, thus requiring reorientation, renegotiation, and renavigating toward establishing a new routine culture (2009, 230–36). "Although the people may physically survive, culturally what was is no more" (Downing and Garcia-Downing 2009, 230).

Dissonant culture in the advent and immediate duration of involuntary displacement and resettlement entails such manifestations as the loss of a safety net for those who are most vulnerable, differential exposure to the risk of increased impoverishment due to differences in income, demography, and location for some parts of the population, disruption of production activities and other temporal routines formerly predictable throughout the seasonal cycle, temporary or permanent severing of social relationships, and change in social positions of households, families, or entire villages in relation to others. Dissonant culture brings breakdown in the provisioning of food, loss of land and/or jobs, cessation of schooling and other social events, sharing of common goods, the emergence of "ephemeral dissonance norms" which might be unacceptable relative to routine norms, dissonance overload which paralyzes the ability to respond appropriately to new risks in cultural terms, a decreased ability to rely on kin and social networks for aid and assistance, the erosion of support and coping mechanisms, increased morbidity and mortality due to new diseases, and the redefinition of access to routinely allocated resources, and an increased frequency of rituals to reestablish and reaffirm collective identity (Downing and Garcia-Downing 2009, 230–34). All of this is to say that involuntary displacement is an unmitigated disaster for those facing displacement. But given the dynamic nature of social organization and interaction within communities, as evidenced in both the Las Margaritas example and the empirically informed theoretical and conceptual discussion above, are these responses and degrees of dissonance uniformly distributed among all members of a community faced with involuntary displacement?

Forced displacement and resettlement are always perceived as a disaster by displaced people. But human communities are not homogeneous, and neither are their responses to disaster. Scudder documented that among the first responses to involuntary displacement and resettlement is the closing up of the social and cultural system, conservative clinging to that which is most familiar, avoiding taking risks, and making only incremental changes in the process of coping and adjusting to the stress of the new physical and social environmental conditions (Scudder 2005, 35; Scudder and Colson 1982). This accounts for, at least, the intensification or increase of ritual activity. Displacement and resettlement may result in the temporary or permanent severing of kin ties and social networks (Downing and Garcia-Downing 2009, 230); it may also result in reuniting kin, if those overseeing resettlement operations allow resettlers "to recreate the security formerly provided by familiar structures, institutions, and symbols," such as "replicating former house types; transferring crops and productive techniques, regardless of their relevance to the new habitat; and relocating in social units of resettlers' own choice, including extended groups, residential units within communities, and entire communities as well as networks of communities linked by marriage, ritual, or other ties. Such a preference makes sense because it allows resettlers to adapt to new conditions with the support and assistance of familiar people." In the Kariba case, brothers who had separated due to normal fissioning processes within kin groups as new families and lineages were formed or because of previous conflicts, were reunited in the stressful conditions of resettlement. In such contexts, resettled people will go to great lengths to recreate previously established cultural patterns (Scudder 2005, 35). Communities resettled to make way for the Zimapan Dam in Mexico, for example, attempted to align themselves residentially along the new community main street that replicated the previous alignment in the original settlement along the river (Downing 1996, 42).

Eventually, as resettlers are well along in the process of reconstituting their lives and livelihoods, and in some cases sooner rather than later, the system begins to reopen. Generally, at this point, the elite take their money and leave, rather than be subjects of a government resettlement program. At the other end of the spectrum, some of the most vulnerable will fail for lack of capacity to take advantage of new opportunities which may present themselves in the wake of displacement and resettlement. Some may be unable to recover from the social, economic, and cultural trauma. Many, if not most, however, often discover a silver lining in the disaster. The effect of the exit of often corrupt elites—large landowners, commercial middlemen, shopkeepers, money-lenders—is like taking the lid off a boiling pot. The capable, hardworking majority are liberated to make the most of new opportunities represented by the resettlement investments, opportunities that would previously have been captured by the elite (Partridge 2013, 159, 1989).

The Las Margaritas example presented above, one among many, demonstrates that communities almost invariably exhibit differential capacities for adaptation, resilience, learning, experimentation, creativity, and innovation. The example reveals and highlights sources of differentiation based on gender, age, wealth, livelihood strategies, command of indigenous or traditional knowledge, and social power, among other factors. Responses and adaptations to resettlement are a product of both forces for change and forces for maintenance (see Mathur 2019, 49–93) reflected in the dynamic social relationships, collective activity, and economic strategies employed by corporate groups as members of communities.

As we pointed out in the introduction of this book, it is impossible to restore, reconstruct, or reestablish the routine culture and traditional community that have been erased by forced displacement and resettlement (Downing and Garcia-Downing 2009; Oliver-Smith 2018, 28). More precisely, it is impossible for external development "experts" tasked with implementing resettlement operations to restore, reconstruct, or reestablish a community's routine culture. We would argue that it is entirely possible, however, for the displaced and resettled people themselves to do so. That this is possible is, given the evidence presented in this chapter, only because *they have always done so.* And they have always done so on their own terms. What eventually emerges may look to an outsider to be a dramatically changed culture; what eventually emerges will and should be defined by the people themselves. Downing and Garcia-Downing point out that reestablishment of a new routine culture begins quickly, depending on the degree of disruption, lest chaos and dissonance reign supreme. "Some elements of a new routine culture begin to rearticulate almost immediately. Relationship by relationship, decision by decision, block by block, group by group, new routines crystallize" (2009, 235). Certainly, not everything crystallizes at once. As discussed above, risk aversion and inward orientation, clinging to the familiar, and incremental steps toward reestablishing various forms of security and previous social and cultural patterns sooner or later give way, at different times and for different individuals and groups, to more active adaptation, risk-taking, experimentation, and innovation. Some adaptive strategies or situational adjustments will succeed while others fail; some will be discarded, and some retained. Individuals and families may place a differential priority on what strategies for reestablishment are to be employed, whether it be pursuing livelihood options, recommencing children's education, rebuilding desired public infrastructure, and so on. The ebb and flow, wax and wane, the flux in timing and intensity of these activities will vary between and among individuals, families, extended kin, and larger corporate groups, with differential results. The point is that the resettlers themselves will (or should be allowed to) determine the course(s) of action as they see fit.

The active, dynamic depiction of culture as an endogenous result of social collaboration, cooperation, and conflict set out above might be best seen as congruent to Hobsbawm's (1983) notion of "invented traditions." Traditions are seldom, if ever, archaic holdovers from time immemorial. Rituals may persist through time, for example, but their form and content are subject to revision as different practitioners carry them on or as conditions change. Traditions are the emic result of interaction, practical activity, subjective experiences, and collective action, and the adaptation of these through time to changing environmental constraints and opportunities. Corporate adaptations merge to become the new order, or tradition.

Such an assertion is often puzzling to those carrying the conceptual baggage of culture as a determinant force. New patterns and traits are seen by outsiders as indications of acculturation, assimilation, integration and modernization, or loss of tradition, while they are continually asserted by their bearers to be traditional. Conceptualizations which depict culture as blueprint are much less effective in accounting for change and adaptation.

The guidelines to achieving successful resettlement and community social, human, and economic development are, according to Downing and Garcia-Downing: rejecting the five fallacies of implementing resettlement programs—specifically, the dictums that (i) compensation is enough; (ii) tick-box compliance and nontransparent agreements are satisfactory, (iii)

PAPs are responsible for their own failures due to stereotypical characterizations mentioned above, (iv) that liability for failure rests not with designers, planners, financers, architects, technical personnel, and (v) that all obligations and responsibility cease upon the moment construction is completed (2009, 237–40).

The remedies for overcoming these fallacies include strengthening baseline studies, ensuring that vulnerable peoples are protected, providing procedures that encourage displaced persons to participate actively in displacement and resettlement decisions, and actively promoting sociocultural and psychological innovations that directly address the rebuilding of a new routine (Downing and Garcia-Downing 2009, 237). We do not hesitate to add commitment to provide substantial and sufficient financing for resettlement operations in project budgets that extend beyond the end of construction and further.

We submit that such remedies can be found precisely and firmly ensconced in the International Standard for Involuntary Resettlement, that body of empirically derived provisions, principles, and directives contained in all previous safeguard policies and current performance standards promulgated by the MDFIs. Most importantly, it is the implementation of these provisions, principles, and directives, supervised by competent, committed resettlement expert social scientists in close and continual collaboration and with the active participation of PAPs, throughout the duration of resettlement operations and beyond. As important, it is essential that these professionals work in collaboration with country counterparts to translate the International Standard for Involuntary Resettlement into legally binding national and subnational laws, regulations, and policies to help ensure the successful achievement of resettlement programs that are culturally acceptable to the PAPs as they themselves define.

The next series of chapters present case examples of both successful and unsuccessful application of the International Standard in MDFI financed projects. Successful case examples largely involved creative and innovative thinking, designing, planning, and implementation. Those examples that were unsuccessful largely overlooked, neglected, ignored, or willfully subverted the Standard.

Chapter 5

Avoiding, Minimizing, and Anticipating Resettlement

Where the physical or economic displacement of communities risks impoverishment of the affected people, the first directive of the International Standard for Involuntary Resettlement is to avoid or minimize displacement and resettlement of people to the extent possible. This can be achieved by focusing more intently in the planning and design phases of a project on options assessment and design alternatives. Scudder has advocated that options assessment "must precede selection of any specific development plan" (2005, 309). Referring specifically to the hydropower sector, such options assessment will require additional funding upfront, and close supervision by oversight committees comprised of multiple government departments and disciplines. But because options assessment and designing alternatives tend to be dominated by those in charge of a project, it is essential that all stakeholders, including affected communities, be involved in the process (Scudder 2005, 289).

On the other hand, in a context of climate change and/or related increased need for disaster risk reduction, climate change adaptation, and mitigation strategies, where resettlement is absolutely necessary and the only viable alternative available to remove people from high risk and vulnerable areas, such as those prone to flood or landslides, and relocate them to safer conditions, the challenge is to anticipate and plan for preventive resettlement, so as to enhance and optimize development benefits. Resettlement is increasingly being considered as a potential mitigation and adaptation strategy for reducing negative impacts (de Sherbinin et al. 2011). The significant increase in disaster-forced displacement has elevated consideration of what has come to be variously termed "preventive resettlement" (Correa 2011a, b), "anticipatory resettlement" (Oliver-Smith 2020), and "planned resettlement" or relocation (Wilmsen and Rogers 2019) as a disaster risk reduction option or strategy. There are many efforts underway to confront these coming crises; many of them were noted in chapter 1.

Oliver-Smith (2020) has summarized the state of knowledge, policy, guidelines, and practice regarding resettlement and disaster risk reduction and its inherent complexities. While the necessity of preventive resettlement is likely to increase over the coming years, several analysts have, based on the record of DFDR, advised caution in terms of embracing resettlement as a climate change adaptation, or mitigation strategy as well as a disaster risk reduction option (de Sherbinin and Oliver-Smith 2014; Price 2019b; Wilmsen 2019; Wilmsen and Webber 2015; Wilmsen and Rogers 2019). Price, for example, notes that "[r]isk to people arising from climate change may be exaggerated and manipulated for political reasons. People may be moved from their land as a 'protective measure' that actually masks ulterior motives—land grabbing, a desire to control certain groups of people, a wish to build up a docile base of domestic consumers who can be policed and serviced more easily and cheaply in urban centers than in far flung, remote locations" (Price 2019b, 197). Because national and state governments, whether alone or in conjunction with private developers, are more likely to oversee these types of resettlement, they may use "the threat of disaster and climate change to target the vulnerable . . . or control the undesirable or politically marginalized through resettlement, rather than addressing underlying inequalities." In this context, "forced displacement intersects with the discourse on 'land grabbing'" (Price 2019b, 197). Wilmsen and colleagues have echoed much the same concern in the case of China, where planned resettlement is viewed "as the answer to a multitude of social ills, including poverty, environmental change, low levels of domestic consumption, and most recently, climate change, providing impetus to the normalization of resettlement as adaptation" (Wilmsen and Rogers 2019, 118; see chapter 1 regarding PAR in China).

The need for caution and involvement of resettlement social science experts in insisting on the application and implementation of the International Standard for Involuntary Resettlement in such instances is borne out by the case, eerily reminiscent of failed DFDR examples presented in chapter 2, of La Yerbabuena, La Becerrera, and surrounding villages in Colima, Mexico. After a series of evacuations beginning in 1998 due to an active volcano, most residents reluctantly agreed in 2002 to be resettled further away, only to find their new homes poorly designed, situated on much smaller lots than their original homes, which "averaged 1,500 square meters, with space for household gardens and small animals," travel distance to their fields, markets, and schools increased. Some families who refused resettlement continued to be harassed by government authorities. Many residents, both those who moved and those who refused to move, suspected that volcanic risk was used as a means to relocate them out of the way to enable more powerful economic and political interests, particularly the luxury resort hotel Hacienda de San Antonio, only a few kilometers from La Yerbabuena, which was not pressured to move, to acquire the land (Oliver-Smith 2020, 206; Cuevas-Muniz and Lujan 2005; Cuevas-Muniz and Gavilanes-Ruiz 2018; see Rodriguez Garcia, Cuevas-Muniz, and Arellano Ceballos 2016 for a similar case in Michoacan).

Those displaced as a result of the 2004 Indian Ocean tsunami were permanently resettled without any involvement in the process. The outcomes included poorly designed houses with cheap materials, thereby increasing the profit of building contractors, absence of functioning public infrastructures such as schools and public transport, lack of rainwater and wastewater drainage systems for both houses and the resettlement site as a whole, exposing the new settlement to new risks of flooding during the monsoon, lack of public garbage collection and appropriate waste treatment, thereby jeopardizing community health, relocation far away from original villages, a decline in living conditions due to disruptions in income generation, increased costs of commuting, accessing schools, hospitals, and utilities, the latter of which were disconnected when resettlers could not pay, and conflicts between hosts and newcomers. Resettlement houses were closed, sold, or rented out as some moved back to their original locations (Oliver-Smith 2020, 207–09).

In contrast, the resettlement of Guatemalan Tz'utjil Maya communities of Panabaj and Tz'anchaj in the aftermath of an avalanche from the Toliman volcano caused by Hurricane Stan, which resulted in the deaths of 600 people, the destruction of 205 houses, possessions and crops, was carried out with the full participation of the indigenous people. The government's reconstruction plan emphasized economic and social development and reducing vulnerability, and focused on rebuilding culturally appropriate houses, schools, health centers, water and sanitation systems, and other public infrastructure, supporting agriculture, livestock raising, agroforestry, and handicraft enterprises. Land for the new communities with low hazard exposure and access to roads, markets, services, and other facilities was selected in consultation with affected community members. It turned out that the land selected was the original, pre-Columbian settlement, reinforcing the deep cultural ties to the site and ancestors, as well as permitting the fulfillment of the Maya preference to live out their entire lives on traditional land. By 2010, 700 families had been resettled in the new communities (Oliver-Smith 2020, 209–11, citing Aguirre Cantero 2011).

Below, case examples are presented wherein design alternatives, such as changing the location of a project, result in reductions in the amount of land expropriated which, in turn, reduces the total number of people physically displaced who must then be resettled.

It bears repeating here that the case examples presented and in subsequent chapters do not necessarily imply that the projects cited were free of flaws or exemplary in all respects.

CASE EXAMPLES

As seen in the case examples below, in many instances of involuntary resettlement caused by development projects, it has been possible to reduce or eliminate altogether the need for population displacement through small changes in the location or design of projects. Avoidance or minimization is achieved by analysis of design alternatives that will optimize project benefits while simultaneously minimizing land acquisition requirements, avoiding or reducing the need for involuntary resettlement, and bringing total project costs down.

Pakistan: Power Transmission Enhancement Investment Program

The project design team made small deviations in the location of power transmission towers within the existing right-of-way in order to avoid involuntary resettlement. Demolition and relocation of 117 houses was avoided, including twenty-two sharecroppers with no titles to their houses, and, hence, no right to compensation under domestic law. Avoidance of resettlement was accomplished with no increase in project costs and with significant cost savings (Asian Development Bank 2009b).

Thailand: Pak Mun Hydroelectric Project

During feasibility-level engineering studies conducted by the Electricity Generating Authority of Thailand (EGAT) it was estimated that some 10,000 properties would have to be acquired for the future reservoir displacing some 40,000 people. The affected area included not only agricultural land and house sites of farmers but also substantial numbers of residences on the outskirts of a populous town at the tail end of the future reservoir. However, in design-level studies EGAT lowered the dam crest by several meters, thereby reducing the number of displaced people to about 1,000 and avoiding completely flooding part of the nearby town (World Bank 1998a).

India: Western Transport Corridor Project

The project is located in the state of Karnataka and built by the National Highways Authority. It starts at 75 kilometers north of Bangalore, ends 340 kilometers north of Haveri town, and transverses four districts and thirty-two villages. The works were divided into four sections, and during implementation engineers and resettlement officials reduced land acquisition requirements by 35, 13, 48, and 51 percent, respectively (from total 1,092.7 ha to 577.26 ha), by making pragmatic changes in the alignment of the highway to avoid cultivated land, utilize wasteland, and to reduce the amount of land for interchanges (Asian Development Bank 2007).

El Salvador: Logistical Infrastructure Project

Pre-Feasibility-Level planning studies for modernization and amplification from two to four lanes of a major intra-city highway included three roundabout interchanges or *glorietas*. Each roundabout would have required expropriation of tens of hectares of land and displacement of scores of informal commercial businesses traditionally located at the intersections of the old highway (grocery stores, restaurants, mechanic workshops, fruit/vegetable vendors, and so forth). During feasibility-level planning studies, however, the roundabouts were eliminated and traffic signals were substituted. This change entirely avoided the need for significant land acquisition and consequent population displacement and resulted in considerable cost savings (Millenium Challenge Corporation 2015).

Where resettlement is aimed at relocating people living in risk-prone areas to safer and more secure conditions, the challenge is to optimize the development opportunities that can be provided in the new location. This necessarily entails facilitating free, prior and informed participation of the beneficiaries, direct participation of community organizations, as well as the local authorities in the risk-prone areas and the receiving areas.

El Salvador: Precarious Urban Settlements in the Metropolitan Area of San Salvador

Nine urban communities composed of poor and extremely poor people were identified as periodically subject to disasters such as landslides and flooding. The project was designed to provide civil works to mitigate the risks of landslides and/or manage the evacuation of floodwaters, as well as to improve the quality of life through investments in the provision of potable water, drainage and sewers, paved streets, community meeting centers, and public schools. But where local conditions and/or technical limitations did not permit the construction of civil works, many families had to be moved away from areas prone to landslides or flooding and resettled in more stable conditions. The resettlement planning process entailed working with local municipal governments, community organizations made up of residents of the communities, and the people to be resettled to identify municipal lands in the same communities where house plots could be allocated free of charge to those who had to be resettled. The project owner, the Ministry of Public Works of the Government of El Salvador, appointed a planning team composed of an engineer and a social worker who were present in each of the affected communities at least once a week, every week, for a period of two years conducting consultations, assessment of alternatives, and design studies. In this way, the design team interacted continuously throughout the resettlement planning processes with the stakeholders and people to be resettled. The project eventually presented to and approved by the Inter-American Development Bank was, therefore, the product of two years of participatory planning with the community, local authorities, and the persons to be resettled (Inter-American Development Bank 2011).

Colombia: Moravia Resettlement from Garbage Dump in Medellin

Throughout the 1970s and 1980s, a vacant area of about 43 hectares in between two major highways in the city of Medellin was utilized as a garbage dump, and waste occupying about 7 hectares accumulated to a height of 30 meters by 1984 when the dump was closed. During this same period, hundreds of families displaced from rural areas by violence and armed conflict migrated to the city and settled on the garbage dump, earning their poor livelihoods by recycling waste that could be sold. Some 1,745 families came to occupy the area, despite the instability of the soils and continuous emissions of toxic gases from the garbage. In 1990, the municipal government declared the area one of public calamity and initiated a program of resettlement of some 800 families living in the most noxious conditions, planted the largest botanical garden in the city with over 50,000 ornamentals of 46 species to combat the gases, built a cultural center and pedestrian paths to tour the garden, and constructed a primary school. An NGO, Corporación Antioquia Presente, was contracted to supervise and accompany the resettlement by the municipality, providing apartments with ownership titles in a multistory building called Nuevo Occidente in the same area but away from the garbage dump, carried out job training for the 800 resettled plus 884 families not resettled, established 92 new artisan and manufacturing enterprises, provided 184 microcredits for creating new businesses, and delivered technical assistance and capacity building programs in small business management, administration of microcredit and seed capital, and publicity and marketing. Today, the community and its botanical gardens are an attraction visited by over 3,000 tourists curious to learn how ragpickers on a garbage dump were transformed into a normal working-class community (Antioquia Presente 2013; *El Colombiano* 2018).

Colombia: The Rebirth of La Tebaida

On January 25, 1999, the municipality of Tebaida in the department of Quindio was struck by an earthquake that destroyed 92 percent of the municipality's capital town of 28,000 inhabitants. Some 3,196 homes had to be reconstructed, repaired, or resettled. The NGO Antioquia Presente was given the task of guiding the resettlement and reconstruction of two new neighborhoods: El Canarito of 952 families and Fundaciones with 85 families. Utilizing donations from Medellin business corporations, foundations, and private donors, the NGO launched a program of self-construction of the new neighborhoods by the affected people themselves, utilizing local and own labor and materials provided by donors and house plots purchased by the NGO. In addition, the NGO organized and delivered training and capacity building programs to stimulate new enterprises and employment. The quality of life was dramatically improved as all the families resettled became owners of their new self-built houses, whereas before they had been renters (Antioquia Presente 2018).

Chapter 6

Identifying Social, Economic, and Cultural Impacts

The second directive of the International Standard for Involuntary Resettlement is, where population displacement is unavoidable, to identify the nature and extent of the socioeconomic impacts of a project which will require involuntary resettlement, such as the taking of land, shelter, assets, and/or other means of livelihood. Such impacts may affect persons with formal legal rights to land and other assets, persons with no such rights but whose claims to land and other assets are recognized in other ways under national laws, and persons who have no recognizable legal right or claim to the land or other assets upon which they depend. The first two categories of displaced persons are to be provided compensation for their losses and other assistance to resettle and reestablish their livelihoods under the terms of the RAP. The third category of displaced persons is to be provided assistance to resettle and reestablish their livelihoods under the terms of the RAP in lieu of compensation for the land and assets they occupy.

The International Standard for Involuntary Resettlement calls for resettlement assistance for those who lack formally recognized land rights because, in many cases, these people have had no viable, legal avenue to assert formal land claims, for example, those living in areas where long-standing communal or customary tenure regimes operate but where the state has failed to formalize their rights. Persons displaced from land being acquired who have no legal right or claim to that land are often actually long-term occupants whose informal right to possess and use the land has been respected by neighbors and local authorities for generations. The failure to formalize such rights can usually be attributed to the inefficiency of land administration systems of many governments rather than to the long-term occupants. This is frequently the case, for example, in urban slum areas and remote rural regions where the state has had little or no presence in the past. Similarly, many governments have failed to formalize and protect the hereditary rights of subsistence farmers, pastoralists, hunters-and-gatherers, and other traditional communities who have lived on their land from time immemorial. It is the legitimate, albeit informal, rights of long-term occupants that are recognized by the International Standard for Involuntary Resettlement, rights that can be verified by neighbors and local authorities, and not the cases of opportunistic squatters seeking to exploit the situation to extract cash compensation.

SOCIAL IMPACT ANALYSIS ON THE GROUND

Delineating the impacts of a project includes mapping out the areas of direct and indirect impacts for multiple project components. Sometimes, impacts have been overlooked and estimates of resettlement requirements and costs are too low. It is important to include all project components that will require land acquisition and potential population displacement, including items that may not appear to be major components such as access roads, workforce housing, contractor camps, materials depots, warehouses, offices, workshops, service roads, laydown areas, borrow pits, waste disposal areas, and other ancillary facilities.

In addition, participatory mapping conducted with PAPs can help identify secondary and tertiary rights that people depend upon for livelihoods that are often missed by routine surveys. Such participatory mapping efforts are particularly important for women, indigenous people, and others that hold rights under customary tenure systems and whose patterns of resource use may be easily overlooked. These groups often hold rights to use common property, to use certain parcels within a community, to use property at particular times of the year, or they may hold leasehold rights—formal and informal. Surveying may not capture these rights unless supplemented by adequate ethnographic interviewing and observation, including community mapping exercises.

CASE EXAMPLES

People's Republic of China: Shaanxi Highway Development Project

Land acquisition requirements increased by 29 percent in the PRC Shaanxi Highway Development Project. The reason is that the resettlement plan was based only on the design studies for the main highway and neglected the several connecting highways, interchanges, bypasses, and service areas. Some

290 families and 1,334 persons were ultimately resettled, compared to the planned 262 families and 1,093 persons (Asian Development Bank 2005a).

India: Sardar Sarovar Project

The project consisted of a multipurpose dam on the Narmada River in the state of Gujarat, the reservoir of which flooded portions of Gujarat and parts of the neighboring states of Maharashtra and Madhya Pradesh. The Resettlement Action Plan accepted by the World Bank at appraisal addressed land acquisition requirements at the dam construction site and in the future reservoir area but failed to take into account land acquisition for thousands of kilometers of irrigation canals, service roads, bridges, and water control and distribution works in the irrigated command area. The additional land acquisition requirements of this enormous amount of unaccounted-for civil works increased the involuntary resettlement impacts and project costs dramatically. The unaddressed project resettlement impacts were unmanageable under the terms of the Resettlement Action Plan agreed with the World Bank and widely condemned by international human rights nongovernmental organizations. The outcry ultimately caused the withdrawal of World Bank support for the project (Morse and Berger 1992).

ESTABLISHING THE SOCIAL AND CULTURAL BASELINE

A Social Impact Analysis in the context of involuntary resettlement encompasses (i) identification of stakeholders and interests; (ii) baseline demographic data collection including the census of population and properties affected; (iii) identification of socioeconomic income levels; and (iv) the cultural production and distribution systems that generate such incomes. Not only the displaced people but also the host population among whom they may be relocated are affected. Further, affected people often have complex livelihood strategies that combine farming, gathering, livestock rearing, and occasional off-farm employment (Smyth et al. 2015, 222).

Vulnerable parties especially may depend upon access to common property resources such as firewood, fodder, water, and natural resources such as honey to support livelihoods. Women may not be named on property titles but have subsidiary rights to manage certain parcels held in the names of fathers or husbands. Project analyses need to account for these important secondary rights. In other words, baseline studies should seek to capture the full spectrum of income earned by displaced people and the variety of tenure/ usufructuary rights that exist in a location.

Similarly, where communities are partially affected, those not losing land or housing and who remain behind may also be affected if economic and social support networks or systems are disrupted. A good practice is to consider the displaced, those who remain behind, and host populations as affected people that should be included in the Social Impact Analysis to a degree commensurate with the impacts stemming from the project. Whether displaced or not, or part of a host community, the right of women and other vulnerable groups should be carefully identified in baselines.

Census

There is an absolute necessity for first-hand, on-the-ground documentation. This work almost always requires field research and an empirical census of the affected populations rather than reliance upon secondary data. National census data are an often-used secondary data source, but they are notoriously inaccurate and incomplete. As seen in the case of the Arenal Hydroelectric Project in Costa Rica (see below), entire segments of the affected population may be missed by the government census takers. In other instances racial, social class, or religious prejudice can exclude certain groups, as one of the authors experienced in India when he noticed that a hamlet of indigenous people living in brick houses on the outskirts of a Hindu village were not being counted in the census then being executed. When he asked why, the Hindu manager of the census team explained, "Oh, they are Banjaras. They are pagan nomads that roam over the whole country. They don't belong to this village." The manager did not explain how the nomads could carry their brick houses around the country on their backs. In still another instance, one of the authors discovered in a Turkish hydroelectric dam project proposed for World Bank financing that many of the minority Kurdish villages to be resettled by the project's resettlement plan were completely vacant. The census figures given in the resettlement plan were copied from an earlier outdated census and did not reflect the fact that, ten years earlier, the Turkish Army had evacuated the villagers in an effort to cut off Kurdish guerrilla fighters from their bases of support in the countryside.

Asset Evaluation

Accompanying the census, there must be an inventory of assets upon which the displaced people depend for their livelihood that will be lost because of the displacement. Delineating the impacts of a project includes mapping out the areas of direct and indirect impacts for multiple project components. Many times impacts have been overlooked and estimates of resettlement requirements and costs are too low. It is important to include all project components that will require land acquisition and potential population displacement, including items that may not appear to be major components such as access roads, workforce housing, contractor camps, materials depots, warehouses, offices, workshops, service roads, laydown areas, borrow pits, waste disposal areas, and other ancillary facilities.

The census and property inventory should produce accurate empirical information on the nature and magnitude of project resettlement requirements, but these should not be considered a straitjacket. Project planners should use common sense to take into account predictable changes such as the spontaneous in-migration of workers in addition to those brought by contractors as well as new shops, restaurants, bars, and other businesses enterprises attracted to the developing area.

Production Systems and Resource Base

Beyond the census data and assets inventory, it is important to carry out an analysis of production and distribution systems that sustain the livelihoods of affected people. Such systems usually entail management of multiple production activities generating multiple income streams. For example, peasant small farm holders throughout the world cultivate field crops of grains and tubers such as maize, rice, cassava, or potatoes, and keep gardens producing a great variety of vegetables, herbs, and medicinal plants; as well as planting fruit trees like banana, pear, mango, citrus, and avocado; rearing small livestock like pigs, chickens, and goats as well as sheep, cattle or llamas for meat, milk, fur, and hides; and in China's farming communities one always finds a village fish pond. In addition to the consumption of the produce from these activities, farmers almost always produce in surplus, which is bartered in kind with neighbors or marketed for cash. Finally, thanks to greater opportunities for training and education, many young people from these communities who do not wish to continue farming their parents' land find employment in nearby towns and cities, contributing to household incomes of siblings, parents, and grandparents through remittances. The sheer complexity of the multifaceted production system managed by peasant farmers cannot be captured in any census of inventory of assets, but understanding it is key to designing livelihood improvement or restoration projects in resettlement operations.

Turning to the other end of the spectrum, urban poor communities threatened with displacement, in towns and cities throughout Latin America, Africa, and Asia, seemingly obtain their livelihoods partly from wage labor. But a closer look reveals several income streams to complement wage labor. This is especially the case for those earning at or below the minimum wage in the country. Such multiple income streams often include planting vegetables and herbs in kitchen gardens, part-time fishing, rearing hogs or poultry, gathering wild plants from commons grasslands or forests, manufacture of artisanal crafts, as well as the sale of fruit from trees planted in the patio. In addition, all urban slum dwellers are engaged in social support networks that entail the inequivalent but reciprocal exchange of services based in kin, fictive kin, and patron-client relationships, such as emergency loans, child care, short-term employment, attention to the elderly, and security of person and property. In addition, some operate service businesses out of their homes, such as beauty parlors, barbershops, tailoring and repair of garments, servicing of appliances, sale of home-cooked food, and shops, bars, and bakeries. The urban poor must be understood to be dependent on multiple income streams without which they could not survive on a miserable minimum wage.

Pastoralists in Kenya, Uganda, and Tanzania surely depend upon the milk and blood drawn from their nomadic herds of cattle, ranging over hundreds of square kilometers of pasture, and tended by the teenage and young adult males. Such pastoralists recognize and have names for a dozen types of grass upon which they and the cattle depend for survival during different times of the year. But a central part of the overall production system entails a semi-sedentary home base where lactating cows and their calves are kept in pens. These semi-sedentary settlements are comprised of shelters made of wooden poles, cow dung, mud, and grass thatch constructed by the women, and they are shifted periodically from one location to another as the surrounding pasture is depleted and sanitary conditions deteriorate. The milk and blood which are dietary staples of all the community are drawn by adult males and females from the penned animals in the semi-sedentary settlement. Similarly, small livestock like goats and chickens are reared by females and their juvenile offspring in the settlements. These and milk, meat, and hides from the cattle are bartered or exchanged with farmers nearby the semi-sedentary settlements for grains, fruits, and vegetables. In addition, from practically every extended family household, males and females venture out to find employment for wages in nearby villages and towns. So even an apparently simple production system like herding cattle entails multiple facets.

In many communities one encounters the landless poor, indigenous minorities, and other vulnerable households who derive much of their livelihoods from common property, in productive activities such as livestock rearing, hunting, gathering, and/or fishing. It is important to emphasize the frequent loss of such common property resources for several reasons. First, empirical field studies in India, for example, have shown that a disproportionate percentage of the landless poor and vulnerable households among the displaced population depend upon common property resources—grasslands, forests, and so-called "wastelands"—for up to 80 percent of their income from livestock rearing and gathering wild vegetation (Jodha 1986). Second, land acquisition legal frameworks inherited from former European colonial administrations usually do not provide for recognition, compensation and/or replacement of common properties expropriated by the state and upon which the landless poor, indigenous peoples, and other vulnerable groups often depend for their survival.

The Social Impact Analysis identifies the social impacts caused by land acquisition, calculates the numbers of people and properties expected to be impacted, assesses the incomes and livelihoods of displaced people, and provides a gender-disaggregated analysis of the present economic and socio-economic conditions of the host and displaced populations. Social impacts may include harms that flow from loss of areas that have special cultural, religious, or environmental significance for affected peoples. These impacts may be particularly difficult to value but are extremely important to take into account in order to attempt to minimize social harms.

The Myth of Land Tenure Registries and Records

Although in most countries the right to property ownership is guaranteed to all citizens by a constitution, in a great many countries, the formal system through which rights to property are registered, titled, and enforced is incomplete. Important components of this framework may be missing; it may contain ambiguous or contradictory provisions; officials may lack critical capacity; financial resources may not be sufficient to support administrative activities or efforts to enact needed policies; laws and implementing regulations may be stalled and tied up in long-standing negotiations; and, of course, many land administration systems are corrupt. A recent report notes that while local communities hold upward of 65 percent of the world's land area under customary tenure systems, national governments recognize a small fraction of this land (Rights and Resources Initiative 2015). In a survey of nineteen sub-Saharan African countries, this study found that only 2.75 percent of community and indigenous lands are legally recognized as owned by local communities and indigenous peoples. In Latin America, the governments of Brazil, Colombia, Honduras, Paraguay, and others have failed for decades to issue ownership titles to as much as 50 percent of peasant small farm holders who have worked their lands for generations. In cases such as these, land tenure security is only obtained informally, through de facto respect for and recognition of the legitimacy of a family's claim to the land by neighbors, other villages, and local authorities.

Because secondary data are almost always inaccurate and unreliable, resettlement planning must entail first-hand field research and empirical investigation on the ground. Demographic, socioeconomic, and cultural data may be collected from community leaders, women, representatives of groups that may use resources in an area (migrants, pastoralists, fishermen, and so forth), electoral lists, municipal authorities, cadastral maps, aerial photographs, tax records, land registries, and the national census, but such secondary data must always be verified by field surveys, project censuses, and property inventories conducted by the resettlement planning team (see, e.g., Mathur 2011a). The property inventory should include not only private land, structures, crops, and trees but also commons or communal property such as wells, ovens, prayer houses, schools, clinics, forests, grazing areas, fishing areas, fuel wood lots, and others, which are not usually recorded in secondary sources. The inventory should also make note of plots which are not titled in women's names, but which women use and control to feed their families and to produce crops for market.

Accurate baseline data of this kind are central to the formulation of a practical Resettlement Action Plan. Where the time lapse between the Social Impact Analysis and the beginning of construction is long (several years), the census and property inventory require updating prior to beginning resettlement operations. One reason to update the census and property data is that impacts may have changed by the time detailed design-level engineering studies are completed. Another reason is that a Social Analysis conducted several years prior to the actual displacement cannot reflect the formation of new households through marriage, the deaths of titleholders, and transmission of rights to heirs, or out-migrations, separations, and divorces.

The baseline should determine a cut-off date after which no further changes are acceptable. This date should be widely disseminated among PAPs using appropriate local methods that may include announcements posted in local government offices, in community centers, and meeting areas, via radio or via social media. It is important that this date be widely shared in order to avoid problems associated with opportunistic squatting as well as legitimate actions PAPs may take to maintain livelihoods (such as planting crops). The date of completion of the updated census and property inventory often serves as the cut-off date for resettlement assistance eligibility. Dissemination of the cut-off date throughout the project area also helps to discourage in-migration of squatters. Persons taking up residence in the project area after that date are not eligible for compensation or resettlement assistance. Similarly, loss of fixed assets, such as built structures, crops, trees, and others, established after the cut-off date are not compensated. Seasonal resource users absent from the project area at the time of the census, such as nomadic pastoralists or seasonal migrants to cities, should receive special consideration regarding impacts upon their properties or livelihoods and included as appropriate in resettlement planning.

CASE EXAMPLES

Costa Rica: Arenal Hydroelectric Project

The storage reservoir created by the Costa Rica Electrification Institute to generate electricity flooded two towns and many cattle ranches, displacing some 2,500 people. The national census conducted twelve months prior to the initial planning for the project counted the townspeople but failed to count the workers living on the cattle estates. In fact, the national census missed 32 percent of the population that would be displaced by the project who were documented in the Social Impact Analysis conducted as part of the resettlement planning process by the Costa Rica Electrification Institute (Partridge 1993).

Peoples Republic of China: Ertan Hydroelectric Project

This dam on the Yalong River in Sichuan Province was the largest dam in the PRC until Three Gorges was built. The Resettlement Plan delineated land to be acquired for the access road, construction site internal roads, main dam, coffer dam, diversion tunnel, powerhouse, reservoir, rock quarry, sand borrow pits, laydown areas, batching plant, contractor camp (housing, workshops, warehouses, offices, kitchens, vehicle and machinery parking lots), and government officials camp (housing, offices, kitchen, vehicle parking lot). For each of these components, the amount/type of land to be acquired was measured together with the number of households that would lose (1) house plots and houses; (2) kitchen gardens, patios, wells, and latrines; (3) shops, offices, workshops, restaurants, and hotels; (4) rice paddy terraces; (5) livestock pens; (6) fishponds; (7) orchards; (8) dry farmland; and (9) pasture. In addition, common property resources pertaining to villages and towns to be acquired were also delineated, including (10) grasslands; (11) fuel wood lots; (12) minor forest products collecting areas; (13) wastelands; (14) riverine fisheries; (15) government offices; (16) access roads; (17) internal roads; (18) wells and water supply systems; (19) electricity power stations and grid; (20) temples; (21) schools; (22) clinics; and (23) community meeting halls. All of the assets and properties, including common property resources, were identified and were replaced by the project in new settlement areas (World Bank 1991a, 1995b).

Population increase through migration stimulated by project works should be anticipated in order to adequately plan for necessary infrastructure, housing, services, and the like. In the Ertan project in Sichuan Province, the Social Impact Analysis demonstrated that a relatively small town of about 15,000 people had to be relocated as part of the planned resettlement. The Sichuan authorities and project planning team were advised by the World Bank resettlement specialist to design the new town to accommodate two or three times that number of residents, due to a predictable influx of spontaneous migrants looking for employment in construction and in new business attracted by the massive development investment in the region. This advice was rejected by the authorities. The town was designed and built for 15,000 people. By the end of project construction, the new town had a population of 40,000 people, inadequate infrastructure, overloaded public services, and a shortage of decent housing (World Bank 1995b).

Peoples´ Republic of China: Shanxi Road Development II Project

The main highway and local roads land acquisition affected over fifty villages in thirteen townships in three counties. The Second Highway Design and Research Institute (SHDRI) conducted initial feasibility-level surveys from February 1998 to June 1999. The Social Impact Analysis was carried out November–December 2001 by local village committees formed for the purpose, composed of both displaced people and host villagers, together with staff from county government offices working under the supervision of the SHDRI and the Shanxi Communications Department. The village-based Social Impact Analysis involving direct participation of the affected people showed only twenty houses had to be demolished and rebuilt elsewhere, but some 3,532 households (15,187 people) would lose irrigated land, vegetable gardens, orchards, wood lots, and others, which had to be replaced. Village committees composed of host and displaced people agreed upon redistribution of farmlands, increasing productivity through irrigation, reclaiming wastelands, and innovating processing industries to resettle the displaced people within the same villages. Based on the participatory Social Impact Analysis the impacts were accurately identified, acceptable income restoration plans were designed with each village committee and resettlement and rehabilitation agreements were formally signed with each affected household (Asian Development Bank 2008).

Guinea: Simandou Project

The Simandou Project is the largest proposed mining and infrastructure project in sub-Saharan Africa. It seeks to develop 650 kilometers of railway from an open-cut iron ore mining site at Pic de Fon and Oueleba to the south of the Simandou Mountain Range to a port site south of Conarky in Forecariah prefecture. The project is being developed by Rio Tinto and involves the physical displacement of 343 households and the economic displacement of 5,520 households. In total, affected people in the 2-kilometer area will be compensated. Rio Tinto has developed agreement and certificate templates that are specific to physical and economically displaced households. Templates provide for compensation for loss of crops and trees; replacement compensation for loss of land and housing; and community project compensation at the community level. Compensation is assessed at the individual level but agreed at the household level to take the needs of women and vulnerable groups into consideration. A Government Land Commission is working with customary authorities and other local stakeholders to identify and acquire rights to the replacement land. The project uses participatory village mapping, along with GIS photo interpretation, to identify land features and to provide a basis for compensation. A census and household questionnaire are administered along with focus group discussions and a GPS-based land survey. This results in a "Village Profile Report" that provides a summary of key village-level information. Early activities have introduced new farming techniques and technologies to some communities reportedly resulting in increases in crop yields and in commercial salt production (Rio Tinto 2014).

Thailand: Pak Mun Project

Fisherfolk whose livelihoods were drastically affected by the Pak Mun Dam were not included in the Social Impact Analysis carried out by an engineering firm during project planning. Scores of fisherfolk families economically displaced by the project were missed. As a result, resettlement plans were severely under-designed, and costs were significantly underestimated. The project had to allocate significant additional resources to reestablish those affected by the decline in incomes from fishing, and the project was subjected to national and international condemnation by human rights nongovernmental organizations (World Bank 1998a).

In some countries, like the PRC, Uruguay, and Thailand, local and national government entities maintain continuously updated property and population records, such as land titles, cadastral maps which include information related to valuation and tax rate, property transfers, inheritance, usufruct rights, encumbrances, location of common property resources, and so forth, so that secondary data tend to be reliable. But complete and accurate records of land rights information is relatively rare. In many countries, land administration records are not updated upon transfer, and cadastral maps do not reflect subdivisions or encumbrances such as easements. For example, in India, land registries in some districts are ten to twenty years out of date. In other cases, data related to customary land holdings are simply nonexistent.

India: Sardar Sarovar

Resettlement planning was based on census data that were ten years old and therefore inaccurate. Likewise, land registry records, which theoretically should include updated information on sales, purchases, inheritances, and so forth, that were utilized in planning had not been updated for twenty years in some districts. No empirical field surveys were undertaken to verify and update the secondary data contained in official records. In addition, many of the PAPs were tribal people who did not appear in the registries because they had no titles to their ancestral lands. They were, therefore, not legally entitled to compensation and/or resettlement under Indian law at that time. Their ancestral lands were legally registered as "government land," and there existed no records of hereditary usufruct rights and no knowledge of cultural, customary land-use patterns of the indigenous households that depended upon ancestral lands and had done so for centuries. The result was a completely deficient resettlement operation that failed to capture reality on the ground and proved unworkable (Morse and Berger 1992).

Bangladesh: Jamuna Bridge

Jointly financed by Asian Development Bank and the World Bank, the resettlement operation provides a cautionary case illustrating the importance of documenting impacts and precisely determining eligibility in the analysis of impacts. The land areas subject to acquisition were flood prone and not densely populated, but shortly before construction was to begin, thousands of opportunistic squatters invaded the project impact area and erected makeshift shelters in the hope of securing compensation money. The project had conducted a detailed census and taken aerial photographs of the project impact area during the analysis of impacts and was able to use these as evidence that many claims for indemnification and resettlement were unjustified (World Bank Inspection Panel 1996).

Chapter 7

The Resettlement Action Plan

The International Standard for Involuntary Resettlement requires that Resettlement Action Plans (RAPs) be conceived, designed, financed, and implemented as socioeconomic development projects. That is to say that, like any development project, the RAP must

- identify the development objectives the project is designed to achieve, as well as the benefits expected for the communities participating;
- set out a concrete legal and policy framework for the operation, which may depart from and go considerably beyond domestic policy frameworks but without violating such statutes;
- describe the steps taken to ensure free, prior, and informed participation of the population affected in preparation and implementation of the project;
- detail the dimensions of the operation, including a demographic census of households to benefit and properties affected;
- present the process wherein the locations and technical designs for new production systems, creation of employment opportunities, and other activities to ensure income streams have been consulted with and are acceptable to the communities involved;
- disaggregate and target by gender, age, and where necessary skills or capabilities the income producing activities agreed with the affected people; and
- establish the institutional resources being dedicated to execution, the technical skills being assigned, the managerial responsibility for administration, the training requirements needed and being offered, the monitoring, feedback, and grievance mechanisms in place, and the budget and financing arrangements.

The International Standard for Involuntary Resettlement requires that all people displaced, not just property owners, must be included in the RAP. They are all to be resettled and assisted in reestablishing their livelihoods and, if possible, improve their standards of living, irrespective of whether they are physically displaced or economically displaced or both from the resources upon which they depend for their livelihood. That means that those who may be labeled by some states as "squatters" or "possessors" or "occupants" of their lands are to be considered eligible for resettlement and reestablishment of their livelihoods in accord with the International Standard for Involuntary Resettlement.

Where population displacement is unavoidable, a RAP should be conceived, developed, and executed as a sustainable development project, providing sufficient investment resources to enable the persons displaced by the project to share in project benefits This means displaced persons have to be supported and assisted in their efforts to improve their livelihoods and standards of living or at least restore them, in real terms, to pre-displacement levels or to levels prevailing prior to the beginning of project implementation whichever is greater. Care must be taken to consult and listen to affected people in order to provide, that is to design, staff, and finance, such assistance in socially and culturally compatible ways. Livelihood improvement or restoration programs, measures, or instruments will be successful to the extent that they mesh with the knowledge, skills, capabilities, and aspirations of the displaced people. And the only way to accomplish that is to ensure from the outset that displaced people are active and direct participants in the design and implementation of the livelihood improvement or restoration projects. In other words, in a very real, practical sense, the people being resettled must come to own the development project called resettlement.

CASE EXAMPLES

Costa Rica: Arenal Hydroelectric Project

The reservoir created by this dam project flooded, in addition to the two towns of Arenal and Tronadora, thousands of hectares of land devoted to cattle ranches. The cattle ranch owners were mostly absentee, but living on their land were their employees and ranch hands who worked the cattle. These workers, according to long-standing cultural tradition, were paid a small salary, but they were also provided farming plots on the ranch to grow staple foods as well as a house plot where they constructed their dwelling. When the cattle ranches were expropriated, the landowners were duly compensated for the expropriation of their property by the state. But their employees and ranch hands, who were legally landless, received no compensation with which to resettle themselves elsewhere. The project owner, the Costa Rica Electrification Institute, recognizing the risk of impoverishment of the displaced workers, devised a RAP to resettle the workers to one of three different sites selected by the workers, where they were allocated farming plots and house plots to replace those expropriated by the project upon which they depended. In addition, the Institute provided coffee tree seedlings, cut-fodder plantings for livestock, and a choice among seven different kinds of house designs and materials. An independent evaluation of the outcomes documented the fact that the livelihoods of the resettled people were not only restored to previous levels but significantly improved (Partridge 1993). These findings were largely confirmed twenty years later by Stocks (2014).

Peoples´ Republic of China: Xiaolangdi Resettlement Project

Care needs to be taken to ensure that RAPs are realistic and the measures designed to rebuild livelihoods are socially and culturally compatible as well as economically feasible and sustainable. The People's Republic of China (PRC) Xiaolangdi Resettlement Project provides an illustration of the proper focus on enhancing livelihoods through realistic planning that is compatible with local social, cultural, and economic conditions. Over 90 percent of the people displaced by a flood-control dam on the Yellow River were farmers. The World Bank expressed doubts during preparation (1990–1993) concerning the feasibility and sustainability of a PRC-proposed focus on industrial resettlement (creation of numerous industries to provide employment) but accepted it initially as a method of improving living standards because of the prior strength of the industrial sector which grew at 15 percent per year during the period 1980–1992. But by appraisal (1994) the Bank's initial doubts proved to be correct, and this component was replaced with a land-for-land-and-agriculture-based program because macroeconomic changes had caused the rural industry sector to become unstable, and, therefore, risky as a basis for achieving the objective of rebuilding livelihoods. So the government changed the approach from a focus on county-based industrial employment to one focused on village-level industries, commercial farming (cash crops, livestock, fishery, agro-processing), off-farm employment, and land-based agriculture through redistribution of host village wastelands, drylands, and pasture lands. Hosts were compensated and included in income improvement schemes such as irrigation, terracing, topsoil deposit, and green manuring, thus increasing the carrying capacity of the land to support both settlers and hosts (World Bank 2004b).

Indonesia: Kedung Ombo Irrigation Project

Experience shows that programs designed for other purposes may not be suitable or transferable to involuntary resettlement operations. Such was the case in the Indonesia Kedung Ombo Project where the World Bank accepted the *Transmigrasi* or Transmigration legal and policy framework to resettle some 3,000 families from the future reservoir area of an irrigation project. The Indonesian Transmigration Program had over the years successfully recruited hundreds of thousands of farm families from the densely populated island of Java and resettled them to the less populated "outer islands" of the country, both to relieve population pressure on the scarce farmlands of Java and to bring new lands under cultivation in the outer islands. Most independent evaluations found the new farming settlements to be viable and the colonists' lives better than before, so the World Bank accepted this model for the Kedung Ombo involuntary resettlement. The negative consequences were quite unexpected. Throughout several years of implementation, the Transmigration Program resettled some 3,000 families from the future Kedung Ombo reservoir area to several newly established farming settlements in the outer islands. A total of some 40 million US dollars were budgeted and spent during that period in the preparation of the new farms and village sites, mobilization and transport of the displaced people, and the provision of farm tools, seeds, and resettlement assistance packages. All was duly monitored and reported by the government every year to the satisfaction of the World Bank. Yet a few months prior to filling the reservoir, a local nongovernmental organization reported that there were still thousands of people living in the reservoir area who had not been resettled. It was discovered belatedly that the Transmigration Program, in accordance with long-standing internal practices, recruited only able-bodied young couples with young children to the new farming communities. It did not permit the allocation of farmlands and houses to single adult individuals, or families with older children, or to the aged. Thus, the Transmigration Program left behind aged parents, families with adult children, and single siblings of the affected people. In effect, the program broke up the affected families. Those left behind were dispersed to the city slums on an emergency basis by the military prior to reservoir filling, where they were compelled to find their own way with only a token transition allowance and cut off from family and community social support networks (World Bank 1998b).

Paraguay: Integrated Program to Clean the Bay Area of Metropolitan Asunción

In contrast to previous examples, some existing programs can fit well and meet the needs of involuntary resettlement operations when they have the necessary experience and personnel. An example is the Habitat Program in Paraguay. The project owner is the National Secretariat of Housing of the Government of Paraguay that designed a program to provide water treatment facilities and a sewerage system for the slum areas bordering the Bay of Asunción on the Paraguay River. Recognizing its lack of experience and human resources to carry out the necessary resettlement of a score of families occupying the site needed to construct a water treatment plant named San Lorenzo, the Secretariat signed an agreement with the UN-HABITAT program in Asunción to design and carry out the resettlement plan. The UN-HABITAT team had ample experience and human resources to accomplish the task and drew upon policy guidance based on experience elsewhere with population displacement and resettlement (du Plessis 2011; Inter-American Development Bank 2014; UN-Habitat, UNHCHR and Farha 2011).

Whether or not existing programs can achieve the objectives of involuntary resettlement and restoration of livelihoods as specified in the International Standard for Involuntary Resettlement is a judgment call to be negotiated among the project owners, the project financiers, and the affected communities.

VULNERABLE GROUPS AND SPECIAL MEASURES REQUIRED

Vulnerable groups among the PAPs, such as those below the poverty line, the landless, the elderly, women-headed households, indigenous peoples, ethnic minorities, or other displaced persons who may not be protected through national land acquisition and compensation legislation, require special measures to ensure their condition is not worsened. The principal lesson from international experience is that the vulnerable among the PAPs need special, targeted attention designed to improve their livelihoods and living standards.

Indigenous and Tribal Peoples

Indigenous and tribal peoples are often deeply dependent on and adapted to an ancestral territory which they know and understand intimately and which is synonymous with their cultural identity, as pastoralists, hunter-gatherers, fisherfolk, or horticulturalists. Their displacement from their ancestral homes is extremely risky not because their cultural adaptation is fragile but because it is so strongly rooted in the specific conditions of their environment as to be practically nonreplicable elsewhere. Unless an equivalent set of conditions can be found in the vicinity to which they might move, it is extremely unlikely that indigenous people can be successfully relocated to a new and different environment. For this reason, the International Standard for Involuntary Resettlement requires that particular efforts are made to ensure that there is "broad community support" among the affected indigenous people for the proposed resettlement operation. By this is meant that although some will resist the proposed resettlement, the bulk of the affected population accepts that the resettlement is necessary, that the destination to which they will move is suitable, that the host community or neighboring people are not opposed, and that they believe they will be able to rebuild their livelihoods, social support networks, and community. While the active and direct participation of displaced people in their own resettlement is always desirable, in the case of resettlement of indigenous peoples it is vital. Once again, in a very real, practical sense, the indigenous community being resettled must come to own the development project called resettlement.

Gender

Women-headed households are considered vulnerable in part because of ubiquitous discrimination resulting in lower incomes for the same work, denial of equal access to education, and because they are burdened with childrearing in addition to having to work outside the home. But equally important is the vulnerability of their social support networks, involving the reciprocal exchange of services among women, to disruption in the process of displacement and resettlement. Single mothers depend heavily on the mutual support of a network of other single mothers, as well as their own siblings, to manage employment outside the home, childcare, housekeeping, meal preparation, care for aged parents, and running the bureaucratic gauntlet of health, finance, police, and education institutions to obtain services for their families. In the context of involuntary resettlement, women-headed households require special attention by carefully locating resettlement sites to protect social support networks, by offering training opportunities to enhance skills and earning capacity, by providing start-up money for entrepreneurs to open new businesses, by ensuring priority targeting of women-headed households for delivery of education and healthcare services, and by giving transition support (jobs, food allowances) during training and start-up periods of new jobs or businesses.

The Extreme Poor, Landless, Elderly, and Disabled

Each of these categories of vulnerable people faces discrimination and similar constraints, disadvantages, and dependencies. All are impoverished, many suffering from chronic illness, most are illiterate and lacking skills needed to increase income, living chaotic, unpredictable lives dependent on irregular, intermittent short-term employment as well as the support of mutual help networks. Most are characterized by other segments of society as largely responsible for their own poverty, prone to criminality, prone to abuse of alcohol and drugs, and prone to sending their children out into the streets to beg. Such derogatory stereotypes are generally not applied to the elderly and disabled; however, all the categories of vulnerability mentioned above share a fragile dependence upon social support networks. The networks link higher-strata families to lower-strata vulnerable people through ties of kinship, fictive kinship, and patron-client relationships that entail the inequivalent but recipro-cal exchange of services. It is through such networks, that the vulnerable obtain short-term employment, credit for emergencies, healthcare, school supplies, and security of person and property which they cannot otherwise obtain on their own. As in the case of women-headed households, displacement and resettlement can rupture such networks deepening impoverishment and even threatening survival. To lessen such risks, special attention is required to care-fully locate resettlement sites so as to protect social support networks and to prioritize and target delivery of essential services to the vulnerable.

Ensuring Successful Implementation through Effective Management and Adequate Financing

A major challenge in many involuntary resettlement operations is that power-ful, highly centralized governmental institutions that execute development projects often have little experience with implementing involuntary resettle-ment operations. Due to this lack of experience, in almost all instances, there is a pressing need for training and capacity-building of the staff of the institutions assigned the responsibility for designing and implementing resettlement plans.

Capacity-Building

When responsibility for resettlement is delegated to lower-level local and regional institutions, the challenge may be even greater. Therefore, it is almost always necessary to consider whether existing institutional capacity and human resources available are adequate and, if not, to design programs for strengthening that capacity. Issues to be addressed in programs that assess existing capacity include the following: (i) ensuring there is clear responsibility and accountability for involuntary resettlement planning and implementation at top management levels; (ii) ensuring the management of resettlement planning and implementation has been adequately integrated into overall project management; (iii) ensuring the borrower/client's execut-ing agencies have the human, technical, and financial resources, including external experts, to meet the demands of resettlement planning and imple-mentation; (iv) clearly articulating the responsibilities and accountability of personnel who perform or ensure quality work entailed in resettlement;

(v) ensuring the performance or contribution of departments, ministries, or agencies beyond the executing agency; (vi) establishing a process of periodic review of resettlement management system performance; and (vii) assessing and evaluating the borrower/client's previous experience with resettlement planning and implementation. Programs for strengthening capacity should address the following: (i) identifying and evaluating the borrower/client's mechanism for identifying and addressing staff training needs; (ii) assessing how training needs of specific job functions are analyzed; (iii) assessing whether the need for training contractors is warranted; (iv) ensuring that training is reviewed and periodically updated as needed; and (iv) ensuring the tracking and documentation of training (Partridge 2009, 16–17).

As a matter of good management practice for large scale and complex resettlement projects, an independent internationally recognized involuntary resettlement expert should be appointed as a member of an Advisory Group or Panel of Experts (POE) to the project. Such a panel may include as well technical specialists in rural and/or urban socioeconomic development as needed, depending upon the nature of income generation challenges being faced, such as agricultural production, small business development, livestock rearing, education, and job training.

Creating a Stand-Alone Institution Devoted Solely to Resettlement Operations

It may be beneficial in cases of large and complex projects for there to be established a stand-alone institution—a division, department, or office— either wholly independent or within a government agency or ministry, solely devoted to and responsible for resettlement operations. The Papaloapan project, for example, created the Office of Population Relocation (OPR) within the Commission, and it was given the responsibility of planning and implementing the resettlement program for the Aleman Dam. Likewise, the Indian Narmada Sagar Dam project, a companion project to Sardar Sarovar as part of the Narmada River Complex, created a separate body charged with implementing resettlement operations in that case. Such institutions should be adequately financed and staffed with competent professionals and have at least semiautonomy in terms of decision-making and operational procedures.

CASE EXAMPLES

Colombia: Sagamoso Hydroelectric Project

The reservoir that permits the generation of 820 megawatts of electricity displaced 141 families from their farms and homes. The electricity-generating agency of Colombia, ISAGEN, in dialogue with the affected families and local government representatives established an RAP in which (i) owners with titles to farms were eligible to receive replacement farmland equal to that lost up to a maximum of 20 hectares and a minimum of 5 hectares and a replacement house; (ii) occupants of farms with no title but whose neighbors testified had possessed and worked the land for more than three years were eligible to receive replacement farmland equal to that lost up to a maximum of 20 hectares and a minimum of 5 hectares and a replacement house; and (iii) renters, sharecroppers, and resident farm laborers with no land rights but whose neighbors testified had lived on the land for more than five years were eligible to receive replacement farmland of 5 hectares and a house. Female-headed households were allocated and received titles to the replacement farmland and houses exactly as male-headed households in accord with the eligibility criteria established by the RAP. All affected people also had the option of negotiating a cash compensation payment and resettling themselves to a place of their own choice without any further government assistance, which the large landowners preferred. Smallholders, occupants without title, and renters, sharecroppers, and laborers preferred the resettlement entitlement of replacement land and house. The later renters, sharecroppers, and laborers, a vulnerable segment of the displaced population not protected by national land acquisition statutes, clearly had their living standards and livelihoods improved as a result of the RAP (Euler-Hermes and Banco de Santander 2011).

India: Mumbai Urban Transport Project

Legally landless slum dwellers numbering approximately 19,220 households, who under Indian land acquisition legislation at the time were not entitled to monetary compensation or resettlement, were assisted to become owners of apartments. The resettlement planners used a participatory and consensus-building approach among project stakeholders. As a result, a working partnership was established between the government, Mumbai Metropolitan Regional Development Authority, NGOs, and the affected communities. The objectives of the resettlement and rehabilitation policy adopted by the government were to (i) minimize resettlement by exploring all viable alternative project designs; (ii) to develop and execute resettlement plans in such a manner that displaced persons are compensated for their losses at replacement cost prior to the actual move, where displacement was unavoidable; (iii) to accord formal housing rights to project-affected households at the resettlement site (such rights were in the form of leasehold rights to the cooperative society of project-affected households and occupancy rights of built floor space); (iv) to develop and implement the details of the resettlement program through active community participation; (v) to endeavor either to retain the existing community social networks or to integrate the resettled population with the host community and to minimize any adverse impact on the host community; and (vi) to improve the environmental health and hygiene of resettled people and the host community at the resettlement sites. In this way, the most vulnerable of displaced persons, who were not protected under land acquisition legislation at the time, were incorporated into the benefit streams of the investment project by a development-oriented RAP (World Bank 2002).

The budget for involuntary resettlement operations should be detailed in the Resettlement Action Plan to ensure adequate financial resources are made available. In a simple lineal project, such as a highway or pipeline, resettlement operations may be completed in a few months and budget projections are quite simple. But in large and complex resettlement operations, such as the Xiaolangdi Resettlement Project in China, the budget must be projected over a period of years.

People's Republic of China: Xiaolangdi Resettlement Project

Project resettlement operations spanned approximately two years of planning, five years of implementation following the start of construction, plus three years of independent external monitoring follow-up to ensure corrective actions if the objective of rebuilding livelihoods was not achieved. The budget calculated and updated annually spanned ten years to ensure the financial resources required were identified and committed to resettling over 172,000 people into 227 new villages and 12 towns (World Bank 2004b). Appendix 2 summarizes the general categories of expense budgeted for the project during each of its phases.

The monitoring system is a project management tool. It provides monthly or quarterly reports to project management regarding the outcomes of the involuntary resettlement operation and the well-being of the resettled population. The purpose is not only to document success but also to identify the need for corrective actions if things are not going well.

Swaziland: Komati Basin Maguga Dam

This hydropower dam on the Komati River was a joint endeavor with South Africa which affected 155 households of farmers and pastoralists, some 65 of which were resettled to new farms and houses and 90 of which lost farmland that was replaced with new lands. The government of Swaziland established in 1996 a Resettlement and Compensation Policy that included the requirement for retaining consultants to conduct independent monitoring of the implementation of the resettlement program. In 2001, the University of

Swaziland was retained to design and develop a program for monitoring the socioeconomic, health, and land-use impacts of the construction and operation of the Maguga Dam. The University of Swaziland, in turn, approached the Environmental Evaluation Unit at the University of Cape Town and the Institute of Natural Resources at the University of Kwazulu-Natal to assist them with the project. The aim of the independent monitoring program was to assess over a five-year period whether the resettlement program was achieving its overall objective of improving the livelihoods of the people who were forced to relocate. The monitoring team identified three program components to be monitored: financial and in-kind compensation associated with loss of assets or access to assets; financial and in-kind restoration and development associated with the forced removal of the affected households; and the overall success and ability of the resettlement program to improve living standards of the affected parties. Its findings regarding overall success in improving living standards were positive (United Nations Environment Programme 2006).

A good monitoring system has two components. First, monitoring focuses upon the timely delivery of planned works, goods, and services to the displaced population. Information should be disaggregated by gender and special attention paid to the poor and vulnerable. Good monitoring involves resettlement committees at the local level and local governance structures verifying and reporting progress. The implementation plan in the resettlement documentation provides the schedule of activities and the monitoring report documents progress in each activity. The second aspect of the system is assessing outcomes as measured against baseline conditions. The focus is on the well-being of the displaced people and whether or not the objectives of the resettlement operation are being achieved. The evaluation of outcomes should be gender disaggregated and concentrated on a few sensitive indicators.

One useful example of sensitive indicators of the well-being of PAPs is that designed by the Shaanxi Academy of Social Sciences for the Shaanxi Highway Development Project (Asian Development Bank 2005a). These include the following:

- Abnormal sales of livestock—may indicate economic distress, increased costs of production, increased costs of services, or greater demand for ritual and ceremonial events;
- Children dropping out of school—may indicate child labor needed to generate income, absence of teachers, poor quality of education, or violence in the school;
- Increased morbidity and mortality—may indicate problems with public health conditions, infectious disease, nutritional stress, or increase in accident rate; and

- Declines in household income—may indicate job loss, failed crops, no access to markets, failure to master new technologies, elevated costs of inputs, transport or processing, inadequate support services from the project, or a lack of short-term credit.

As shown above, changes in sensitive indicators do not in themselves explain anything because there can be many factors that account for such changes. The indicators should be thought of as an early warning system which functions to alert management that something is going wrong. A change in indicators means there is need for a detailed investigation to determine what accounts for the change observed and how its causes can be addressed and corrected.

Monitoring and evaluation may be either internal or external, depending on the sensitivity and complexity of the operation. Monitoring continues until resettlement objectives are achieved. A post-implementation evaluation or audit report prepared by an independent research institution to capture lessons learned to be applied in future projects is recommended as best practice.

Chapter 8

Free, Prior, and Informed Participation of Project-Affected Communities

Social Impact Analysis (SIA) identifies the project stakeholders, including but not limited to displaced people, to whom information regarding the proposed involuntary resettlement plan must be disclosed. The International Standard for Involuntary Resettlement requires prior and informed participation of displaced people and other stakeholders in the preparation of draft resettlement plans, a participation process that continues through the formulation of final resettlement plans and any revisions or updates thereto. Such participation must take place in a form, manner, and language understandable to the displaced people. The International Standard for Involuntary Resettlement requires formal disclosure and dissemination of the official resettlement action plan that has been agreed among displaced people and project authorities in the same form, manner, and language understandable as the draft resettlement plan.

Resettlement plans are usually prepared by highly educated professionals, written in official languages, presented in lengthy and complex formats, and expressed in legalistic terminology with which ordinary citizens are often unfamiliar. Therefore, it is usually important to disseminate simplified and easy to understand summaries of resettlement plans to the displaced and host populations in their own language(s) and at site(s) that are accessible to them. Disclosure of resettlement plans and other documents should be free of cost to the affected people and other stakeholders, prior to the initiation of any project works or elements of the proposed plan, and describe the policies, steps, and procedures that will ensure informed participation in decision-making into the future.

The objectives of the International Standard for Involuntary Resettlement are to reconstruct the livelihoods of all displaced persons in real terms relative to pre-project levels and to improve the standards of living of the displaced poor and other vulnerable groups. Achieving these objectives requires engaging the displaced people in a transparent, public, and deliberative process of participation in planning their resettlement. Since development entities are significantly more powerful than displaced people, they have a duty toward them that stems from the asymmetry of power, meaning the powerful have the responsibility to help those who cannot defend themselves (Sen 2009). *This means posting skilled professionals to the field where the affected people live* to work in a participatory fashion, often with poor, illiterate, and vulnerable affected people, in carrying out consultations and preparations for the necessary studies to plan the resettlement operation.

PARTICIPATION VERSUS CONSULTATION

We deliberately use the term "participation" here as distinguished from "consultation." While the provisions and directives of the International Standard for Involuntary Resettlement include both terms, they are usually conceptually differentiated from one another, such that provisions call for "free, prior and informed consultation" with PAPs while also advocating their "participation." The debate over "consultation" has been a long, intense, and often heated one. Our reason for focusing on the term "participation" is due to the frequent tendency to subvert the concept of consultation by project proponents and authorities. Such subversions may be inadvertent and innocent repetitions of top-down bureaucratic "business as usual," which of course is highly undesirable in resettlement operations, or they may be the product of egregious attempts to bypass the requirement, such as minimal posting of announcements on poles and buildings throughout towns in the project area, which may be long distances away from affected communities, thus potentially limiting access to such information by community members. Another common practice which subverts a truly participatory process is to place written copies of resettlement plans in government offices in the regional towns or state capital or to publish resettlement plans on a government website, ignoring the fact that many PAPs may not be able to access them because of distances and costs of travel, do not have access to the internet, and cannot understand them in any case because they are illiterate.

Another common "consultation" strategy is to hold public meetings, again usually held in towns which may be distant from affected communities. Attending such meetings requires expensive travel costs from community members, many of whom may not be able to afford it. Affected community members are forced to come to meetings held by project authorities or proponents, rather than authorities or proponents going out to affected communities. Moreover, in public meetings, the agendas are set by project authorities and proponents, who control the proceedings and time allotted for public comments. Thus, not every voice has an equal chance of being heard or have their concerns expressed. Even when project authorities or proponents go out to affected communities, such "consultation" too often consists of officials meeting with PAPs to simply tell them what is going to happen to them, asking if they have any questions and, in extreme cases, duping them into signing papers which, unbeknownst to them, signify that they have given their approval or consent for a project to proceed. It is for these reasons that we emphasize the term "participation," which entails, when it is carried out properly, *collaboration* and *negotiation* with PAPs as equals and fellow citizens, on a level playing field.

To overcome these common errors made by authorities in structuring consultations and participation, it is highly recommended to organize forums with PAPs in which authorities may table their ideas, listen to questions and suggestions from the PAPs, collaborate in identifying points of convergence and those of contrast, and negotiate resolution of these in a manner agreeable to both parties. It is to be expected that in some instances the concerns of the authorities and the concerns of the PAPs may diverge while in others they may converge. But the point of the collaboration in both cases is to negotiate an agreement on the way forward that is acceptable to PAPs and authorities alike.

It is worth remembering at this point that beyond participation in the planning of their resettlement, PAPs should also participate in the implementation of agreed policies and plans. Establishing the roles PAPs can play in carrying out the resettlement plan, those of the authorities responsible for the resettlement, and those of the other parties to the operation such as contractors, local government officials, and NGOs, is part and product of the collaborative resettlement planning process. For example, PAPs should be engaged in resettlement site selection, be employed in the construction of new houses and installation of infrastructure, participate in land clearing and preparation, work in planting nurseries to grow seedlings for fruit trees, gardens, and field crops, monitor the delivery of services by contractors, public institutions, and NGOs, track and report on the well-being of the more vulnerable, and myriad other contributions to the participatory execution of the resettlement program. Of course, all these forms of participation in implementation cannot always be achieved in all aspects of the operation. But the point is that PAPs should not be seen nor be made to feel like passive observers but active, direct, responsible participants in carrying out their parts of the overall resettlement program.

GRIEVANCE REDRESS MECHANISM

The International Standard for Involuntary Resettlement requires that an efficient and effective grievance redress mechanism be established on a project-by-project basis. A grievance redress mechanism is a vital part of stakeholder engagement. It should provide a process for receiving and addressing project-related complaints from affected people. A grievance redress mechanism normally consists of three phases: registering and investigating the complaint at the project level, negotiating a resolution by project management with an appeal to an independent third-party arbiter if the complainant is not satisfied, and, as a last resort, if still not satisfied, appeal to the country's judicial system. The grievance redress mechanism should be in place early in the resettlement planning process. The scope, form, and level of complexity of the process should be proportionate to the impacts on the displaced and host populations.

In the case of large projects with potentially complex and significant impacts, the mechanism should be formally established and easily accessible at the design stage and maintained in place for several months after the end of project construction. Accessibility is based on physical location close to displaced people, access to communication and transportation, and language, literacy, and education levels. In smaller projects with relatively straightforward issues, the client should consider designating a point of contact, such as a community liaison officer, to whom project-related views and concerns of the displaced people can be addressed.

The responsibility for receiving grievances should be handled by experienced and qualified personnel with the authority to respond. The project should establish a procedure for receiving grievances, recording and documenting them (e.g., name of the individual or organization filing the complaint, the date and nature of the complaint, any follow-up investigation or actions taken, the final decision on the complaint, how and when relevant project decisions were communicated to the complainant, and whether management action has been taken to avoid recurrence of community concerns in the future), and responding in a reasonable period of time. This procedure should ensure that the confidentiality of the persons raising the complaint is protected. Responses should involve deliberations and collaborations with displaced people and the local leaders the people perceive to be legitimate authorities.

The grievance mechanism should be designed to take into account specific cultural attributes as well as traditional mechanisms for raising and resolving issues. If the project-affected community groups have significant cultural differences, tailored approaches may be needed to ensure that each group (especially women) is able to raise concerns. Planners should be aware of administrative mechanisms available in the country for resolution of disputes and should not impede access to these mechanisms. Almost always arrangements are required to permit appeal to a higher authority should the aggrieved party not be satisfied with the initial solution proposed.

CASE EXAMPLES

People's Republic of China: Daguangba Multipurpose Project

The Daguangba Dam on the Changhua River on Hainan Island was built to provide electricity generation and transmission as well as irrigation from a 16 kilometers canal. The reservoir displaced 27,800 Li and Miao national minority people (indigenous) from their farms and homes. The Resettlement Plan provided for 2,300 hectares of irrigated replacement farmland from redistributed host community landholdings and, in compensation, the project provided irrigation to an additional 12,700 hectares of host community land, thus doubling the carrying capacity of the land. The two engineers who carried out the planning studies for the resettlement of each village were native to Hainan Island and proficient in the local languages and consulted with both host and displaced communities during the preparation of the Resettlement Plan over a period of two years. Nevertheless, the draft Resettlement Plan, written in Mandarin, could not be readily understood by the mostly illiterate and monolingual national minority people, so the Hainan Provincial Electric Power Company prepared visual presentations, conducted consultation meetings with the displaced people in their own villages and languages, and established information offices in the field staffed by employees who spoke the local languages to facilitate information dissemination, consultation, and participation. The field officers accompanied the displaced people from the planning through the implementation of the project (World Bank 1991b).

El Salvador: Precarious Urban Settlements in the Metropolitan Area of San Salvador

Nine urban communities composed of poor and extremely poor people were identified as periodically subject to disasters such as landslides and flooding. The project was designed to provide civil works to mitigate the risks of landslides and/or manage the evacuation of floodwaters, as well as to improve the quality of life through investments in the provision of potable water, drainage and sewers, paved streets, community meeting centers, and public schools. But where local conditions and/or technical limitations did not permit the construction of civil works, many families had to be moved away from areas prone to landslides or flooding and resettled in more stable conditions. The resettlement planning process entailed working with local municipal governments, community organizations made up of residents of the communities, and the people to be resettled to identify municipal lands in the same communities where house plots could be allocated free of charge to those who had to be resettled. The project owner, the Ministry of Public Works of the Government of El Salvador, appointed a planning team composed of an engineer and a social worker who were present in each of the affected communities at least once a week, every week, for a period of two years conducting consultations, assessment of alternatives, and design studies. In this way, the design team interacted continuously throughout the resettlement planning processes with the stakeholders and people to be resettled. The project eventually presented to and approved by the Inter-American Development Bank was, therefore, the product of two years of participatory planning with the community, local authorities, and the persons to be resettled (Inter-American Development Bank 2011).

India: Upper Krishna II Irrigation Project

At the outset, the project resettlement office to which displaced persons had to report their grievances was located over 250 miles away from the project site in the Karnataka state capital city of Bangalore. The distance and the costs in time and money to traverse it effectively barred displaced people from expressing grievances to project authorities. This is one reason project authorities remained unaware of the utter failure of the resettlement operation and the severe harm suffered by the affected people until a year had gone by (World Bank 1998c).

India: Mumbai Urban Transport Project

Where NGOs are effective and honest interlocutors, they can very well assist in the function of the grievance mechanism. In this case, the Project Implementation Agency designated a senior officer at the local level to consider any grievance of displaced people in consultation with local NGOs accompanying the displaced people in the resettlement program. If the aggrieved displaced person is not satisfied with the decision of the grievance officer and local NGO, a final appeal is made to the Grievance Redressal Committee appointed by the Project Management Unit comprised of its officials and representatives of several independent regional NGOs. Decisions are made in accordance with the Resettlement and Rehabilitation Policy adopted by the project, outlined in the Resettlement Action Plan, and distributed throughout the project impact area in pamphlets and posted on bulletin boards (World Bank 2002).

Chapter 9

Rebuilding Livelihoods

The Cornerstone of Successful Resettlement and Development

The overarching objectives of involuntary resettlement, according to the International Standard for Involuntary Resettlement, are to rebuild the livelihoods of all displaced people in real terms relative to pre-project levels and to improve the standards of living of the displaced poor and other vulnerable groups. Care should be taken to ensure that entitlements, assistance, and benefits designed to enhance or at least restore livelihoods are socially and culturally compatible as well as economically feasible and sustainable. Income restoration measures should be allocated among the displaced people in proportion to their losses and in relation to their needs. For this purpose, it is helpful to break down kinds of displaced persons and their eligibility for livelihood restoration measures, assistance, and benefits. Appendix 1 presents a matrix formulated for a transportation infrastructure project in Costa Rica to show how income restoration measures, assistance, and benefits are delineated for different types of displaced people and degrees of impact (Inter-American Development Bank 2013). It should be noted here that for Appendix 1, cash compensation is due for all property losses but is retained by the project to pay a portion of the costs of providing land, housing, and resettlement assistance. When displaced people are legally ineligible for cash compensation (landless) their resettlement costs fall entirely to the project.

It must be emphasized that involuntary resettlement projects that do not provide livelihood restoration measures, such as replacement farmland and pasture for agriculturalists or training for alternative employment or opening a new business, are inevitably failures. We must also recognize, however, that it is not possible to fully or completely restore livelihoods as they were lived prior to the displacement and resettlement, including production, distribution, and consumption systems. Clearly, what has been destroyed or dismantled by displacement cannot be simply reproduced or replicated in a new environment. Key socioeconomic conditions will have changed: the presence of new social actors such as new creditors, local markets, clients, or customers, new transport and distribution systems, new demands for technical or management skills, or new services such as agricultural extensions. From the point of view of many displaced people, such changes imply venturing into the unknown and are threatening, suspicious, traumatic, and stressful. Largely for this reason, at least at the outset, many displaced people attempt to overcome the unknown and lessen the stress by falling back on proven and traditional practices with which they are comfortable. Other displaced people welcome the new opportunities the project can bring, such as new opportunities for women to work for wages, opportunities for secondary education for youth, new labor-saving production technologies such as grain grinding mills or motorized crop cultivation, the introduction of higher value crops, and new opportunities for participation in the governance of their communities with the departure of the corrupt elite.

ESSENTIAL FIRST STEPS TOWARD
REBUILDING LIVELIHOODS

Fair and just compensation for lost assets is an essential first step toward rebuilding livelihoods. The constitutions of all countries provide for the exercise of eminent domain, the right of the government to take private property for public use by virtue of the superior dominion of the sovereign power over all lands within its jurisdiction, which carries with it the obligation to compensate owners for such expropriations. The principle of eminent domain over all lands extends to government acquisition of community, commons, and corporate properties as well. Almost universally such properties taken by the government are to be compensated by money paid to property owners. A common basis for financing the implementation of resettlement plans is to apply such monetary compensation to cover the costs of resettlement.

Where free and open markets for land and housing exist, fair and just compensation can be the payment in cash for assets taken, such as land, structures, orchards, wells, at their replacement value. The former property owners can then purchase replacement properties in the market and relocate themselves and reestablish their homes, farms, jobs, or businesses. This is often the preferred resettlement alternative in many projects both by governments and by wealthier property owners, because the rich usually do not want to be subject to a government resettlement scheme. But where property markets do not exist or replacement assets cannot be bought because there is an insufficient supply of land and housing, then payment of cash compensation alone is not a viable resettlement alternative. In the latter cases, the project must provide replacement properties equivalent to those lost to the PAPs for them to relocate and reestablish their homes, farms, jobs, or businesses. Where this occurs, it is not uncommon for a project to retain compensation money to be paid to those opting for resettlement by the project to cover part of the resettlement costs.

When the livelihoods of PAPs are dependent upon land-based production systems, such as farming, livestock rearing, or hunting, and gathering, equivalent land must be made available to replace that lost. Equivalency is assessed in terms of productive potential, locational advantages, and other factors considered important to the PAPs like spaces for gardens, fruit trees, and livestock pens in addition to houses. Such lands to be allocated to the PAPs should be cleared and/or prepared prior to their arrival, or, that failing, PAPs can be paid to prepare the land and be provided transitional support until the productive potential can be realized in terms of putting food on the table or generating income from sales.

Housing should replicate to the extent possible the customary materials, designs, and sizes of that being replaced. Frequently, the best solution is to allow the PAPs to construct their own replacement houses utilizing materials provided by the project combined with those that can be salvaged from the old houses. Such a strategy implies a transition allowance that may include the provision of food, salaries, and so forth until the residence is completed and habitable. Such a strategy ensures that housing will be culturally and environmentally appropriate. What is certain is that radical, culturally insensitive, top-down changes in housing, such as moving rural villagers into apartment blocks or nomadic pastoralists into sedentary villages designed by urban architects, will be totally unacceptable to the PAPs. Finally, the International Standard for Involuntary Resettlement laid out here stipulates that PAPs shall not be displaced until their replacement housing in the receiving area is ready for occupancy.

Existing social and cultural institutions of the PAPs should be respected to the extent possible, and the most effective way to do that is to engage their active participation in choosing resettlement sites, laying out new farms and neighborhoods, preparing lands for productive use, designing and building residences and commons areas like parks and playgrounds, and contracting for the reconstruction and delivery of public services such as educational facilities, healthcare clinics, and potable water, electricity, and sanitation systems. This is also a way to foster ownership and initiative and dampen tendencies toward dependency, as when one of the authors asked a villager resettled one year earlier why a broken water pump handle was not repaired, to which the man replied: "the pump was installed by government and they have not come back to fix it."

Rebuilding or innovating new production systems begins with establishing a good measure of subsistence security, almost always through falling back upon traditional skills, jobs, crops, technologies, and forms of work organization. In a process Arensberg (1978) called reciprocal accommodation, innovations are gradually grafted onto the traditional once subsistence security has been established. It is only then that PAPs have the leeway to take risks, to experiment, to innovate. It is only then that PAPs will have the time and energy to take advantage of training and capacity building opportunities that may be required to adopt innovative production systems. Such educational opportunities should always be built into resettlement projects once subsistence security is achieved to foster improvements in livelihoods and standards of living by empowering the next generation, and girls in particular. As we have pointed out earlier, forcing PAPs into promising new production systems at the outset will dramatically heighten the risks of failure, poisoning the wells for further innovation, and often lead to impoverishment.

Wherever and whenever projects generate revenue or profit, the International Standard for Involuntary Resettlement requires that project-affected communities must be entitled, *with priority*, over and above compensation and other forms of restitution, to receive a fair proportion of project revenues as full beneficiaries (Cernea 2007, 2008, his emphasis; see Cernea and Kanbur 2008 for case examples; van Wicklin 1999). Benefit-sharing mechanisms and agreements should be negotiated with the participation of PAPs at the earliest stages prior to project construction and relocation and be legally binding.

CASE EXAMPLES

India: Upper Krishna II Irrigation Project

The reservoir flooded several villages of agriculturalists and their landless laborers. The project provided for the construction of six new villages with modern houses that had concrete floors, metal roofs, drainage, potable water, electricity, and sanitary facilities, which taken together were interpreted by project authorities as an improvement over traditional mud and stick structures, with dirt floors, roofed with palm thatch, and with no water, electricity, or latrines. One year following the completion of these villages a World Bank supervision mission reported that the six new, beautiful villages were entirely empty. The new houses were vacant. This is because the project did not provide replacement agricultural land and pasture for livestock, so the displaced farmers and their laborers had no means of making a living and had fled to nearby city slums (World Bank 1998c).

It should also be emphasized that promises of livelihood reconstruction measures made in Resettlement Action Plans (RAP) which are not based on and verified by hard evidence presented in the RAP may turn out to be unworkable on the ground. Such was the case in the Ahafo Mine Project in Ghana.

Ghana: Ahafo Mine Project

This gold mining project presented a RAP to the International Finance Corporation promising that affected people would be provided a choice between cash compensation for loss of agricultural land, houses, fruit trees, wells, fences, and so forth or replacement agricultural land and new houses in resettlement villages to be built by the project. Of 1,700 affected households about 400 chose the latter and were moved into new houses in the Kenyase and Ntotroso settlements. The rest preferred cash compensation and resettled themselves. An independent monitoring investigation several years later reported that 53 percent of settlers in Kenyase and 37 percent of settlers in Ntotroso did not have access to agricultural land and were likely to abandon their new homes due to lack of income. The project owner and financier had failed to verify that the promised farmland was, in fact, available. Local chiefs refused to make the promised land available to the displaced (International Finance Corporation 2005).

The common assertion that it is difficult or even impossible to find replacement lands for displaced people has been proven wrong by decades of experience. Land to replace that lost has been allocated, created, or purchased in many instances through the exercise of creativity, intelligence, and diligence on the part of project engineers, government officials, resettlement specialists, and the displaced people themselves. The following are a few examples showing what can be done when serious people put their minds to the task of allocating, creating, or purchasing replacement land.

People's Republic of China: Shiman Expressway Project

Over 113 hectares of arable land were created in three ways. The most common method (some 93 hectares) was by using waste earth from the construction activities to fill ravines. After leveling, they were provided topsoil to become cultivated lands. Waste earth was also used to fill barren waste and cold spring paddy fields which changed them from low-yield to high-yield farmland. Finally, in conjunction with the contractors, construction machinery was used to convert barren slopes into terraces. These newly created lands were distributed to farmers who lost arable land, enabling them to reconstruct their livelihoods without any extra charges or deductions from compensation funds (World Bank 2008).

People's Republic of China: Shanxi Road Development II Project

The objective of livelihood improvement, or at least restoration, was achieved through two kinds of income restoration plans prepared with the participation of host and displaced villagers. The first kind entailed redistribution of village land, improvement of irrigation systems, and developing aquatic and live-stock products breeding. Improved irrigation alone raised average output by 67 percent. The second kind of income restoration was applied where villages could not undertake land redistribution because there was no land available. In one case by reclaiming wasteland displaced farmers increased their veg-etable production by four times and increasing incomes relative to those prior to resettlement. In another case the displaced were assisted in obtaining motor vehicles to transport construction materials for the Yellow River Bridge. In another case, some 300 villagers from settlements close to major cities received skills training. In 2006, an independent external evaluation report documented the tripling of average per capita income of the affected villages compared to baseline incomes in 2001. In the five villages that suffered the largest productive land losses, net income increases per capita ranged from a low of 20 percent to a high of 160 percent (Asian Development Bank 2008).

India: Land Made Available by Irrigation

When irrigation is introduced into a formerly rain-fed farming area, large landowners sell off parts of their holdings in order to pay the costs of land lev-eling, digging water delivery channels, installing sluice gates, and purchasing new machinery. A study by MYRADA documented such land sales in the future command area of the Upper Krishna II Irrigation Project beginning a year before the irrigation waters began to flow and continuing for another year. The data show that some 30 percent of the command area was sold dur-ing that two-year period, mostly to the wealthy in nearby cities. MYRADA concludes that there is little justification for not freezing such sales until displaced people have the opportunity to purchase replacement farmlands in the command area and transform themselves from victims into project ben-eficiaries (Fernandez n. d.).

People's Republic of China: Xiaolangdi Resettlement Project

Because of the scale, complexity, and difficulty of the resettlement required, this separate stand-alone project was created parallel to the loan for the main dam and civil works (the Xiaolangdi Multipurpose Project). Some 172,487 people or 51,969 households were resettled between 1992 and 1997. A total of 227 new villages and 12 new towns were constructed. Over 90 percent of the displaced people were farmers, so tens of thousands of hectares of farm-lands had to be created from host community wastelands, pastures, and dry farmlands, through the provision of irrigation, the rescue of topsoil, and terracing with soil enhancement through green manure. Host communities were compensated for land lost and provided benefits such as improved irrigation, innovations to produce high-value crops, improvement livestock rearing, and nonfarm ventures. Hundreds of township industries such as agro-processing, fishponds, and livestock rearing were reestablished in the new settlements. New settlements were supplied with improved infrastructure such as potable water supplies, electricity, and drainage which was also extended to host communities to include them in the benefit streams of the project. Whereas many displaced people previously lived in caves, new resettlement houses made of brick and concrete block made a major contribution to improving living standards. The income restoration programs were remarkably successful: average per capita income increased from Y485 in 1992 to Y1,104 in 1997. About 70 percent of the displaced people achieved higher or the same incomes in 1997 as before the project, and the remaining 30 percent achieved 80 percent of former incomes by 1997. The latter were the subject of follow-up corrective actions to improve incomes for another three years (World Bank 2004b).

Where replacement farmland is allocated, created, or purchased, special care should be exercised to ensure that new income restoration systems are economically sustainable. Technical viability alone in the absence of consideration of marketing, processing, and transportation constraints is inadequate. An example is the resettlement operation associated with the Shuikou Hydroelectric Project in China.

People's Republic of China: Shuikou Hydroelectric Project

The resettlement operation resettled 67,000 people displaced by the reservoir of the Shuikou Dam, most of whom were rice and wheat farmers from low-lying riverine settlements. They were allocated wastelands on sloping hillsides which had been reclaimed by terracing with green manure and topsoil deposit. While a variety of crops were planted for subsistence purposes, the climate was judged ideal for fruit production and farmers were encouraged by the project to establish fruit tree plantations for nearby urban markets. Thousands of resettled farmers did so. The displaced people were assisted during the three- to four-year period before the fruit trees began to produce fruit by employment in project civil works. Unfortunately, the nearby urban markets were quickly saturated, prices plummeted, and hopes of anticipated cash incomes were dashed. The project was forced to assist the farmers further by designing agricultural diversification projects throughout the resettlement zone. The latter measures were ultimately successful in improving livelihoods but at the cost of sacrificing significant sunk investments that failed to pay off (World Bank 2000).

Improving the living standards of the displaced vulnerable groups presents special challenges. The vulnerable are those who are limited in their capacity to take advantage of resettlement assistance and development opportunities because of their poverty, race, age, gender, ethnicity, language, religion, or other sociocultural characteristics. Special targeting of the vulnerable is needed because they are typically socially excluded, often burdened by education and health deficiencies, and frequently disadvantaged by discriminatory practices or social norms. They may need to be engaged with separately from others so that they feel more at liberty to raise concerns without fear of recrimination.

People's Republic of China: Shaanxi Highway Development Project

In the 119 villages affected by land acquisition, poverty was endemic and farming plots were extremely small. Village committees agreed to redistribute cultivated land so as provide those losing land a livelihood. But because the land of the whole village was affected, per capita cultivated land was reduced from 0.94 mu to 0.67 mu or 28.7 percent, thus threatening deepening impoverishment. The Resettlement Plan was based on (i) enlarging cultivated areas through the reclamation of wastelands and ravines, construction of terraces, and top soil deposit and increasing orchard and cash cropping; (ii) industrial restructuring by increasing output of cattle, pigs, and sheep; and (iii) assisting women in establishing homespun cloth production cooperatives to make tourism market products. The women's hand-woven cloth and embroidery yielded yearly household incomes four times more than before. The livelihoods of both host and resettled households were improved (Asian Development Bank 2005a, b).

People's Republic of China: Hubei Shiyan-Manchuangan Expressway Project

Poverty is ubiquitous in the project impact area to the extent that all displaced people were considered vulnerable. In addition to the creation of new farmlands to replace lost lands, special efforts were made to improve living conditions. Before resettlement houses of affected villagers were of earth-wood, all resettlement housing was of brick-concrete. Prior to the project, 28 percent had floor areas below 100 square meters and only 18 percent had more than

180 square meters; afterward, only 9 percent were below 100 square meters and 80 percent were over 180 square metes. The number of households with access to houses through formal roads was increased from 41 percent to 75 percent. The number of households with tap water increased from 64 percent to 76 percent. At the end of the project, all households had access to electricity. Post-project external monitoring surveys show satisfaction with the improved conditions was 95 percent (World Bank 2008).

Self-relocation using cash compensation, if paid at replacement value as required by the International Standard for Involuntary Resettlement, is also an option preferred by many of the better off displaced people. Where land, housing, and labor markets exist and work well, self-relocation using cash compensation may be preferred by people privileged by wealth, political influence, education, and accustomed to managing cash to acquire replacement assets, capabilities, or productive activities on their own. In such cases, resettlement assistance may then be limited to helping the negotiation of prices, providing legal services, and paying transportation and subsistence allowances.

For most displaced people who are not privileged by wealth, political influence, education, and experience in managing cash, however, money alone is not a satisfactory means of reducing the risks of impoverishment and other harms produced by involuntary resettlement. This is true for several reasons:

- Cash compensation goes quickly to moneylenders, shopkeepers, and landlords that provided credit to small farmers and small business people in the past. Field studies show that the poor and vulnerable displaced people are immediately stripped by such creditors of any cash compensation (Mahapatra 1986; Nagi Reddy 1986a, b).
- Assessment of compensation is usually based on sales records over a period of several years. But sales records do not reflect replacement values because buyers and sellers often collude to report smaller amounts to reduce taxes (Bose 1990).
- Cash compensation is paid only to those with legal ownership rights, which leaves many landless displaced people with insufficient resources to pay the expenses of resettling themselves without assistance (Bose 1990).
- Cash compensation is not paid for common property resources expropriated (forests, grasslands, rangelands, fisheries, and others) that may provide as much as 80 percent of the income of the poor derived from livestock, non-timber forest products, hunting, and fishing (Bose 1990).

Transition period support and assistance to the most vulnerable displaced people are required by the International Standard for Involuntary Resettlement. The transition period is that interval between physical relocation to newly established resettlement sites and the moment when new production activities, new employment, or new business enterprises restore income streams to levels that existed prior to the move or better. Transition period assistance can be short-term jobs, subsistence support, salary maintenance, or similar arrangements.

Colombia: Sagamoso Hydroelectric Project

In addition to a policy and program designed to protect and improve living standards of the most vulnerable, Colombia´s national electricity agency ISAGEN established a policy of paying a transition allowance during the period when the former production activities ceased and the new activities resumed creating new income streams. The transition allowance was equivalent to the national minimum wage in Colombia. Vulnerable resettled people were thereby employed in clearing new farmlands, building new houses, constructing settlement infrastructure, and so forth until income from cash crops of cacao and citrus became available to complement that from subsistence gardens of manioc, corn, squash, banana, and other staple foods (Euler-Hermes and Banco de Santander 2010).

Part III

CONCLUSIONS

Chapter 10

Resettlement as Social, Economic, and Human Development

As we pointed out in the introduction, the intensifying global competition for economic dominance, combined with the current state of human-induced planetary warming and the associated increase in disastrous extreme weather events, virtually guarantees that megaprojects and environmental processes will increasingly entail the involuntary displacement and resettlement of millions. Recognizing this fact, our message is simple: we have at our disposal a body of knowledge and principles, embodied in the International Standard for Involuntary Resettlement, to guide the resettlement process such that it enhances the possibility that the affected communities with whom we work in collaboration can realize sustainable social, economic, and human development as they themselves define and envision it.

It has often been pointed out by development and organizational scholars alike that large organizations with complex bureaucracies suffer from a lack of institutional memory. The MDFIs are not immune. Consider, briefly, the example of the World Bank, the innovator of involuntary resettlement safeguard policy. After forty-six years of operational experience with involuntary resettlement, numerous portfolio reviews, and internal and independent evaluations of performance, its Inspection Panel published in April 2016 a report on "Emerging Lessons" in involuntary resettlement (Inspection Panel 2016). Examining twenty-two Bank-financed projects involving resettlement, the report discussed seven lessons that could be taken from experience with those projects: three from the preparation phase, three from the implementation phase, and one regarding long-term impacts. The first lesson is that accurate scoping of risks is the foundation of successful resettlement programs; the second is that meaningful consultation and participation are essential elements of involuntary resettlement programs; the third is that the choice of the appropriate resettlement instrument is the cornerstone of effective resettlement; the fourth lesson is that active supervision is necessary to effectively identify and resolve problems; the fifth is that the compensation for PAPs needs to be timely and based on sound valuation methodologies; the sixth is that a grievance mechanism needs to be accessible, reliable and transparent to be effective; and finally, the seventh is that livelihood restoration works best when transitional support, development assistance, and culturally appropriate resettlement alternatives are provided (Inspection Panel 2016). That these lessons are presented as "emerging" strikes us as incredulous.

The lessons identified have been embodied in the very provisions and directives of the Bank's own safeguard policies from OMS 2.33 to OP/BP 4.12. In this book, we have noted that the lessons are embedded in the policies, frameworks, and performance standards of the World Bank, the International Finance Corporation, the Inter-American Development Bank, the Asian Development Bank, the African Development Bank, the European Bank for Reconstruction and Development, and the Organization for Economic Cooperation and Development. Taken together, they have come to constitute an International Standard for Involuntary Resettlement. We also note that after more than four decades of experience, there exist hundreds upon hundreds of independent, internationally recognized resettlement specialists who are intimately familiar with the Standard who serve as consultants to these MDFIs and their member country governments. We conclude that the reason cases continue to be brought to the Inspection Panel by people harmed by development projects is not the lack of lessons or experience with them but the *institutional failure to apply the requirements* of the International Standard for Involuntary Resettlement on which all seem to agree. That failure is shared by the MDFIs and their member governments.

One of the central tenets of the present volume, in accordance with the central policy proscriptions contained in virtually all prior safeguard policies, frameworks, and performance standards which we have defined as the International Standard for Involuntary Resettlement, is that the objective of resettlement operations must be enabling the sustainable social, economic, and human development of resettled communities, entailing the freedom to choose among alternative development opportunities that may present themselves in the new circumstances following resettlement and reestablishment. Achieving resettlement with development, however, is in a very real sense not to be found in any policy or performance standard provision or directive per se. Successful resettlement with development will only have a greater chance of being realized when the provisions and directives in the International Standard for Involuntary Resettlement are enforced by the MDFIs and translated into binding laws, regulations, and policies at the national and subnational levels. Only in this fashion will the Standard be effectively implemented on the ground by professionals who are competent and committed to the human, social, and economic development of resettled communities, with the full participation and collaboration of displaced people with the human right to culturally define what development means to them, and working together to formulate and implement strategies that will realize that vision of development in a manner that is culturally appropriate and mutually acceptable. This concluding chapter briefly considers the challenges resettlement professionals face and what is entailed in successfully confronting those challenges.

CHALLENGES AHEAD

The challenges faced by resettlement practitioners today, whether in development projects or disasters or urban gentrification, are largely the same as those that have always been faced—the priority placed on throwing massive amounts of money at the problem, inadequately financed resettlement operations, recalcitrant project managers and borrower country officials, and institutionalized social exclusion, to name just a few (see Partridge 1995, 2013). The difference lies in the fact that such challenges have intensified in a context in which it is apparent that many if not most countries have not yet overcome institutional, economic, social, and cultural exclusion of many of their citizens affected by physical and/or economic displacement, nor do they yet have the legal and policy architecture in place to adequately deal with involuntary resettlement at a time when the exponential increase in the displacement and resettlement of communities is a reality.

To confront these challenges, we remind the reader that there also exist supportive staff, colleagues, managers, and administrators within the financing institutions and borrower country governments or ministries who are well aware of the International Standard for Involuntary Resettlement. They together with the cadre of independent internationally recognized and experienced resettlement specialists around the world, host country universities, research institutes, and the like are committed to fulfilling the promise of the Standard (again, see Partridge 1995, 2013). Resettlement specialists in the MDFIs, their member countries, and independents bring the capacity to analyze the myriad stakeholders, countervailing forces, and vested interests of a society that perpetuate the structural obstacles that exclude the poor, the vulnerable, and the indigenous. But analysis is merely the first step. To confront the challenges mentioned, we must go beyond analysis and apply the lessons learned on the ground.

We assert that there has emerged a well-documented *praxis* of involuntary resettlement, the actual doing, and the regularly repeated actions and practices of all successful resettlement operations as contrasted with the conceptual stipulations of policy. That *praxis* comprises the actionable measures, instruments, and processes that have proven time and time again efficacious in achieving resettlement as development. We reiterate here the key steps of that *praxis*:

- designing and implementing involuntary resettlement as a participatory development project;
- identifying impacts, compensation requirements, and persons physically and/or economically displaced in a census;
- conducting a socioeconomic analysis of the culture and communities to target and engage constituent social groups;
- carrying out programs to improve or at least restore livelihoods of affected people that match their capabilities and development aspirations;
- providing special attention to those vulnerable to the disruption of social support networks;
- establishing effective management, monitoring, and finance systems to move the resettlement operation forward.

The history of applied social science, including that on involuntary displacement and resettlement, is filled with insightful analyses, too voluminous to cite here, both qualitative and quantitative, brilliant syntheses, elegant conclusions, and very precise recommendations—too often ignored. The quality of analytical work on sociocultural issues is not the issue. The issue revolves around the receptor, the administrator, and the manager who chooses to act or not act on *empirically derived, concrete, actionable recommendations* to make better decisions. Resettlement social scientists' problem is not one of analysis or lessons derived therefrom; it is one of *taking ethically and politically effective action* on recommendations that fly in the face of powerful vested interests (Partridge 1985). Sociocultural analysis with any practical value at all in resettlement operations is grounded in complex socioeconomic systems that delimit the options and field of action and must be understood as such. This requires professionals who speak the language of the actors within these systems—actors with whom they can collaborate in employing the formal and informal methods and analytical tools to generate conclusions based on primary data rather than secondary myth, prejudice, and putative theories. The issue is gaining or insisting on access to policymakers, managers, and officials at all levels to convince them of the importance of including the excluded in the resettlement and development process.

"Putting people first" (Cernea 1985, 1991) is not simply a catchy social science slogan. It is a call to action based on decades of empirical observation and results that challenge us to eschew the monopoly of the development process by powerful groups that control the state and have traditionally captured the MDFIs. Putting people first challenges social scientists, administrators, and managers in these international organizations and in their member state governments to understand the development process as largely one of social groups contending for legitimacy, the state being only one, albeit the most powerful, of the stakeholders engaged in that struggle. In that struggle for legitimacy—the right to a piece of territory, the right to full participation, the right to be included as fellow citizens, the right to development as defined by local communities, the right to be given the freedom to choose—people affected by development must come first. This means that the MDFIs and their member governments must increasingly enter into negotiations with all groups involved in population displacement and involuntary resettlement (Aronsson 2002). To the extent that development projects consist in the transactions between a powerful center and less powerful local communities, putting people first means tipping the scale toward the less powerful by giving them ample voice and vote in the negotiation of their future. If resettlement with development is to work to the benefit of either, it must ultimately benefit both (Partridge 1995).

Overcoming the challenges entails going beyond the normal functioning of government institutions. It is not that government institutions do not function well but that they do so only for their clients. The excluded are not and have never been their clients. Reaching the poor, vulnerable, and indigenous at risk of impoverishment as a result of involuntary displacement requires designing innovative mechanisms, processes, and instruments that permit and facilitate the flow of services, goods, and works to those who have never had access to development resources (see, e.g., Price 2018). It means going beyond business as usual to correct the institutionalized social exclusion that perpetuates persistent poverty. As Cernea (2008) and others have warned, failure to do so risks increasingly massive protests. As pointed out in chapter 2, the tide of increasingly well-informed affected peoples' and civil society's defiance, mobilization, and resistance will not be deterred (Oliver Smith 2010). The tide may very well grow into a tsunami. Affected people are increasingly prepared to fight for their rights and social justice.

The current nationalistic political agendas, with their increasingly xenophobic tendencies and exclusionary views of the poor and indigenous/tribal, have led in recent times to the convenient branding of dissenters, protesters, and activists of all stripes as terrorists or enemies of the state. Resistance movements have more frequently confronted violent reprisals, including detention, disappearances, murder, assassination, and further repression (e.g., Honduras, India, Brazil, among other examples). Resettlement operations that continue to fail to incorporate affected people into the planning, design, and implementation of their own development as they define and conceive it will only add more fuel to the flames and potentially risk the escalation of violent conflict.

Resettlement specialists, whether institutional staff or consultants, depend on empirical investigation. It is only through *in vivo* field investigation that the institutionalized structural obstacles that perpetuate poverty in any given society can be addressed. While resettlement consultants and specialists on the staff of MDFIs do not conduct lengthy ethnographic research themselves in any given project´s area of influence, they identify, recruit and commission in-country specialists, academic or otherwise, who have conducted an in-depth investigation, who are familiar with the languages and cultures of their societies, and who manifest an ethical commitment to people's participation in the development decisions that will affect their lives. Together, resettlement specialists, in-country social scientists, and the PAPs themselves have the requisite knowledge and skills to tailor development interventions involving involuntary resettlement to what is socially and culturally acceptable, practicable, and therefore workable.

Social science involvement in resettlement operations, be it from the inside or outside, demands unwavering commitment, persistence and insistence on the part of practitioners to recognize the human rights of those displaced and resettled, and to achieving the sustainable social, economic, and human development of resettled communities. It demands that resettlement social science and its practitioners be involved at the very outset, not at the tail end of the process to simply provide ex post assessments of what went wrong. It is essential that a resettlement social specialist lead or at least closely supervise the development of effective resettlement action plans. Leaving the preparation of resettlement action plans to office-bound contractors, corporate divisions, construction, architectural, infrastructure and energy consulting and engineering firms, which have little first-hand, on-the-ground knowledge and experience with the social, cultural, and economic systems of the communities they seek to resettle, will inevitably be inadequate and harmful.

Over the last four decades, significant progress has been made in addressing the risks of displacement and resettlement of human communities. The evolution of the widely accepted International Standard for Involuntary Resettlement and the examples of both positive and negative experiences with these, as shown in the many examples cited throughout this book, are evidence that we have come a long way since the Kariba Dam resettlement disaster. Yet many challenges remain, and much remains to be learned. What is certain is that if the coming generation of scholars, practitioners, and policymakers approach those challenges by systematically applying the lessons learned from experience, the rewards will ultimately be of immense importance to development professionals, developing country governments, and the people threatened by forced displacement and resettlement.

Appendix 1

Table A.1   **Matrix for Rebuilding Livelihoods Based on the Types of Displaced Persons and the Degrees of Impact**

	Lose all land and lose house	*Lose all land but not house*	*Lose part land and house*		*Lose part land not house*	
			Greater than 10 percent	*Less than 10 percent*	*Greater than 10 percent*	*Less than 10 percent*
Owners with freehold title	Land equal or better House equal or better Productivity investment[1] Transport allowance[2] Subsistence allowance[3] Health and education services	Land equal or better Productivity investment Subsistence allowance Health and education services	Land equal or better House equal or better Productivity investment Transport allowance Subsistence allowance Health and education services	House equal or better Transport allowance Subsistence allowance Health and education services	Land equal or better Productivity investment Subsistence allowance Health and education services	Subsistence allowance Health and education services
Occupants more than three years	Land equal or better House equal or better	Land equal or better	Land equal or better House equal or better	House equal or better	Land equal or better	

Renters, tenants, sharecroppers, wage laborers				
Lose job and lose house	Land or training and employment; House equal or better; Transport allowance; Subsistence allowance; Health and education services	Productivity investment; Transport allowance; Subsistence allowance; Health and education services	Productivity investment; Transport allowance; Subsistence allowance; Health and education services	Productivity investment; Subsistence allowance; Health and education services
Lose job but not house	Land or training and employment; Subsistence allowance; Health and education services	Productivity investment; Subsistence allowance; Health and education services	Productivity investment; Subsistence allowance; Health and education services	

NOTES

1. Productivity investment may include farmland leveling, top soil rescue, terracing with green manure, drip irrigation, and so forth; planting fruit, nut, or oil tree seedlings; installing processing facilities (e.g., milk-chilling plant); introducing soils testing for high-value cropping, improved livestock fodders, modern veterinary services, and so forth.

2. A transport allowance provides for the cost of the physical moving of displaced people, household belongings, livestock, and productive equipment such as tools, inventories, machinery, and so forth.

3. A subsistence allowance, made up of food, fuel, and fodder, is distributed to all displaced people until such time as their income streams are at least restored or, if possible, improved relative to pre-project levels.

Appendix 2

Table A.2   General Categories of Project Expense Budgeted in Correspondence to Project Stage, Xiaolangdi Resettlement Project

Implementation stage	Resettlement activity	Personnel salaries and benefits		Equipment, materials, supplies		
		Person months	Unit cost	Items	Unit cost	Total cost
Resettlement planning phase 1	Establishment of resettlement office, staff, vehicles, computers, training, and so forth					
	Initiate land acquisition studies, updating of cadastre maps					
	Updating land records and regularization of recognizable property claims					
	Issuance of moratorium on new construction					
	Identification of potential resettlement sites and Alternative income restoration strategies					
	Social analysis of displaced population and host population					
	Definition of impact categories and entitlements					

(Continued)

171

Implementation stage	Resettlement activity	Personnel salaries and benefits		Equipment, materials, supplies		Total cost
		Person months	Unit cost	Items	Unit cost	
	Consultations with affected people on choices of resettlement sites and income restoration measures					
	Policy and legal framework formulation, dissemination to affected people					
	Independent advisory panel appointed					
	Internal and/or external monitoring system established					
	Administrative overhead, managers, support staff, and so forth					
	Price and physical contingencies					
Resettlement planning phase 2	Feasibility studies of resettlement sites (geographic, topographic, soils, water, and so forth)					
	Feasibility studies for new structures (houses, shops, market buildings, community buildings, prayer houses, and so forth)					
	Feasibility studies for new infrastructure (access roads, drainage, sewers, electricity, and so forth)					
	Feasibility studies for income/ livelihood restoration or improvement modules or subprojects					
	Environmental Assessment of proposed plan components					
	Preparation, dissemination, consultations of simplified draft resettlement plan					
	Information office functioning; grievance system established					

Implementation stage	Resettlement activity	Personnel salaries and benefits		Equipment, materials, supplies		
		Person months	Unit cost	Items	Unit cost	Total cost
	Internal and/or external monitoring system					
	Independent advisory panel					
	Administrative overhead, managers, support staff, and so forth					
	Preparation of draft resettlement based on choices of displaced people					
	Dissemination draft resettlement plan					
	Appraisal resettlement plan					
	Price and physical contingencies					
Resettlement detailed design phase 3	Initiate transfer, donation, purchase, or acquisition of final resettlement sites					
	Site-specific design-level studies for infrastructure of new settlement					
	Site-specific design-level studies for new farmlands preparation					
	Site-specific design-level studies for new houses, business locales, shops, and so forth					
	Census and property inventory finalized					
	Establish and disseminate cut-off date					
	Consultations with displaced people on final resettlement plan					
	Information office functioning; grievance system functioning					
	Internal and/or external monitoring system					
	Independent advisory panel					
	Administrative overhead, managers, support staff, and so forth					

(Continued)

Implementation stage	Resettlement activity	Personnel salaries and benefits		Equipment, materials, supplies		
		Person months	Unit cost	Items	Unit cost	Total cost
	Price and physical contingencies					
Contracts awarded phase 4	Final resettlement plan submitted, approved, disseminated to displaced people; contracts awarded					
	Payment of compensation for land, structures, crops, wells, trees, etc. expropriated					
	Construction of new settlement sites, houses, infrastructure, community buildings, shops, vendor stalls, and so forth					
	Preparation of new farmlands, terraces, irrigation, planting trees, and so forth					
	Subsistence allowance paid (food, fodder, fuel)					
	Transportation allowance paid for moving people, belongings, livestock, equipment, and so forth					
	Transaction costs of land titling, house titling, and so forth					
	Transfer of people and belongings to New settlement sites					
	Capital inputs provided by project (tools, seeds, livestock, machinery, tree seedlings, and so forth)					
	Technical assistance (agricultural extension, soils testing, marketing, and so forth)					
	Services provided (veterinary, credit, health, education, and so forth)					

Implementation stage	Resettlement activity	Personnel salaries and benefits		Equipment, materials, supplies		
		Person months	Unit cost	Items	Unit cost	Total cost
	Training programs (carpenter, machine operator, electrician, and so forth)					
	Employment office (placement in project or outside project)					
	Grievance system functioning					
	Internal and/or external monitoring system					
	Independent advisory panel					
	Administrative overhead, managers, support staff, and so forth					
	Price and physical contingencies					
Construction stage 5	Technical assistance (agricultural extension, soils testing, marketing, and so forth)					
	Services provided (veterinary, credit, health, education, and so on)					
	Training programs (machine operator, electrician, and so on)					
	Employment office (placement in project or outside project)					
	Grievance system functioning					
	Internal and/or external monitoring system functioning					
	Administrative overhead, managers, support staff, and so forth					
	Price and physical contingencies					

Note: Stage 5 resettlement activities continue annually until incomes and livelihoods have been enhanced or at a minimum restored as documented in monitoring reports.

References Cited

African Development Bank. 2003. *Operational Safeguard No. 2 Involuntary Resettlement: Land Acquisition, Population Displacement and Compensation.* Abidjan/Tunis.

African Development Bank. 2013. *African Bank Group's Integrated Safeguard System: Policy Statement and Operational Safeguards.* Safeguards and Sustainability Series, Volume 1, Issue 1. December. Abidjan.

African Development Bank. 2015. *The African Development Bank's Involuntary Resettlement Policy: Review of Implementation.* Safeguards and Sustainability Series, Volume 1, Issue 3. Abidjan.

Agrawal, Arun, and Kent Redford. 2009. "Introduction: Conservation and Displacement: An Overview." *Conservation and Society* 7 (1), 1–10.

Aguirre Beltran, Gonzalo. 1973. *Regiones de Refugio.* Instituto Nacional Indigenista, Mexico.

Aguirre Cantero, E. 2011. "Guatemala: The First Tz'utujil City of the Twenty-First Century." In *Preventive Resettlement for Populations at Risk of Disaster: Experiences from Latin America.* E. Correa, ed. Pp. 85–106. World Bank and Global Facility for Disaster Risk Reduction and Recovery, Washington, D.C.

Alaniz, Ryan. 2017. *From Strangers to Neighbors: Post-Disaster Resettlement and Community Building in Honduras.* University of Texas Press, Austin.

Alcorn, Janis B. 1984. "Development Policy, Forests, and Peasant Farms: Reflections on Huastec-Managed Forests' Contribution to Commercial Production and Resource Conservation." *Economic Botany* 38 (4), 389–406.

Amaral, A. R. P., and J. M. dos Santos. 2019. "The Construction of the Sobradinho Dam and the Relocation of the Residents of Velha Sento-Se to Nova Sento-Se/ Bahia." *International Journal of Advanced Engineering Research and Science* 6 (8), 249–256.

Antioquia Presente. 2013. "Moravia, de la Incertidumbre del Morro de Basuras a la Conquista de Nuevo Occidente." Presentation at Celebration of the NGO's 25th Anniversary, Medellin, Colombia.

Antioquia Presente. 2018. "El Renacer de La Tebaida." Presentation at Celebration of the NGO's 30th Anniversary, Medellin, Colombia.

Appel, H. 2019. *The Licit Life of Capitalism: U. S. Oil in Equatorial Guinea.* Duke University Press, Durham.

Appel, H., A. Mason, and M. Watts, eds. 2015. *Subterranean Estates: Life Worlds of Oil and Gas.* Cornell University Press, Ithaca.

Arensberg, C. M. 1942. "Report on a Developing Community, Poston, Arizona." *Applied Anthropology* 2, 2–21.

Arensberg, C. M. 1978. "Theoretical Contributions of Industrial and Development Studies." In *Applied Anthropology in America.* E. Eddy and W. Partridge, eds. Pp. 49–78. Columbia University Press, New York.

Aronsson, Inga-Lill. 2002. *Negotiating Involuntary Resettlement: A Study of Local Bargaining During the Construction of the Zimapan Dam.* Uppsala University Department of Cultural Anthropology and Ethnology Occasional Papers 17. Uppsala.

Asher, M., and Y. Atmavilas. 2011. "Special Economic Zones: The New 'Land' Mines." In *Resettling Displaced People: Policy and Practice in India.* M. H. Mathur, ed. Pp. 317–335. Routledge and the Council for Social Development, New Delhi.

Asian Development Bank. 1994. *Handbook for Incorporation of Social Dimensions in Projects.* Manila.

Asian Development Bank. 1995. *Involuntary Resettlement Policy.* Revised 2003, 2006, 2009. Manila.

Asian Development Bank. 1998. *Handbook on Resettlement: A Guide to Good Practice.* Manila.

Asian Development Bank. 2001. *Policy on Social Protection.* Manila.

Asian Development Bank. 2005a. *External Monitoring Report on Land Acquisition and Resettlement. Shaanxi Highway Development Project.* Consulting Expert Team Shaanxi Academy of Social Sciences, Manila.

Asian Development Bank. 2005b. *PRC: Shaanxi Highway Development Project. External Monitoring Report on Land Acquisition and Resettlement (No. 6).* Shaanxi Academy of Social Sciences, Manila.

Asian Development Bank. 2007. *Capacity Building for Resettlement Risk Management: Country Report—India.* Manila.

Asian Development Bank. 2008. *Completion Report. PRC: Shanxi Road Development II Project.* Manila.

Asian Development Bank. 2009a. *Safeguard Policy Statement.* Manila.

Asian Development Bank. 2009b. *Pakistan: MFF Power Transmission Enhancement Investment Program Tranche 3—Revised Land Acquisition and Resettlement Plan (LARP).* Manila.

Asian Development Bank. 2009c. *Mainstreaming Land Acquisition and Resettlement Safeguards in the Central and West Asia Region.* Technical Assistance Report. Manila.

Asian Development Bank. 2012. *Involuntary Resettlement Safeguards: A Planning and Implementation Good Practice Sourcebook—Draft Working Document.* Manila.

Asian Development Bank. 2014. "News Release: ADB's Social and Environmental Safeguards, with Improvements, Can Be a Benchmark." November 11. http://www.adb.org/news/adb-s-social-and-environmental-safeguards-improvements-can-be-benchmark.

Asian Infrastructure Investment Bank. 2016. *Environmental and Social Framework.* Beijing.

Bailey, F. G. 1969. *Stratagems and Spoils.* Blackwell, Oxford.

Barnett, H. G. 1952. *Innovation: The Basis of Cultural Change.* McGraw-Hill, New York.

Barrios, Roberto. 2017. *Governing Affect: Neoliberalism and Disaster Reconstruction.* University of Nebraska Press, Lincoln.

Barry, Andrew. 2013. *Material Politics: Disputes Along the Pipeline.* Wiley-Blackwell, UK.

Bateson, Gregory. 1935a. *Naven.* Stanford University Press, Stanford.

Bateson, Gregory. 1935b. "Culture Contact and Schismogenesis." *Man* 35, 178–183.

Bebbington, Anthony, and Jeffrey Bury, eds. 2015. *Subterranean Struggles: New Dynamics of Mining, Oil, and Gas in Latin America.* University of Texas Press, Austin.

Beckford, G. L. 1999. *Persistent Poverty: Underdevelopment in Plantation Economies of the Third World.* Second Edition. University Press of the West Indies, Mona.

Belshaw, C. 1976. *The Sorcerer's Apprentice: An Anthropology of Public Policy.* Permagon, New York.

Bennett, John W. 1969. *Northern Plainsmen: Adaptive Strategies and Agrarian Life.* Aldine, Chicago.

Binford, Leigh. 2016. *The El Mozote Massacre: Human Rights and Global Implications.* Revised and Expanded Edition. University of Arizona Press, Tucson.

Bose, S. 1990. *India Land Acquisition and Resettlement: Processes and Procedures in Four States.* Asia Technical Department, World Bank, Washington, D.C.

Bray, D. B., L. Merino-Perez, and D. Barry, eds. 2005. *The Community Forests of Mexico: Managing for Sustainable Landscapes.* University of Texas Press, Austin.

Brechin, S. R., P. Wilshusen, C. Fortwnagler, and P. West, eds. 2003. *Contested Nature: Promoting International Biodiversity with Social Justice in the Twenty-first Century.* State University of New York Press, Albany.

Brockington, Dan. 2002. *Fortress Conservation: The Preservation of the Mkomazi Game Reserve, Tanzania.* Indiana University Press, Bloomington.

Brokensha, D. 1963. "Volta Resettlement and Anthropological Research." *Human Organization* 22, 286–290.

Brokensha, D., and T. Scudder. 1968. "Resettlement." In *Dams in Africa: An Interdisciplinary Study of Man-Made Lakes in Africa.* N. Rubin and W. Warren, eds. Pp. 20–62. Augustus M. Kelley Publishers, New York.

Brookings Institution, Georgetown University, and United Nations High Commission for Refugees. 2015. "Guidance on Protecting People from Disasters and Environmental Change through Planned Relocation."

Brosius, J. P., A. Tsing, and C. Zerner, eds. 2003. *Communities and Conservation: Histories and Politics of Community-Based Natural Resource Management.* Altamira Press, Walnut Creek.

Bugalski, N. 2016. "The Decline of Accountability at the World Bank?" *American University International Law Review* 31 (1), 1–56.

Bunker, S. G. 1983. *Underdeveloping the Amazon.* University of Chicago Press, Chicago.

Butcher, D. A. P. 1970. "The Social Survey." In *The Volta Resettlement Experience.* R. Chambers, ed. Pp. 78–103. Pall Mall Press, London.

Butcher, D. P. 1990. *A Review of the Treatment of Environmental Aspects of Bank Energy Projects.* Industry and Energy Department Working Paper, Energy Series Paper No. 24. World Bank, Washington, D.C.

Camara Barbachano, F. 1955. "Comentarios Sobre Antropología y Administración en la Cuenca del Papaloapan." In *Anais de XXXI Congreso Internacional de Americanistas.* Pp. 447–460. Sao Paulo.

Cancian, Frank. 1972. *Change and Uncertainty in a Peasant Economy: The Maya Corn Farmers of Zinacantan.* Stanford University Press, Stanford.

Castile, G. P., and G. Kushner, eds. 1981. *Persistent Peoples: Cultural Enclaves in Perspective.* University of Arizona Press, Tucson.

Castro, A. P., D. Taylor, and D. Brokensha, eds. 2012. *Climate Change and Threatened Communities: Vulnerability, Capacity and Action.* Practical Action Publishing, UK.

Cepek, Michael L. 2018. *Life in Oil: Cofan Survival in the Petroleum Fields of Amazonia.* University of Texas Press, Austin.

Cernea, M. M., ed. 1985. *Putting People First: Sociological Variables in Rural Development.* Revised Second Edition Published 1991. Oxford University Press, New York.

Cernea, M. M. 1986. *Involuntary Resettlement in Bank-Assisted Projects: A Review of the Application of Bank Policies and Procedures in FY 79-85 Projects.* Agriculture and Rural Development Department, The World Bank, Washington, D.C. February.

Cernea, M. M. 1993a. "Anthropological and Sociological Research for Policy Development on Population Resettlement." In *Anthropological Approaches to Resettlement: Policy, Practice, and Theory.* Michael M. Cernea and Scott E. Guggenheim, eds. Pp. 13–38. Westview Press, Boulder.

Cernea, M. M. 1993b. "The Sociologist's Approach to Sustainable Development." *Finance and Development* 30 (4), 11–13.

Cernea, M. M. 1997. "The Risks and Reconstruction Model for Resettling Displaced Populations." *World Development* 25 (10), 1569–1589.

Cernea, M. M., ed. 1999. *The Economics of Involuntary Resettlement: Questions and Challenges.* World Bank, Washington, D.C.

Cernea, M. M. 2000. "Risks, Safeguards, and Reconstruction: A Model for Population Displacement and Resettlement." In *Risks and Reconstruction.* M. Cernea and C. McDowell, eds. Pp. 11–55. World Bank, Washington, D.C.

Cernea, M. M. 2005a. "'Restriction of Access' Is Displacement: A Broader Concept and Policy." *Forced Migration Review* 23, 48–49.

Cernea, M. M. 2005b. "The 'Ripple Effect' in Social Policy and its Political Content: A Debate on Social Standards in Public and Private Development Projects." In *Privatising Development: Transnational Law, Infrastructure and Human Rights.* M. Likosky, ed. Pp. 65–101. Martinus Nijhoff Publishers, Leiden.

Cernea, M. M. 2006. "Population Displacement Inside Protected Areas: A Redefinition of Concepts in Conservation Policies." *Policy Matters* 14 (March), 8–26.

Cernea, M. M. 2007. "Financing for Development: Benefit-Sharing Mechanisms in Population Resettlement." *Economic and Political Weekly* (March 24), 1033–1046.

Cernea, M. M. 2008. "Compensation and Benefit Sharing: Why Resettlement Policies and Practices Must Be Reformed." *Water Science and Engineering* 1 (1), 89–120.

Cernea, M. M. 2016a. "Foreword—Social Impact Assessment and Safeguard Policies at a Fork in the Road: The Way Forward Should Be Upward." In *Assessing the Social Impact of Development Projects: Experience in India and other Asian Countries.* H. M. Mathur, ed. Pp. vii–xxiv. Springer, Dordrecht.

Cernea, M. M. 2016b. "Foreword—State Legislation Facing Involuntary Resettlement: Comparing the Thinking in China and India on Development-Displacement." In *Development-Induced Displacement in China and India.* F. Padovani, ed. Pp. vii–li. Lexington Books, Lanham.

Cernea, M. M., and J. Friedenberg. 2007. "'Development Anthropology Is a Contact Sport': An Oral History Interview with Michael M. Cernea." *Human Organization* 66 (4), 339–353.

Cernea, M. M., and S. Guggenheim, eds. 1993. *Anthropological Approaches to Resettlement: Policy, Practice, and Theory.* Westview Press, Boulder.

Cernea, M. M., and J. Maldonado. 2018. "Challenging the Prevailing Paradigm of Displacement and Resettlement: Its Evolution, and Constructive Ways of Improving It." In *Challenging the Prevailing Paradigm of Displacement and Resettlement: Risks, Impoverishment, Legacies, Solutions.* M. Cernea and J. Maldonado, eds. Pp. 1–42. Routledge, New York.

Cernea, M. M., and H. M. Mathur, eds. 2008. *Can Compensation Prevent Impoverishment? Reforming Resettlement Through Investments and Benefit-Sharing.* Oxford University Press, New York.

Cernea, M. M., and C. McDowell, eds. 2000. *Risks and Reconstruction: Experiences of Resettlers and Refugees.* World Bank, Washington, D.C.

Cernea, M. M., and K. Schmidt-Soltau. 2006. "National Parks and Poverty Risks: Policy Issues in Conservation and Resettlement." *World Development* 34 (10), 1808–1830.

Cernea, M. M., V. Thomas, and R. van den Berg. 2016. "The Controversy Over Safeguard Policies." *Resettlement News* 33–34, 1–2.

Chambers, R., ed. 1970. *The Volta Resettlement Experience.* Pall Mall Press, London.

Chambers, Robert. 1985. "Shortcut Methods of Gathering Social Information for Rural Development Projects." In *Putting People First: Sociological Variables in Rural Development.* M. Cernea, ed. Pp. 399–415. Oxford University Press, New York.

Chapin, Mac. 2004. "A Challenge to Conservationists. *Worldwatch* 17 (6), 17–31.

Chatty, D., and M. Colchester, eds. 2002. *Conservation and Mobile Indigenous Peoples: Displacement, Forced Settlement and Sustainable Development.* Berghahn Books, New York.

Clark, D. 2009. "An Overview of Revisions to the World Bank Resettlement Policy." In *Displaced by Development: Confronting Marginalization and Gender Injustice.* L. Mehta, ed. Pp. 195–224. Sage Publications, New Delhi.

Clawson, D. L. 1978. "Intravillage Wealth and Peasant Agricultural Innovation." *Journal of Developing Areas* 12 (3), 323–336.

Clay, J., and B. Holcomb. 1985. *Politics and the Ethiopian Famine, 1984–1985.* Cultural Survival, Cambridge.

Clay, J., S. Steingraber, B. Holcomb, and P. Niggli. 1988. *The Spoils of Famine: Ethiopian Famine Policy and Peasant Agriculture.* Cultural Survival, Cambridge.

Cliggett, L. 2000. "Social Components of Migration: Experiences from Southern Province, Zambia." *Human Organization* 59 (1), 125–135.

Cliggett, L. 2005. *Grains from Grass: Aging, Gender, and Famine in Rural Africa.* Cornell University Press, Ithaca.

Cliggett, L. 2014. "Access, Alienation, and the Production of Chronic Liminality: Sixty Years of Frontier Settlement in a Zambian Park Buffer Zone." *Human Organization* 73 (2), 128–140.

Cochrane, G. 2017. *Anthropology in the Mining Industry.* Palgrave-Macmillan, Cham.

Cohen, R., and F. Deng. 1998a. *Masses in Flight: The Global Crisis of Internal Displacement.* Brookings Institution Press, Washington, D.C.

Cohen, R., and F. Deng. 1998b. *The Forsaken People: Case Studies of the Internally Displaced.* Brookings Institution Press, Washington, D.C.

Collier, G., and E. Quarantillo. 2005. *Basta! Land and the Zapatista Rebellion in Chiapas.* Third Edition. Food First Books, Oakland.

Colson, E. 1971. *The Social Consequences of Resettlement.* Manchester University Press, Manchester.

Colson, E., and T. Scudder. 1988. *For Prayer and Profit: The Ritual, Economic, and Social Importance of Beer in Gwembe District, Zambia, 1950–1982.* Stanford University Press, Stanford.

Compliance Advisor Ombudsman (CAO). 2003. *A Review of IFC's Safeguard Policies. Core Business: Achieving Consistent and Excellent Environmental and Social Outcomes.* January. Washington, D.C.

Concha-Holmes, A., and A. Oliver-Smith, eds. 2020. *Disasters in Paradise: Natural Hazards, Social Vulnerability, and Development Decisions.* Lexington Books, Lanham.

Correa, E. 2011a. *Populations at Risk of Disaster: A Resettlement Guide.* The World Bank and Global Facility for Disaster Reduction and Recovery, Washington, D.C.

Correa, E., ed. 2011b. *Preventive Resettlement of Populations at Risk of Disaster: Experiences from Latin America.* The World Bank and Global Facility for Disaster Reduction and Recovery, Washington, D.C.

Cuevas-Muniz, A., and J. C. Gavilanes-Ruiz. 2018. "Social Representation of Human Resettlement Associated with Risk from Volcan de Colima, Mexico." In *Observing the Volcano World: Volcano Crisis Communication*. C. Fearnley, et al., eds. Pp. 321–334. SpringerOpen, New York.

Cuevas-Muniz, A., and J. L. S. Lujan. 2005. "Reubicacion y Desarticulacion de la Yerbabuena: Entre el Riesgo Volcanico y la Vulnerabilidad Politica." *Descatos* 19 (September–December), 41–70.

Curran, B., T. Sunderland, F. Maisels, J. Oates, S. Asaha, M. Balinga, L. Defo, A. Dunn, P. Telfer, L. Usongo, K. von Loebenstein, and P. Roth. 2009. "Are Central Africa's Protected Areas Displacing Hundreds of Thousands of Rural Poor?" *Conservation and Society* 7 (1), 30–45.

Dafeamekpor, Rockson-Nelson. 2019. "Statement on the Role of the Volta River Authority Resettlement Trust Fund Vis-a-Vis the Situation of the Resettlement Communities by Hon." Rockson-Nelson E. K. Dafeamekpor, Esq. https://ir.parliament.gh/bitstream/handle/123456789/1343/2019_07_12_15_57_19.pdf. Accessed 2/22/20.

Danner, M. 1994. *The Massacre at El Mozote*. Vintage, New York.

Davis, G., and H. Garrison. 1988. *Indonesia: The Transmigration Program in Perspective*. World Bank, Washington, D.C.

Davis, S. 1977. *Victims of the Miracle*. Cambridge University Press, New York.

de Sherbinin, A., M. Castro, F. Gemenne, M. Cernea, S. Adamo, P. Fearnside, G. Krieger, S. Lahmani, A. Oliver-Smith, A. Pankhurst, T. Scudder, B. Singer, Y. Tan, G. Wannier, P. Boncour, C. Ehrhart, G. Hugo, B. Pandey, and G. Shi. 2011. "Preparing for Resettlement Associated with Climate Change." *Science* 334, 456–457.

de Waal, A. 2005. *Famine that Kills: Darfur, Sudan*. Revised Edition. Oxford University Press, New York.

de Wet, C. 2006. "Risk, Complexity and Local Initiative in Forced Resettlement Outcomes." In *Development-Induced Displacement: Problems, Policies and People*. C. de Wet, ed. Pp. 180–202. Berghahn Books, New York.

de Wet, C. 2009. "Does Development Displace Ethics? The Challenge of Forced Resettlement." In *Development and Dispossession*. A. Oliver-Smith, ed. Pp. 77–96. School for Advanced Research Press, Santa Fe.

Denevan, W. M. 1983. "Adaptation, Variation and Cultural Geography." *The Professional Geographer* 35 (4), 399–407.

Department of Foreign Affairs and Trade (DFAT), Government of Australia. 2015. *Displacement and Resettlement of People in Development Activities*.

Department of Foreign Affairs and Trade, Government of Australia. 2019. *Environment and Social Safeguard Operational Procedures*.

DeWalt, B. R. 1979. *Modernization in a Mexican Ejido*. Cambridge University Press, New York.

Displacement Solutions. 2014. *The Peninsula Principles in Action: Climate Change and Displacement in the Autonomous Region of Gunayala, Panama*. Mission Report. Displacement Solutions, Geneva.

Doughty, P. 1999. "Plan and Pattern in Reaction to Earthquake: Peru, 1970–1998." In *The Angry Earth*. A. Oliver-Smith and S. Hoffman, eds. Pp. 234–256. Routledge, New York.

Dowie, M. 2009. *Conservation Refugees: The Hundred-Year Conflict Between Global Conservation and Indigenous Peoples.* MIT Press, Cambridge.

Downing, T. 1996. "Mitigating Social Impoverishment When People Are Involuntarily Displaced." In *Understanding Impoverishment: The Consequences of Development-Induced Displacement.* C. McDowell, ed. Pp. 33–48. Berghahn Books, Oxford, UK.

Downing, T. 2002a. *Avoiding New Poverty: Mining-Induced Displacement and Resettlement.* International Institute for Environment and Development, London.

Downing, T. 2002b. "Creating Poverty: The Flawed Economic Logic of the World Bank's Revised Involuntary Resettlement Policy." *Forced Migration Review* 12, 13–14.

Downing, T. 2008. "Annex C: Spiritual Significance in Busoga Culture." In *Investigation Report: Uganda Private Power Generation (Bujagali) Project (Guarantee No. B0130-UG).* Pp. 220–226. World Bank Inspection Panel, Washington, D.C.

Downing, T. 2016. "Foreword." In *Global Implications of Development, Disasters and Climate Change: Responses to Displacement from Asia-Pacific.* S. Price and J. Singer, eds. Pp. x–xiii. Routledge, New York.

Downing, T., and C. Garcia-Downing. 2009. "Routine and Dissonant Culture: A Theory About the Psycho-Socio-Cultural Disruptions of Involuntary Displacement and Ways to Mitigate Them Without Inflicting Even More Damage." In *Development and Dispossession.* A. Oliver-Smith, ed. Pp. 225–253. School of American Research Press, Santa Fe.

Downing, T., S. Hecht, H. Pearson, and C. Garcia-Downing, eds. 1992. *Development or Destruction: The Conversion of Tropical Forest to Pasture in Latin America.* Westview Press, Boulder.

Drucker, C. 1985. "Dam the Chico: Hydropower Development and Tribal Resistance." *The Ecologist* 15 (4), 149–157.

du Plessis, J. 2011. *Losing Your Home: Assessing the Impact of Eviction.* United Nations Human Settlements Programme (UN-Habitat) and United Nations High Commissioner for Human Rights, Nairobi, Kenya.

El Colombiano. 2018. "En Moravia Nacio el Nuevo Medellin." March 15.

Ensor, M., ed. 2009. *The Legacy of Hurricane Mitch: Lessons from Post-Disaster Reconstruction in Honduras.* University of Arizona Press, Tucson.

Euler-Hermes and Banco de Santander. 2010. *Sagamoso Hydroelectric Project Resettlement Program Due Diligence Assessment.* Hamburg and Madrid.

Euler-Hermes and Banco de Santander. 2011. *Social Due Diligence Analysis of Resettlement and Downstream Impacts of the Sagamoso Dam, Bucaramanga, Colombia.* Hamburg and Madrid.

European Bank for Reconstruction and Development (EBRD). 2014. *Environmental and Social Policy.* Updated and Re-Issued in 2019. London.

European Bank for Reconstruction and Development. 2017. *Resettlement Guidance and Good Practice.* London.

Ewell, P., and T. Poleman. 1980. *Uxpanapa: Agricultural Development in the Mexican Tropics.* Permagon, New York.

Fahim, H. 1983. *Egyptian Nubians: Resettlement and Years of Coping*. University of Utah Press, Salt Lake City.

Falla, R. 1994. *Massacres in the Jungle: Ixcan, Guatemala, 1975–1982*. Westview Press, Boulder.

Farha, L. 2011. *Forced Evictions: Global Crisis, Global Solutions*. United Nations Human Settlements Programme (UN-Habitat), Nairobi, Kenya.

Farmer, P. 2011. *Haiti After the Earthquake*. Public Affairs Books, Philadelphia.

Fernandez, A. n.d. *Land Sales in the Shorapur Taluk of the Upper Krishna II Project Command Area*. Mysore Resettlement and Development Agency (MYRADA), Bangalore, Karnataka, India. Unpublished.

Ferris, E. 2014. *Planned Relocations, Disasters and Climate Change: Consolidating Good Practices and Preparing for the Future*. Background Document. For Sanremo Consultation, 12–14 March. United Nations High Commission for Refugees, Brookings Institution and Georgetown University.

Firth, R. 1951. *Elements of Social Organization*. Watts, London.

Fiske, S., and E. Marino. 2020. "Slow-Onset Disaster: Climate Change and the Gaps Between Knowledge, Policy, and Practice." In *Disaster Upon Disaster*. S. Hoffman and R. Barrios, eds. Pp. 139–171. Berghahn Books, New York.

Food and Agriculture Organization. 2012. *Voluntary Guidelines on the Responsible Governance of Tenure of Land, Fisheries and Forests in the Context of National Food Security*. Rome.

Fossgard-Moser, T. 2004. *Social Performance: Key Lessons from Recent Experience Within Shell*. Social Performance Management Unit, Shell International, London. March.

Franke, R., and B. Chasin. 1980. *Seeds of Famine: Ecological Destruction and the Development Dilemma in the West African Sahel*. Allanheld Ossum Publishers, Montclair, NJ.

Fried, M. 1963. "Grieving for a Lost Home." In *The Urban Condition*. L. Duhl, ed. Pp. 151–171. Basic Books, New York.

Gardner, K. 2012. *Discordant Development: Global Capitalism and the Struggle for Connection in Bangladesh*. Pluto Press, London.

Geisler, C. 2009. "Argument-Endangered Humans: How Global Land Conservation Efforts Are Creating a Growing Class of Invisible Refugees." *Foreign Policy*, November 11.

Gjording, C. 1991. *Conditions Not of Their Choosing: The Guaymi Indians and Mining Multinationals in Panama*. Smithsonian Institution Press, Washington, D.C.

Goldman, M. 2005. *Imperial Nature: The World Bank and Struggles for Social Justice in the Age of Globalization*. Yale University Press, New Haven.

Golub, A. 2014. *Leviathan at the Gold Mine: Creating Indigenous and Corporate Actors in Papua New Guinea*. Duke University Press, Durham.

Goodland, R. 1973. *Sobradinho Hydroelectric Project Environmental Impact Reconnaissance*. CHESF/Cary Arboretum of the New York Botanical Garden, New York.

Green, L. 1994. *Fear As a Way of Life: Mayan Widows in Guatemala*. Columbia University Press, New York.

Guha, A. 2011. "Special Economic Zones, Land Acquisition and Civil Society in West Bengal." In *Resettling Displaced People*. H. M. Mathur, ed. Pp. 336–357. Routledge and Council for Social Development, New Delhi.

Hall, A. 1994. "Grassroots Action for Resettlement Planning: Brazil and Beyond." *World Development* 22 (2), 1793–1809.

Halmo, D. 1987. *An Economic Ethnobotany of Resettled Lowland Mazatec Indians: Diversity and Ethnodevelopment*. Unpublished Master's Thesis in Applied Anthropology, Georgia State University, Atlanta.

Halmo, D., and W. Partridge. 1986. "Applied Anthropology Colonization and Development in the Brazilian Amazon. *New Scholar* 10 (1–2), 323–328.

Halmo, D., D. Griffith, and B. Stoffle. 2019. "'Out of Sight, Out of Mind': Rapid Ethnographic Assessment of Commercial Fishermen's Perspectives on Corporate/State Response to the Deepwater Horizon Disaster." *Human Organization* 78 (1), 1–11.

Harnish, A., L. Cliggett, and T. Scudder. 2019. "Rivers and Roads: A Political Ecology of Displacement, Development, and Chronic Liminality in Zambia's Gwembe Valley." *Economic Anthropology* 6 (2), 250–263.

Hatcher, P. 2014. *Regimes of Risk: The World Bank and the Transformation of Mining in Asia*. Palgrave-MacMillan, New York.

Hay, M., J. Skinner, and A. Norton. 2019. *Dam-Induced Displacement and Resettlement: A Literature Review*. FutureDAMS Working Paper 004. University of Manchester.

Hindery, D. 2013. *From Enron to Evo: Pipeline Politics, Global Environmentalism, and Indigenous Rights in Bolivia*. University of Arizona Press, Tucson.

Hinton, A., ed. 2002. *Annihilating Difference: The Anthropology of Genocide*. University of California Press, Berkeley.

Hobsbawm, E. 1983. "Introduction: Inventing Traditions." In *The Invention of Tradition*. E. Hobsbawm and T. Ranger, eds. Pp. 1–14. Cambridge University Press, New York.

Hoffman, S., and R. Barrios, eds. 2020. *Disaster Upon Disaster: Exploring the Gap Between Knowledge, Policy and Practice*. Berghahn Books, New York.

Hoffman, S., and A. Oliver-Smith, eds. 2002. *Catastrophe and Culture: The Anthropology of Disaster*. School of American Research Press, Santa Fe.

Horta, K., S. Nguiffo, and D. Djiraibe. 2007. *The Chad-Cameroon Oil and Pipeline Project: A Project Non-Completion Report*. Environmental Defense, Washington, D.C.

Howes, M., and R. Chambers. 1980. "Indigenous Technical Knowledge: Analysis, Implications and Issues." In *Indigenous Knowledge Systems and Development*. D. Brokensha, et al., eds. Pp. 329–340. University Press of America, Washington, D.C.

Humphrey, C. 2016. *Time for a New Approach to Environmental and Social Protection at Multilateral Development Banks*. Overseas Development Institute Briefing Paper. April.

Hyndman, D. 1994. *Ancestral Rainforests and the Mountain of Gold: Indigenous People and Mining in New Guinea*. Westview Press, Boulder.

Inclusive Development International and International Rivers. 2019. *Reckless Endangerment: Assessing Responsibility for the Xe Pian-Xe Namnoy Dam Collapse.* Asheville and Oakland.

Inspection Panel. 2015. *Kenya Electricity Expansion Project (P103037): Investigation Report.* World Bank, Washington, D.C. July.

Inspection Panel. 2016. *Involuntary Resettlement.* Emerging Lessons Series 1. World Bank, Washington, D.C.

Inter-American Development Bank (IDB). 1997a. *Operations Policy 7.10: Involuntary Resettlement.* Washington, D.C.

Inter-American Development Bank. 1997b. *Involuntary Resettlement Policy and Background Paper.* Washington, D.C.

Inter-American Development Bank. 1999. *Involuntary Resettlement in IDB Projects: Principles and Guidelines.* Washington, D.C.

Inter-American Development Bank. 2001. *Guideline for Resettlement Plans.* Private Sector Department. Washington, D.C. December.

Inter-American Development Bank. 2011. *Precarious Urban Settlements in the Metropolitan Area of San Salvador.* Project Profile. Washington, D.C.

Inter-American Development Bank. 2013. *Transport Infrastructure Project.* Washington, D.C.

Inter-American Development Bank. 2014. *Resettlement Action Plan for the Water Treatment Plan at San Lorenzo.* Washington, D.C.

International Displacement Monitoring Centre (IDMC). 2019. *Global Report on Internal Displacement. IDMC GRID 2019.*

International Finance Corporation. 2002. *Handbook for Preparing a Resettlement Action Plan.* Washington, D.C.

International Finance Corporation. 2005. *Ahafo Mine: Independent Monitoring of Resettlement Implementation.* Washington, D.C.

International Finance Corporation. 2006. *Performance Standard 5: Land Acquisition and Involuntary Resettlement.* Revised and Updated in 2007 and 2012. Washington, D.C.

International Finance Corporation. 2008. *Lessons Learned: Pangue Hydroelectric.* Washington, D.C.

International Finance Corporation. 2012. *IFC Performance Standards for Environmental and Social Sustainability.* Washington, D.C.

IUCN—The World Conservation Union and the World Bank Group. 1997. *Large Dams: Learning from the Past, Looking to the Future. Workshop Proceedings.* Gland, Cambridge UK and Washington, D.C.

Jacka, J. 2015. *Alchemy in the Rainforest: Politics, Ecology and Resilience in a New Guinea Mining Area.* Duke University Press, Durham.

Japan International Cooperation Agency (JICA). 2010. *Guidelines for Environmental and Social Considerations.* Updated in 2012.

Jodha, N. S. 1986. "Common Property Resources and the Rural Poor in Dry Regions of India." *Economic and Political Weekly* (July 5).

Johnson, A. 1972. "Individuality and Experimentation in Traditional Agriculture. *Human Ecology* 1 (2), 149–159.

Johnston, B. R. 2009. "Development Disaster, Reparations, and the Right to Remedy: The Case of the Chixoy Dam, Guatemala." In *Development and Dispossession*. A. Oliver-Smith, ed. Pp. 201–224. School for Advanced Research Press, Santa Fe.

Kabra, A. 2018. "Displacement, Resettlement, and Livelihood Restoration: Safeguard Standards in Practice." *Development in Practice* 28 (2), 269–279.

Kabra, A., and B. Das. 2019. "Global or Local Safeguards? Social Impact Assessment Insights from an Urban Indian Land Acquisition." In *Country Frameworks for Development Displacement and Resettlement*. S. Price and J. Singer, eds. Pp. 195–218. Routledge, New York.

Kamakia, A., S. Guoqing, and M. Zaman. 2017. "Does Kenya's Development-Induced Displacement, and Resettlement Policy Match International Standards? A Gap Analysis and Recommendations. *Journal of Sustainable Development* 10 (5), 162–172.

Kimball, S. T. 1946. "The Crisis in Colonial Administration." *Applied Anthropology* 5, 8–16.

Kimball, S. T., and W. Partridge. 1979. *The Craft of Community Study: Fieldwork Dialogues*. University of Florida Press, Gainesville.

Kimmerling, J. 1991. *Amazon Crude*. Natural Resources Defense Council, New York.

Kircherr, J., and K. Charles. 2016. "The Social Impacts of Dams: A New Framework for Scholarly Analysis." *Environmental Impact Assessment Review* 60, 99–114.

Kircherr, J., M. Ahrenshop, and K. Charles. 2019. "Resettlement Lies: Suggestive Evidence from 29 Large Dam Projects." *World Development* 114, 208–219.

Kirsch, S. 1995. "Social Impact of the Ok Tedi Mine on Yonggom Villages of the North Fly, 1992." *Research in Melanesia* 19, 23–102.

Kirsch, S. 2001a. "Lost Worlds: Environmental Disaster, 'Culture Loss' and the Law." *Current Anthropology* 42 (2), 67–98.

Kirsch, S. 2001b. "Property Effects: Social Networks and Compensation Claims in Melanesia." *Social Anthropology* 9 (2), 147–163.

Kirsch, S. 2006. *Reverse Anthropology: Indigenous Analysis of Social and Environmental Relations in New Guinea*. Stanford University Press, Stanford.

Kirsch, S. 2014. *Mining Capitalism: The Relationship between Corporations and Their Critics*. University of California Press, Berkeley.

Koenig, D. 2009. "Urban Relocation and Resettlement: Distinctive Problems, Distinctive Opportunities." In *Development and Dispossession*. A. Oliver-Smith, ed. Pp. 119–140. School for Advanced Research Press, Santa Fe.

Kohli, K., and D. Gupta. 2016. "Mapping Dilutions in a Central Law: A Comparative Analysis of State-Level Rules Made Under the Right to Fair Compensation and Transparency in Land Acquisition, Rehabilitation and Resettlement (RFCTLARR) Act, 2013." Working Paper. Center for Policy Research.

Korten, D. 1980. "Community Organization and Rural Development: A Learning Process Approach." *Public Administration Review* (September/October), 480–512.

Kottak, C. 1985. "When People Don't Come First: Some Sociological Lessons from Completed Projects." In *Putting People First: Sociological Variables in Rural Development*. M. Cernea, ed. Pp. 325–356. Oxford University Press, New York.

Lahiri-Dutt, K., ed. 2014. *The Coal Nation: Histories, Ecologies and Politics of Coal in India.* Ashgate, Surrey.

Lavell, A. 2016. *Reducing Relocation Risk in Urban Areas.* Bartlett Development Planning Unit, University College, London.

Lazrus, H. 2012. "Sea Change: Climate change and Island Communities." *Annual Review of Anthropology* 41, 285–301.

Lazrus, H., and C. Arenas. 2020. "Islands on an Angry Earth: Climate Change, Disasters, and Implications for Two Island Communities." In *The Angry Earth.* Second Edition. A. Oliver-Smith and S. Hoffman, eds. Pp. 359–370. Routledge, New York.

Leighton, A. 1945. *The Governing of Men: General Principles and Recommendations Based on Experience at a Japanese Relocation Camp.* Princeton University Press, Princeton.

Levien, M. 2011. "Special Economic Zones and Accumulation by Dispossession in India." *Journal of Agrarian Change* 11 (4), 454–483.

Lisansky, J. 1990. *Migrants to Amazonia.* Westview Press, Boulder.

Lo, K., and M. Wang. 2018. "How Voluntary Is Poverty Alleviation Resettlement in China?" *Habitat International* 73, 34–42.

Mahapatra, L. K. 1986. *Resettlement and Rehabilitation Policy and Performance in Orissa II Irrigation Project.* Utkal University, Bhubaneswar, Orissa.

Maisels, S., T. Sunderland, B. Curran, K. von Loebenstein, J. Oates, L. Usongo, A. Dunn, S. Asaha, M. Balinga, L. Defo, and P. Telfer. 2010. "Central Africa's Protected Areas and the Purported Displacement of People: A First Critical Review of Existing Data." In *Protected Areas and Human Displacement: A Conservation Perspective.* K. Redford and E. Fearn, eds. Pp. 75–89. Wildlife Conservation Society, Bronx.

Maldonado, J. 2019. *Seeking Justice in an Energy Sacrifice Zone: Standing on Vanishing Land in Coastal Louisiana.* Routledge, New York.

Manz, B. 1988. *Refugees of a Hidden War: The Aftermath of Counterinsurgency in Guatemala.* State University of New York Press, Albany.

Manz, B. 2006. *Paradise in Ashes: A Guatemalan Journey of Courage, Hope and Terror.* University of California Press, Berkeley.

Marino, E. 2015. *Fierce Climate, Sacred Ground: An Ethnography of Climate Change in Shishmaref, Alaska.* University of Alaska Press, Anchorage.

Mathur, H. M. 2008. "Mining Coal, Undermining People: Compensation Policies and Practices of Coal India." In *Can Compensation Prevent Impoverishment?* M. Cernea and H. M. Mathur, eds. Pp. 260–285. Oxford University Press, Oxford.

Mathur, H. M. 2011a. "Social Impact Assessment: A Tool for Planning Better Resettlement." *Social Change* 41 (1), 97–120.

Mathur, H. M. 2011b. "An Interview with Professor Michael M. Cernea." *Resettlement News* 23–24, 1–4.

Mathur, H. M. 2013. *Displacement and Resettlement in India: The Human Cost of Development.* Routledge, New York.

Mathur, H. M., ed. 2016. *Assessing the Social Impact of Development Projects: Experience in India and Other Asian Countries.* Springer, Dordrecht.

Mathur, H. M. 2019. *Development Anthropology: Putting Culture First.* Lexington Books, Lanham.

McDonald, B. 2006. *From Compensation to Development: Involuntary Resettlement in the People's Republic of China.* Doctoral Dissertation, University of Melbourne, Australia.

McMahon, D. 1973. *Antropologia de una Presa: Los Mazatecos y el Proyecto de Papaloapan.* Instituto Nacional Indigenista, Mexico.

Mejia, M. C. 1999. "Economic Dimensions of Urban Resettlement: Experiences from Latin America." In *The Economics of Involuntary Resettlement.* M. Cernea, ed. Pp. 147–188. World Bank, Washington, D.C.

Mekong River Commission. 2013. *Mekong Basin Planning: The Story Behind the Basin Development Plan.* Phnom Penh.

Millennium Challenge Corporation. 2015. *Logistical Infrastructure Project: Strategic Resettlement Action Plan.* FOMILENIO-Ministry of Public Works, San Salvador.

Moone, J. 1981. "Persistence with Change: A Property of Sociocultural Dynamics." In *Persistent Peoples.* G. Castile and G. Kushner, eds. Pp. 228–242. University of Arizona Press, Tucson.

Moore, S. F. 1975. "Uncertainties in Situations, Indeterminacies in Culture." In *Symbols and Politics in Communal Ideology.* S. F. Moore and B. Myerhoff, eds. Pp. 210–239. Cornell University Press, Ithaca.

Moran, E. F. 1981. *Developing the Amazon.* Indiana University Press, Bloomington.

Morse, B., and T. Berger. 1992. *Sardar Sarovar: Report of the Independent Review.* Resources for the Future, Ottawa.

Muggah, R. 2008. *Relocation Failures in Sri Lanka: A Short History of Internal Displacement and Resettlement.* Zed Books, London and New York.

Murray, G. F. 1997. "A Haitian Peasant Tree Chronicle: Adaptive Evolution and Institutional Intrusion." In *Reasons for Hope: Instructive Experiences in Rural Development.* A. Krishna, N. Uphoff, and M. Esman, eds. Pp. 241–254. Kumarian Press, West Hartford.

Nagi Reddy, C. P. 1986a. *Socioeconomic Survey of Project-Affected Persons Under the Lower Manair Dam.* Centre for Economic and Social Studies, Hyderabad, Andhra Pradesh.

Nagi Reddy, C. P. 1986b. *Rehabilitation of Srisailam Project-Affected Persons.* Centre for Economic and Social Studies, Hyderabad, Andhra Pradesh.

Nahmad Sitton, S. 2019. "Indigenous People, Involuntary Resettlement, International Institutions in Mexico." In *Country Frameworks for Development Displacement and Resettlement.* S. Price and J. Singer, eds. Pp. 168–178. Routledge, New York.

Netting, R. 1993. *Smallholders, Householders: Farm Families and the Ecology of Intensive, Sustainable Agriculture.* Stanford University Press, Stanford.

New Development Bank (NDB). 2016. *Environmental and Social Framework.* Shanghai.

Niederberger, T., T. Haller, H. Gambon, M. Kobi, and I. Wenk, eds. 2016. *The Open Cut: Mining, Transnational Corporations and Local Populations.* Lit Verlag, Zurich.

Norwegian Refugee Council (NRC), and Internal Displacement Monitoring Centre (IDMC). 2015. *Global Overview 2015: People Internally Displaced by Conflict and Violence.* Geneva.

Nugent, J., W. Partridge, A. Brown, and J. Rees. 1978. *An Interdisciplinary Evaluation of the Human Ecology and Health Impact of the Aleman Dam.* Center for Human Ecology and Health, Pan American Health Organization, Mexico.

Ogwang, T., and F. Vanclay. 2019. "Social Impacts of Land Acquisition for Oil and Gas Development in Uganda." *Land* 8, 109. doi:10.3390/land8070109.

Ogwang, T., F. Vanclay, and A. van den Assem. 2018. "Impacts of the Oil Boom on the Lives of People Living in the Albertine Graben Region of Uganda." *The Extractive Industries and Society* 5 (1), 98–103.

Ogwang, T., F. Vanclay, and A. van den Assem. 2019. "Rent-Seeking Practices, Local Resource Curse, and Social Conflict in Uganda's Emerging Oil Economy." *Land* 8, 53. doi:10.3390/land8040053.

Oliver-Smith, A. 1986. *The Martyred City: Death and Rebirth in the Andes.* University of New Mexico Press, Albuquerque.

Oliver-Smith, A. 1991. "Successes and Failures in Post-Disaster Resettlement." *Disasters* 15 (1), 12–23.

Oliver-Smith, A., ed. 2009a. *Development and Dispossession: The Crisis of Displacement and Resettlement.* School of Advanced Research, Santa Fe, New Mexico.

Oliver-Smith, A. 2009b. *Sea Level Rise and the Vulnerability of Coastal Peoples: Responding to the Local Challenges of Global Climate Change in the 21st Century.* United Nations University Institute for Environment and Human Security and Munich Re Foundation Publication Series No. 7.

Oliver-Smith, A. 2018. "Disasters and Large-Scale Population Dislocations: International and National Responses." *Oxford Research Encyclopedia of Natural Hazard Science* 1–40. doi:10.1093/acrefore/9780199389407.013.224.

Oliver-Smith, A. 2020. "Resettlement for Disaster Risk Reduction: Global Knowledge, Local Application." In *Disaster Upon Disaster.* S. Hoffman and R. Barrios, eds. Pp. 198–217. Berghahn Books, New York.

Oliver-Smith, A., and A. de Sherbinin. 2014. "Resettlement in the Twenty-first Century." *Forced Migration Review* 45, 23–25.

Oliver-Smith, A., and S. Hoffman, eds. 2020. *The Angry Earth: Disaster in Anthropological Perspective.* Second Edition. Routledge, New York. First Published 1999.

Oliver-Smith, A., and X. Shen, eds. 2009. *Linking Environmental Change, Migration and Social Vulnerability.* United Nations University Institute for Environment and Human Security and Munich Re Foundation Publication Series No. 12.

Organization for Economic Cooperation and Development (OECD). 1992. *Guidelines for Aid Agencies on Involuntary Displacement and Resettlement in Development Projects.* Paris.

Organization for Economic Cooperation and Development (OECD). 2007. *Revised Council Recommendation on Common Approaches on the Environment and Officially Supported Export Credits.* Paris.

Organization for Economic Cooperation and Development. 2012. *Recommendations of the Council on Common Approaches for Officially Supported Export Credits and Environmental and Social Due Diligence (The "Common Approaches")*. Paris.

Owen, J., and D. Kemp. 2015. "Mining-Induced Displacement and Resettlement: A Critical Appraisal." *Journal of Cleaner Production* 87, 478–488.

Owen, J., and D. Kemp. 2017. *Extractive Relations: Countervailing Power and the Global Mining Industry*. Routledge, New York.

Owen, J., and D. Kemp. 2019. "Displaced by Mine Waste: The Social Consequences of Industrial Risk-Taking." *The Extractive Industries and Society* 6, 424–427.

Owen, J., D. Kemp, E. Lebre, K. Svobodova, and G. P. Murillo. 2019. "Catastrophic Tailings Dam Failures and Disaster Risk Disclosure." *International Journal of Disaster Risk Reduction*. doi:10.1016/j.ijdrr.2019.101361.

Padovani, F., ed. 2016. *Development-Induced Displacement in India and China: A Comparative Look at the Burdens of Growth*. Lexington Books, Lanham.

Parkin, D. 1972. *Palms, Wine and Witnesses: Public Spirit and Private Gain in an African Farming Community*. Chandler Publishing Co., San Francisco.

Partridge, W. 1979. "Banana County in the Wake of United Fruit: Social and Economic Linkages." *American Ethnologist* 6 (3), 491–509.

Partridge, W. L. 1983a. "Desarrollo Agrícola Entre Los Mazatecos Reacomodados." *America Indígena* XLIII (2), 343–362.

Partridge, W. L. 1983b. "Units of Analysis and Priorities of Relevance in Ethnographic Research." Paper presented at the Annual Meeting of the American Anthropological Association, Chicago.

Partridge, W. L. 1984. "The Humid Tropics Cattle Ranching Complex: Cases from Panama Reviewed." *Human Organization* 43 (1), 76–80.

Partridge, W. L. 1985. "Towards a Theory of Practice." *American Behavioral Scientist* 29 (2), 139–163.

Partridge, W. L. 1989. "Involuntary Resettlement in Development Projects." *Journal for Refugee Studies* 2 (3), 373–384.

Partridge, W. L. 1993. "Successful Involuntary Resettlement: Lessons from the Costa Rican Arenal Hydroelectric Project." In *Anthropological Approaches to Resettlement*. M. M. Cernea and S. E. Guggenheim, eds. Pp. 351–369. Westview Press, Boulder.

Partridge, W. L. 1995. "Comments on 'Including Culture in Evaluation Research,' by Klitgaard." In *Proceedings of the World Bank Conference on Evaluation and Development*. Pp. 206–209. World Bank, Washington, D.C.

Partridge, W. L., ed. 2000. *Reasentamiento en Colombia*. Banco Mundial, Alto Comisionado de Naciones Unidas para Refugiados, Red de Solidaridad Social, y Corporacion Antioquia Presente, Bogota.

Partridge, W. L. 2001. "The Population Displaced by Armed Conflict in Colombia." *Social Justice: Anthropology, Peace and Human Rights* 2 (1–2), 25–45.

Partridge, W. L. 2006. "The Guatemala Chixoy Project Resettlement Disaster." In *American Association for the Advancement of Science Workshop on Reparations and Resettlement*. American School of Social Research, Santa Fe, New Mexico. November.

Partridge, W. L. 2008. "Praxis and Power." *Journal of Community Psychology* 36 (2), 161–172.

Partridge, W. L. 2009. *Guidance Note for Safeguard Requirements: Involuntary Resettlement*. Asian Development Bank, Environmental and Social Safeguards Department, Manila.

Partridge, W. L. 2013. "Multilateral Organizations." In *Handbook of Practicing Anthropology*. R. Nolan, ed. Pp. 150–160. John Wiley and Sons, New York.

Partridge, W. L. 2015. *Investigation Report of Consultant Resettlement Specialist, Kenya Electricity Expansion Project*. World Bank Inspection Panel, Washington, D.C.

Partridge, W. L., and A. Brown. 1983. "Desarollo Agricola entre los Mazatecos Reacomodos." *America Indigena* 43 (2), 343–362.

Partridge, W. L., A. Brown, and J. Nugent. 1982. "The Papaloapan Dam and Resettlement Project: Human Ecology Impacts." In *Involuntary Migration and Resettlement*. A. Hansen and A. Oliver-Smith, eds. Pp. 245–263. Westview Press, Boulder.

Petz, D. 2015. *Planned Relocations in the Context of Natural Disasters and Climate Change: A Review of the Literature*. Brookings-LSE Project on Internal Displacement, Washington, D.C.

Piccioto, R. 2013. "Involuntary Resettlement in Infrastructure Projects: A Development Perspective." In *Infrastructure and Land Policies*. G. Ingram and K. Brandt, eds. Pp. 236–262. Lincoln Institute of Land Policy, Cambridge.

Piccioto, R., W. van Wicklin, and E. Rice, eds. *Involuntary Resettlement: Comparative Perspectives*. World Bank Series on Evaluation and Development, Volume 2. Transaction Publishers, New Brunswick.

Pitt, D. 1976. "Development from Below." In *Development from Below: Anthropologists in Development Situations*. D. Pitt, ed. Pp. 7–19. Mouton, The Hague.

Poleman, T. 1964. *The Papaloapan Project*. Stanford University Press, Stanford.

Porter, I., and J. Shivakumar. 2011. *Doing a Dam Better: The Lao People's Democratic Republic and the Story of Nam Theun 2*. The World Bank, Washington, D.C.

Price, D. 1989. *Before the Bulldozer: The Nambiquara Indians and the World Bank*. Seven Locks Press, New York.

Price, S. 2011. "Fifteen Years of ADB Policy on Involuntary Resettlement." *Resettlement News* 23–24, 4–5.

Price, S. 2015. "A No-Displacement Option? Rights, Risks and Negotiated Settlement in Development Displacement." *Development in Practice* 25 (5), 673–685.

Price, S. 2017. "Livelihoods in Development Displacement—A Reality Check from the Evaluation Record in Asia." In *Evaluation for Agenda 2030: Providing Evidence on Progress and Sustainability*. R. van den Berg, I. Naidoo, and S. Tamondong, eds. Pp. 273–289. United Nations Development Programme and International Development Evaluation Association, New York and Manila.

Price, S. 2018. "Legislative Paradigm Shifts for Involuntary People Movement: An Update." *Paradigm_Shift: People Movement* 3 (Autumn), 27–31. College of Asia and the Pacific, Australian National University.

Price, S. 2019a. "Introduction." In *Country Frameworks for Development Displacement and Resettlement*. S. Price and J. Singer, eds. Pp. 1–24. Routledge, New York.

Price, S. 2019b. "Looking Back on Development and Disaster-Related Displacement and Resettlement, Anticipating Climate-Related Displacement in the Asia-Pacific Region." *Asia Pacific Viewpoint* 60 (2), 191–204.

Price, S., and J. Singer, eds. 2019. *Country Frameworks for Development Displacement and Resettlement: Reducing Risk, Building Resiliency*. Routledge, New York.

Raschid-Sally, L., E. K. Akoto-Danso, E. A. K. Kalitsi, B. D. Ofori, and R. T. Koranteng. 2008. "The Resettlement Experience of Ghana Analyzed via Case Studies of Akosombo and Kpong Dams." Paper presented at the 9th Annual Symposium on Poverty Research in Sri Lanka: Exploring Experiences of Resettlement, Colombo. November.

Ravindran, L., and R. Kumar. 2019. "Development Induced Displacement: A Data Mining Approach Towards Vulnerability and Impoverishment Risks." *International Journal of Development and Conflict* 9, 249–290.

Redford, K., and C. Padoch, eds. 1992. *Conservation of Neotropical Forests: Working from Traditional Resource Use*. Columbia University Pres, New York.

Rhoads, R., and O. Muyenyi. 2019. "Safeguarding Community Livelihoods in Uganda: An Analysis of a Country Framework for Land Acquisition, Resettlement, and Rehabilitation." In *Country Frameworks for Development Displacement and Resettlement*. S. Price and J. Singer, eds. Pp. 153–167. Routledge, New York.

Rich, B. 2013. *Foreclosing the Future: The World Bank and the Politics of Environmental Destruction*. Island Press, Washington, D.C.

Richards, P. 1985. *Indigenous Agricultural Revolution*. Hutchison, London.

Richards, P. 1986. *Coping with Hunger: Hazard and Experiment in an African Rice-Farming System*. Allen and Unwin, London.

Richter, B., S. Postel, C. Revenga, T. Scudder, B. Lehner, A. Churchill, and M. Chow. 2010. "Lost in Development's Shadow: The Downstream Human Consequences of Dams." *Water Alternatives* 3 (2), 14–42.

Rights and Resources Initiative. 2015. *Who Owns the World's Land? A Global Baseline of Formally Recognized Indigenous and Community Land Rights*. RRI, Washington, D.C.

Rio Tinto. 2014. "Simandou Resettlement and Compensation Process." Presentation at IAIA Conference. October.

Rodriguez Garcia, H. I., A. Cuevas Muniz, and A. Arellano Ceballos. 2016. "La Reubicacion por Desastre en Anganagueo, Michoacan; Entre la Participacion y Significacion Social." *Politica y Cultura* 45 (Spring), 53–77.

Salisbury, Richard F. *Vunamami: Economic Transformation in a Traditional Society*. University of California Press, Berkeley.

Sanford, V. 2003. *Buried Secrets: Truth and Human Rights in Guatemala*. Palgrave-Macmillan, New York.

Sassen, S. 2014. *Expulsions: Brutality and Complexity in the Global Economy*. Belknap Harvard, Cambridge.

Sawyer, S. 2004. *Crude Chronicles: Indigenous Politics, Multinational Oil, and Neoliberalism in Ecuador.* Duke University Press, Durham.

Sawyer, S., and E. T. Gomez, eds. 2014. *The Politics of Resource Extraction: Indigenous Peoples, Multinational Corporations, and the State.* Palgrave-MacMillan, New York.

Saxena, K. B. 2015. "The Ordinance Amending the Land Acquisition Law (2013): Farmers Lose Out in the Unequal Contest of Power." *Social Change* 45 (2), 324–336.

Schmidt-Soltau, K. 2003. "Conservation-Related Resettlement in Central Africa: Environmental and Social Risks." *Development and Change* 34 (3), 525–551.

Schmidt-Soltau, K. 2005. "The Environmental Risks of Conservation Related Displacements in Central Africa." In *Displacement Risks in Africa.* I. Ohta and Y. Gebre, eds. Pp. 282–311. Kyoto University Press, Kyoto.

Schmidt-Soltau, K. 2009. "Is the Displacement of People from Parks Only 'Purported', or Is It Real?" *Conservation and Society* 7 (1), 46–55.

Schmidt-Soltau, K., and D. Brockington. 2007. "Protected Areas and Resettlement: What Scope for Voluntary Relocation?" *World Development* 35 (12), 2182–2202.

Schumann, D., and W. Partridge, eds. 1989. *The Human Ecology of Tropical Land Settlement in Latin America.* Westview Press, Boulder.

Schwartz, D. 2016. *Transforming the Tropics: Development, Displacement, and Anthropology in the Papaloapan, Mexico, 1940s–1970s.* Doctoral Dissertation, Department of History, University of Chicago.

Scudder, T. 1973. "The Human Ecology of Big Projects: River Basin Development and Resettlement." *Annual Review of Anthropology* 2, 45–55. Annual Reviews, Inc., Palo Alto.

Scudder, T. 1980. "River Basin Development and Local Initiative in African Savanna Environments." In *Human Ecology in Savanna Environments.* D. Harris, ed. Pp. 383–405. Academic Press, London.

Scudder, T. 1983. "Economic Downturn and Community Unraveling." *Culture and Agriculture* 18, 16–19.

Scudder, T. 1984a. "Economic Downturn and Community Unraveling, Revisited." *Culture and Agriculture* 23, 6–10.

Scudder, T. 1984b. *The Development Potential of New Lands Settlement in the Tropics and Sub-Tropics: A State-of-the-Art Evaluation with Specific Emphasis on Policy Implications.* Executive Summary. Program Evaluation Discussion Paper No. 21. USAID, Washington, D.C.

Scudder, T. 1985. "A Sociological Framework for the Analysis of New Lands Settlement." In *Putting People First.* M. Cernea, ed. Pp. 121–153. Oxford University Press, New York.

Scudder, T. 2005. *The Future of Large Dams.* Earthscan, London.

Scudder, T. 2009. "Resettlement Theory and the Kariba Case: An Anthropology of Resettlement." In *Development and Dispossession.* A. Oliver-Smith, ed. Pp. 25–48. School for Advanced Research Press, Santa Fe.

Scudder, T. 2011. "Development-Induced Community Resettlement." In *New Directions in Social Impact Assessment.* F. Vanclay and M. Esteves, eds. Pp. 186–201. Edward Elgar, Cheltenham, UK.

Scudder, T. 2017. "The Good Megadam: Does It Exist, All Things Considered?" In *The Oxford Handbook of Megaproject Management*. B. Flyvbjerg, ed. Pp. 428–450. Oxford University Press, New York.

Scudder, T. 2019a. *Large Dams: Long Term Impacts on Riverine Communities and Free Flowing Rivers*. Springer, Singapore.

Scudder, T. 2019b. "A Retrospective Analysis of Laos's Nam Theun 2 Dam." *International Journal of Water Resources Development* 36 (2–3), 351–370.

Scudder, T., and E. Colson. 1980. *Secondary Education and the Formation of an Elite: The Impact of Education on Gwembe District, Zambia*. Academic Press, New York.

Scudder, T., and E. Colson. 1982. "From Welfare to Development: A Conceptual Framework for the Analysis of Dislocated People." In *Involuntary Migration and Resettlement*. A. Hansen and A. Oliver-Smith, eds. Pp. 267–287. Westview Press, Boulder.

Sen, A. 1981. *Poverty and Famines: An Essay on Entitlement and Deprivation*. Oxford University Press, New York.

Sen, A. 1999. *Development As Freedom*. Knopf, New York.

Sen, A. 2009. *The Idea of Justice*. Harvard University Press, Cambridge.

Sharma, R. 2009. "Displacement for Special Economic Zones and Real Estate Business." In *Beyond Relocation: The Imperative of Sustainable Resettlement*. R. Modi, ed. Pp. 199–217. Sage Publications, New Delhi.

Shearer, C. 2011. *Kivalina: A Climate Change Story*. Haymarket Books, Chicago.

Shi, G. 2018. "Comparing China's and the World Bank's Resettlement Policy Over Time: The Ascent of the 'Resettlement with Development' Paradigm." In *Challenging the Prevailing Paradigm of Displacement and Resettlement*. M. Cernea and J. Maldonado, eds. Pp. 143–161. Routledge, New York.

Shihata, I. F. I. 1993. "Legal Aspects of Involuntary Resettlement." In *Anthropological Approaches to Resettlement*. M. Cernea and S. Guggenheim, eds. Pp. 39–54. Westview Press, Boulder.

Shihata, I. F. I. 2000. "Involuntary Resettlement." In *The World Bank in a Changing World: Selected Essays by I.F.I. Shihata, Vice President and General Counsel, The World Bank*. Martinus Nijhoff Publishers, Dordrecht.

Shihata, I. F. I. 2001. *The World Bank Legal Papers*. Martinus Nijhoff Publishers, The Hague.

Shoemaker, B., and W. Robichaud, eds. 2018. *Dead in the Water: Global Lessons from the World Bank's Model Hydropower Project in Laos*. University of Wisconsin Press, Madison.

Simon, J., and C. Gonzalez Parra. 2019. "Cultural and Political Obstacles to Effective Resettlement: A Case Study of Involuntary Displacement of Pehuenche Families by the Pangue and Ralco Dams in Southern Chile." In *Country Frameworks for Development Displacement and Resettlement*. S. Price and J. Singer, eds. Pp. 247–268. Routledge, New York.

Smith, M. G. 1974. *Corporations and Society: The Social Anthropology of Collective Action*. Duckworth, London.

Smith, N. J. H. 1982. *Rainforest Corridors: The Transamazon Colonization Scheme*. University of California Press, Berkeley.

Smyth, E., M. Steyn, A. M. Esteves, D. M. Fraks, and K. Vaz. 2015. "Five 'Big' Issues for Land Access, Resettlement and Livelihood Restoration Practice: Findings of an International Symposium." *Impact Assessment and Project Appraisal* 33 (3), 220.

Spicer, E. B., ed. 1961. *Perspectives on American Indian Culture Change*. University of Chicago Press, Chicago.

Spicer, E. B. 1971. "Persistent Cultural Systems." *Science* 174 (4011), 795–800.

Spicer, E. H., A. Hansen, K. Luomala, and M. Opler. 1946. *Impounded People*: *Japanese Americans in Relocation Centers*. U.S. Government Printing Office, Washington, D.C.

Stevens, S., ed. 1997. *Conservation Through Cultural Survival: Indigenous Peoples and Protected Areas*. Island Press, Washington, D.C.

Stevens, S., ed. 2014. *Indigenous Peoples, National Parks, and Protected Areas: A New Paradigm Linking Conservation, Culture, and Rights*. University of Arizona Press, Tucson.

Stocks, Gabriela. 2014. *Assessing the Long-Term Effects of Development-Forced Displacement and Resettlement: The Case of New Arenal, Costa Rica*. Doctoral Dissertation, Department of Anthropology, University of Florida, Gainesville.

Swaziland Federal Ministry for Economic Cooperation. 2008. *Dams and Development: The Komati Basin Water Authority Experience*. Mbabane.

Szablowski, D. 2007. *Transnational Law and Local Struggles: Mining, Communities and the World Bank*. Hart Publishing, Oxford.

Tagliarino, N. 2016. *Encroaching on Land and Livelihoods: How National Expropriation Laws Measure Up Against International Standards*. Working Paper. World Resources Institute, Washington, D.C.

Tagliarino, N. 2017. "The Status of National Legal Frameworks for Valuing Compensation for Expropriated Land: An Analysis of Whether National Laws in 50 Countries/Regions Across Asia, Africa, and Latin America Comply with International Standards on Compensation Valuation." *Land* 6 (37), 1–29.

Tagliarino, N. 2018a. "The Need for National Level Legal Protection for Populations Displaced by Expropriation." In *Challenging the Prevailing Paradigm of Displacement and Resettlement*. M. Cernea and J. Maldonado, eds. Pp. 273–292. Routledge, New York.

Tagliarino, N. 2018b. "Avoiding the Worst-Case Scenario: An Assessment of Compensation Eligibility Requirements Applicable to Indigenous Peoples and Local Communities in 30 Countries." In *Rethinking Expropriation Law III: Fair Compensation*. B. Hoops, E. Marais, L. van Schalkwyk, and N. Tagliarino, eds. Pp. 45–86. Seven Eleven International Publishing, The Hague.

Tagliarino, N. 2019. *National-Level Adoption of International Standards on Expropriation, Compensation and Resettlement: A Comparative Analysis of National Laws Enacted in 50 Countries Across Asia, Africa and Latin America*. Seven Eleven International Publishing, The Hague.

Tamakloe, M. 1994. "Long-Term Impacts of Resettlement: The Akosombo Dam Experience." In *Involuntary Resettlement in Africa*. C. Cook, ed. Pp. 99–110. World Bank Technical Paper No. 227. Washington, D.C.

Tate, W. 2015. *Drugs, Thugs and Diplomats: U. S. Policymaking in Colombia.* Stanford University Press, Stanford.

Treece, D. 1987. *Bound in Misery and Iron: The Impact of the Grande Carajas Project on the Indians of Brazil.* Survival International, London.

Tsikata, D., ed. 2006. *Living in the Shadow of the Large Dams: Long Term Responses of Downstream and Lakeside Communities of Ghana's Volta River Project.* Brill, Leiden.

Ulu Foundation, Friends of the Earth-US and Ecological Justice Indonesia. 2014. "World Bank Safeguards Draft Proposes Elimination of Environmental and Social Protections." Comments submitted to the World Bank's Committee on Development Effectiveness (CODE).

United Nations. 1997. *Comprehensive Human Rights Guidelines on Development-Based Displacement.* New York.

United Nations. 2006. "Basic Principles and Guidelines on Development-Based Evictions and Displacement." In *Annex 1 of the Report of the Special Rapporteur on Adequate Housing As a Component of the Right to an Adequate Standard of Living.* New York.

United Nations Commission for Human Rights. 2011. *Guiding Principles on Business and Human Rights.* New York.

United Nations Development Programme. 2014. *Social and Environmental Standards.* New York.

United Nations Environment Programme. 2006. *Independent Monitoring of the Maguga Dam Resettlement.* Nairobi.

United Nations High Commission for Refugees (UNHCR). 1998. *Guiding Principles on Internal Displacement.* 22 July. ADM 1.1, PRL 12.1, PR00/98/109.

United Nations High Commission for Refugees, Georgetown University and International Organization for Migration. 2017. *A Toolbox: Planning Relocations to Protect People from Disasters and Environmental Change.* Washington, D.C.

United States Agency for International Development (USAID). 2016. *Guidelines on Compulsory Displacement and Resettlement in USAID Programming.* Washington, D.C.

van Wicklin, W. 1999. "Sharing Project Benefits to Improve Resettlers' Livelihoods." In *The Economics of Involuntary Resettlement.* M. Cernea, ed. Pp. 231–256. World Bank, Washington, D.C.

Veil, P., and C. Benson. 2004. "When Parks and People Collide." *Human Rights Dialogue* 2 (11), 13–14. Carnegie Council on Ethics and International Affairs, New York.

Villa Rojas, A. 1955. *Los Mazatecos y el Problema Indígena en la Cuenca del Papaloapan.* Instituto Nacional Indigenista, Memorias del INI Vol. VII, Mexico.

Wade, R. 2011. "Muddy Waters: Inside the World Bank As It Struggled with the Narmada Projects." *Economic and Political Weekly* 46 (40), 44–65.

Wade, R. 2016a. "Boulevard to Broken Dreams, Part 1: The Polonoroeste Road Project in the Brazilian Amazon, and the World Bank's Environmental and Indigenous Peoples' Norms." *Revista de Economia Politica* 36 (1), 214–230.

Wade, R. 2016b. "Boulevard to Broken Dreams, Part 2: Implementation of the Polonoroeste Road Project in the Brazilian Amazon, and the World Bank's Response the Gathering Storm." *Revista de Ecnonomia Politica* 36 (3), 646–663.

Wallace, A. F. C. 1954. *Tornado in Worcester: An Exploratory Study of Individual and Community Behavior in an Extreme Situation.* Committee on Disaster Studies, National Research Council, Washington, DC.

Warren, D. M. 1979. "Humanistic Approaches in Applied Anthropology." In *Essays in Humanistic Anthropology.* B. Grindall and D. Warren, eds. Pp. 115–135. University Press of America, Washington, D.C.

Watts, M. 2001. "Petro-Violence: Community, Extraction and Political Ecology of a Mythic Commodity." In *Violent Environments.* N. Peluso and M. Watts, eds. Pp. 189–212. Cornell University Press, Ithaca.

Watts, M. 2004. "Resource Curse? Governmentality, Oil and Power in the Niger Delta, Nigeria. *Geopolitics* 9 (1), 50–80.

Watts, M. 2012. "A Tale of Two Gulfs: Life, Death and Dispossession Along Two Oil Frontiers." *American Quarterly* 64 (3), 437–467.

Watts, M. 2013. *Silent Violence: Food, Famine, and Peasantry in Northern Nigeria.* Second Edition. University of California Press, Berkeley. First Published in 1983.

Watts, M., and E. Kashi, eds. 2008. *Curse of the Black Gold: 50 Years of Oil in the Niger Delta.* PowerHouse Books, Brooklyn.

Weiss, T., and D. Korn. 2006. *Internal Displacement: Conceptualization and Its Consequences.* Routledge, New York.

West, P., and S. Brechin, eds. 1991. *Resident Peoples and National Parks: Social Dilemmas and National Strategies in International Conservation.* University of Arizona Press, Tucson.

Wilmsen, B., and S. Rogers. 2019. "Planned Resettlement to Avoid Climatic Hazards: What Prospects for Just Outcomes in China?" *Asia Pacific Viewpoint* 60 (2), 118–131.

Wilmsen, B., and M. Wang. 2015. "Voluntary and Involuntary Resettlement in China: A False Dichotomy?" *Development in Practice* 25 (5), 612–627.

Wilmsen, B., and M. Webber. 2015. "What Can We Learn from the Practice of Development-Forced Displacement and Resettlement for Organized Resettlements in Response to Climate Change?" *Geoforum* 58, 76–85.

Wilmsen, B., D. Adjartey, and A. van Hulten. 2018. "Challenging the Risks-Based Model of Involuntary Resettlement Using Evidence from the Bui Dam, Ghana." *International Journal of Water Resources Development.* doi:10.1080/07900627.2 018.1471390.

Wilmsen, B., A. van Hulten, X. Han, and D. Adjartey. 2020. "The Environmental and Social Safeguard Policies of the Belt and Road Initiative." In *The Belt and Road Initiative and the Future of Regional Order in the Indo-Pacific.* M. Clarke, M. Sussex, and N. Bisley, eds. Pp. 115–140. Lexington Books, Lanham.

World Bank. 1980. *Social Issues Associated with Involuntary Resettlement in Bank-Financed Projects.* Operational Manual Statement 2.33. Washington, D.C.

World Bank. 1986. *Operations Policy Issues in the Treatment of Involuntary Resettlement in Bank-Financed Projects*. Operations Policy Note 10.08. Washington, D.C.

World Bank. 1990. *Operational Directive 4.30: Involuntary Resettlement.* Washington, D.C.

World Bank. 1991a. *Ertan Hydroelectric Project.* Staff Appraisal Report. Washington, D.C.

World Bank. 1991b. *Daguangba Multipurpose Project.* Staff Appraisal Report. Washington, D.C.

World Bank. 1995a. *Regional Remedial Action Planning for Involuntary Resettlement in World Bank Supported Projects: A Report on One Year of Follow-Up to Resettlement and Development, the Report of the Bankwide Resettlement Review.* Environment Department, Washington, D.C.

World Bank. 1995b. *Peoples' Republic of China: Second Ertan Hydroelectric Project.* Staff Appraisal Report. Washington, D.C.

World Bank. 1996. *Resettlement and Development: The Bankwide Review of Projects Involving Involuntary Resettlement, 1986–1993.* Environment Department Paper No. 032. Washington, D.C.

World Bank. 1998a. *Recent Experience with Involuntary Resettlement: Thailand-Pak Mun Operations Evaluation Study.* Washington, D.C.

World Bank. 1998b. *Recent Experience with Involuntary Resettlement: Indonesia—Kedung Ombo.* Operations Evaluation Study. Washington, D.C.

World Bank. 1998c. *Recent Experiences with Involuntary Resettlement: India—Upper Krishna.* Operations Evaluation Study. Washington, D.C.

World Bank. 2000. *Successful Reservoir Resettlement in China—Shuikou Hydroelectric Project.* Operations Evaluation Department Working Paper. Washington, D.C.

World Bank. 2001a. *Operations Policy 4.12: Involuntary Resettlement.* Revised 2007, 2011, 2013. Washington, DC.

World Bank. 2001b. *Cost of Doing Business: Fiduciary and Safeguard Policies and Compliance.* Report 63081. Washington, D.C. July 16.

World Bank. 2002. *India: Mumbai Urban Transport Project.* Staff Appraisal Report. Washington, D.C.

World Bank. 2003a. *Striking a Better Balance: The World Bank Group and the Extractive Industries.* The Final Report of the Extractive Industries Review, Volume I. Washington, D.C.

World Bank. 2003b. *Striking a Better Balance: Stakeholder Inputs: Converging Issues and Diverging Views on the World Bank Group's Involvement in the Extractive Industries.* The Final Report of the Extractive Industries Review, Volume II. Washington, D.C.

World Bank. 2004a. *Involuntary Resettlement Sourcebook: Planning and Implementation in Development Projects.* Washington, D.C.

World Bank. 2004b. *Xiaolangdi Resettlement Project: Implementation Completion and Results Report.* Washington, D.C.

World Bank. 2008. *Peoples' Republic of China: Hubei Shiyan-Manchuangan Expressway (Shiman) Project.* Project Information Document. Washington, D.C.

World Bank. 2017a. *Environmental and Social Framework*. Washington, D.C.

World Bank. 2017b. *World Bank Environmental and Social Policy for Investment Project Financing*. Washington, D.C.

World Bank. 2017c. *Environmental and Social Standard 5: Land Acquisition, Restrictions on Land Use and Involuntary Resettlement*. Washington, D.C.

World Bank Inspection Panel. 1996. *Report and Recommendation to the Executive Directors of the International Finance Association on Request for Inspection Bangladesh: Jamuna Bridge Project*. Washington, D.C.

World Commission on Dams (WCD). 2000. *Dams and Development: A New Framework for Decision-Making*. Earthscan, London.

Ybarra, M. 2019. *Green Wars: Conservation and Decolonization in the Maya Forest*. University of California Press, Berkeley.

Zaman, M. 2019a. "Rohingya Repatriation: No More Dancing Around Key Issues." *The Daily Star*, November 21.

Zaman, M. 2019b. "NRC and the Larger Crisis Brewing in Assam." *The Daily Star*, December 9.

Zaman, M. 2020a. "ICJ Ruling and the Road Map for Myanmar." *The Financial Express*, February 3.

Zaman, M. 2020b. "Is India Creating Its Own Rohingyas? Op-Ed." *Daily Times*, January 14.

Zaman, M., and H. Khatun, eds. 2019. *Development-Induced Displacement and Resettlement in Bangladesh: Cases and Practices*. Second Revised and Expanded Edition. Nova Science Publishers, New York.

Zarfl, C., A. E. Lumsden, J. Berlekamp, L. Tydecks, and K. Tockner. 2014. "A Global Boom in Hydropower Dam Construction." *Aquatic Sciences*. doi:10.1007/s00027-014-0377-0.

Index

Note: Page numbers followed by "n" refer to notes and page numbers in italics refers to tables.

About the Authors

William L. Partridge is an independent consultant on involuntary resettlement. He recently retired from Vanderbilt University, where he was Professor of Anthropology and Professor of Human and Organizational Development. Before that Partridge served in the World Bank for fifteen years, first as a consultant, then as Senior Anthropologist for the Asia and Pacific Region, and then successively as Principal Anthropologist, Environmental Assessment Manager, Chief of the Environment Division, and finally as Lead Anthropologist for the Latin America and Caribbean Region. Prior to that he was Chairman of the Department of Anthropology at Georgia State University after several years of teaching anthropology at the University of Southern California. He has also served as a consultant to the World Bank, the Inter-American Development Bank, the International Finance Corporation, the Asian Development Bank, the World Bank Inspection Panel, the UN High Commission for Refugees, and several bilateral and national development agencies.

David B. Halmo is an independent researcher and Publications Review Editor for the International Network on Displacement and Resettlement (INDR). He has a PhD in Anthropology from the University of Arizona. He has worked in collaboration with more than fifty American Indian tribes and organizations on numerous social and cultural heritage impact assessment projects. He previously held positions at the National Park Service, Washington, DC, the Institute for Social Research at the University of Michigan and the Bureau of Applied Research in Anthropology in the School of Anthropology at the

University of Arizona. Subsequently, he served as NAGPRA Coordinator and Cultural Preservation Officer for the Chemehuevi Indian tribe in California. He has taught anthropology and international studies at the University of Wisconsin-Parkside and Loyola University-Chicago. He was appointed to the Academic Advisory Committee of the National Research Center on Resettlement, Hohai University, Nanjing, China, in 2019.

www.ingramcontent.com/pod-product-compliance
Lightning Source LLC
Chambersburg PA
CBHW022311280326
41932CB00010B/1059